C000138738

"In a compelling an... demonstrates that the... contribution to revival... the creative tension between religious practices that later revivalists would prize apart. Extempore prayer is nourished by liturgical traditions and the call to repentance finds its goal in the reception of Holy Communion. This is a fascinating and revealing study of one of the great founding fathers of revivalism."

Canon Dr James Steven, academic dean, Centre for Liturgy and Worship, Sarum College

"In his new biography of George Whitefield, Nigel Scotland shows how the eighteenth-century revivalist was one of the most effective preachers of the Christian gospel in world history."

Prof David Bebbington, professor of history, University of Stirling

"George Whitefield is the subject of renewed scholarly interest at the present time, with a regular stream of new books appearing. Whitefield, the 'Elect Methodist', was one of the founders of the evangelical movement in the mid-eighteenth century, and for a time his itinerant preaching made him the most famous figure in the North Atlantic World. This book gives readers an introductory taste of the man and his ministry."

Dr David Ceri Jones, reader in early modern history, Aberystwyth University

George
Whitefield

The First Transatlantic Revivalist

Nigel Scotland

LION

Published by
Lion Hudson Limited
Wilkinson House, Jordan Hill Business Park
Banbury Road, Oxford OX2 8DR, England
www.lionhudson.com

ISBN 978 0 7459 8028 7
e-ISBN 978 0 7459 8027 0

First edition 2019

A catalogue record for this book is available from the British Library

Printed and bound in the UK, July 2019, LH26

To my lovely wife Anne

Acknowledgments

In writing this biography of George Whitefield I am much indebted to a number of people who have helped me along the way. Among them are Dr Ian Maddock, Senior Lecturer in Theology at Sydney Missionary and Bible College, who has a number of publications on Evangelical religion, and Dr Tim Welch, Director of Studies at Bristol Baptist College, who read the manuscript with great care and made a number of helpful suggestions. I owe a huge debt to Professor David Bebbington of Stirling University who very kindly gave my first draft a thorough scrutiny. He helped me to refine and rearrange some of the material and gave much valuable guidance.

I am also enormously grateful to Miranda Lever for her editorial skills. Her meticulous reading, careful attention to detail, and her ability to make awkward and long sentences into smooth reading are second to none.

I am also grateful to Joy Tibbs and Jon Oliver at Lion Hudson for their encouragement. The archivist at the Gloucestershire County Record Office gave me helpful advice on relevant local source material. Over a period of ten years I received stimulus from students at Trinity College Bristol and Bristol Baptist College who took my Durham University MA course on Revivals and Revivalism in England and America. A number of them said they found Whitefield to be a challenging and encouraging role model as they went out to serve in Christian ministry. It is my hope that reading the pages that follow will be a similar inspiration to you.

Dr Nigel Scotland

HONORARY RESEARCH FELLOW, UNIVERSITY OF GLOUCESTERSHIRE

Contents

Preface

Something of the measure of Whitefield's significance as a major figure in the world of the eighteenth century and his enduring impact in the centuries that have followed is seen in the steady flow of biographies and books that have been written about him. The first significant work was from the pen of Dr John Gillies (1712–96). He became the minister of College Church, Glasgow, in July 1742. He knew Whitefield as a personal friend and shared in ministry with him at Cambuslang and elsewhere. The biography, published in 1774, was based on original papers, journals, and letters. It provides interesting and first-hand personal information. Tyerman stated that Gillies' biography gives "the most exact likenesses of the great preacher ever published".[1]

Several biographies and works of significance emerged in the nineteenth century. Among them were a section on Whitefield by Sir James Stephen in his *Essays in Ecclesiastical Biography* (1849) and biographies by Robert Philip (1838) and Joseph Belcher (1857). In his study, the Congregational pastor Philip (1791–1858) drew on the testimony of those who had personal knowledge of his subject and his own study of Whitefield's journals, letters, and sermons. Thus Philip wrote, "This work is chiefly from Whitefield's own pen. So far as it is mine, it is his own spirit."[2] His book is divided into thirty-three relatively short chapters. They are largely in time order and easy to read but the sources on which they are based are rarely specified. Sometimes he includes the number of one of Whitefield's published letters at the end of a paragraph. At other times no sources are given or he contents himself with simply putting "Letters". The essay written by James Stephen (1789–1859) has a strong air of objectivity about it in the way that he highlights

Whitefield's austerity, excessive compulsion to continuous working, and his keeping slaves. Overall he presents a warm picture of his subject. He was however strongly critical of Philip whom he stated, probably with justification, that "he has followed the steps of the great itinerant from the cradle to the grave, in a volume of nearly six hundred closely printed pages, compiled on the principle that nothing can be superfluous in the narrative of the great man's life which was of any real importance to the man himself".[3] Philip's work lacks selectivity and very few sources are given. Joseph Belcher's *George Whitefield: A Biography* is a more concise volume tracing Whitefield's life and labours in a consecutive timeline covering the journeys to the American colonies interlaced with his endeavours in the British Isles. Unlike Philip, the Baptist pastor Joseph Belcher (1794–1859) begins his volume with a chapter on the state of England in the early eighteenth century and makes some attempt to set Whitefield in that context. Following in the wake of Philip, Belcher offers almost no information regarding his sources.

In 1869 J. C. Ryle (1816–1900) published his very short *George Whitefield and His Ministry* in which he lauded his subject with the most fulsome praise. "I believe," he wrote, "[that] no English preacher has ever possessed such a combination of excellent qualifications as Whitefield."[4] He went further, contending, "No Englishman, I believe, dead or alive, has ever equalled him."[5] Ryle, who was the first bishop of the new diocese of Liverpool, was writing at a time when Evangelicals in the Church of England needed encouragement to stand firm and assert their convictions against a background of ritual controversy and growing liberalism. He used Whitefield's rigorous Protestant Reformed evangelism as a model to challenge the clergy "to contend for the faith once for all delivered to all the saints" (Jude verse 3). His short piece was significant in that it prompted a long succession of short inspirational biographies of Whitefield that still continues to the present time. In these studies Whitefield is held up as the ultimate Christian example of leadership, evangelism, and discipleship.

Luke Tyerman (1820–89) who was a popular Victorian Wesleyan Methodist preacher and a fulsome writer, followed Ryle with his *The Life of the Rev. George Whitefield, B.A., of Pembroke College, Oxford* (1876 and 1877). His two-volume biography, which extends to over 1,100 pages, remains the most expansive biography of Whitefield so far published. Tyerman, although Arminian in his theology and ready to point out Whitefield's weaknesses, was nevertheless inspired by his life and ministry. His two volumes are made rich by his wide range of sources, which include many references from the writings of Whitefield's contemporaries, newspapers, and journals of the period.

The twentieth century saw the publication of several Whitefield biographies. They included *George Whitefield the Matchless Soul Winner* (1938) from the pen of the American Edwin Noah Hardy (1862–1950),[6] John Pollock's *George Whitefield the Evangelist* (1973),[7] Arnold Dallimore's two-volume *George Whitefield: The Life and Times of the Great Evangelist of the 18th Century Revival* (1970 and 1980), and Harry Stout's *The Divine Dramatist* (1991). Both Hardy and Pollock's books are in the Ryle tradition with Hardy stating that "the avowed purpose of this new biography is to aid the church to a fuller realization of the opportunities, and privileges of making Christ and his kingdom known".[8] Pollock presents Whitefield as the relentless evangelist through whom God worked in remarkable ways in both England and America to bring numerous people to Christ. The twentieth-century Canadian Baptist pastor, Arnold Dallimore (1911–98), reveals his close sympathies with Whitefield and his theology throughout his work. He is no sycophant however and offers criticisms of Whitefield on matters such as his advocacy of slavery, his marriage, and excessive work ethic. Nevertheless he presents a fulsome, warm, and sympathetic picture of the "great Evangelist". Following Tyerman, from whom he draws a good deal, Dallimore's two volumes give an extensive coverage of Whitefield making abundant use of the six volumes of his subject's published works. He also helpfully examines his interactions with significant individuals including Howell Harris, the Wesleys, the Countess of Huntingdon, and several prominent American clergy including Jonathan Edwards, Gilbert and William Tennent, and Nathan Cole.

In strong contrast to Hardy and Pollock is Harry Stout's *The Divine Dramatist* (1991)[9] and Frank Lambert's *Pedlar in Divinity: George Whitefield and the Transatlantic Revivals, 1737–1770* (1993).[10] Stout's work has been criticized by some who are of the view that he has portrayed Whitefield as a self-serving actor–preacher. Others, however, have commended him for writing a biography which didn't simply amount to a canonization of Whitefield. While that is the case, Stout, it should be said, does commend him for his moral uprightness which resonated well with the biblical saints who were central to his preaching. He also commended his strenuous charitable endeavours and the fact that he was uncorrupted by sex or money. Lambert sets Whitefield in the context of the hugely expanding transatlantic trade markets and the rapid growth in the use of print media. He convincingly demonstrates the way in which Whitefield's effectiveness was boosted by his numerous publications, which included journal extracts, collections of his sermons, press articles, and advertisements.

More recently Thomas Kidd published *George Whitefield: America's Spiritual Founding Father*[11] This is a closely written scholarly book, which, as the title suggests, has its primary focus on Whitefield's impact on the spiritual life of the American colonies. His case for Whitefield being a "spiritual founding father" is convincing. Kidd does not however speculate on how Whitefield would have handled

America's independence.[12] In his book he draws on both Whitefield's published works and a wealth of recent literature and presents a balanced picture of Whitefield.

In this opportunity I have been given to write about Whitefield I have endeavoured to keep to the basic historical sequence of his travels to and from America and his longer spells of ministry in the British Isles. At the same time I have written separate chapters focusing on Whitefield's preaching, his theology and churchmanship, and his spirituality and devotional life which drove and sustained him throughout his ministry. I have also made an attempt to underline his major role in transforming the Methodism of the Oxford-based Holy Club into a national and international movement and examined his role as the leader of the Calvinistic Methodists.

Preface notes

1   L. Tyerman, *The Life of the Rev. George Whitefield* (New York, Anson D. F. Randolph & Company, 1877), Vol. 1, Preface, p. 6.
2   R. Philip, *The Life and Times of the Reverend George Whitefield* (London, George Virtue, 1838), Preface.
3   Sir J. Stephen, *Essays in Ecclesiastical Biography* (London, Longmans, Green, Reader, and Dyer, 1872), p. 385. Sir James Stephen (1789–1859) had links with the Clapham Sect.
4   J. C. Ryle, *George Whitefield and His Ministry* (London, The Banner of Truth Trust, 1959), p. 27.
5   Ibid, p. 28.
6   E. N. Hardy, *George Whitefield the Matchless Soul Winner* (New York, American Tract Society, 1938).
7   J. Pollock, *The Evangelist* (Fearn, Ross-shire, Christian Focus Publications, 1973).
8   E. N. Hardy, op. cit., Preface.
9   H. S. Stout, *The Divine Dramatist: George Whitefield and the Rise of Modern Evangelicalism* (Grand Rapids, William B. Eerdmans Publishing Company, 1991).
10   F. Lambert, *Pedlar in Divinity: George Whitefield and the Transatlantic Revivals, 1737–1770* (New Jersey, Princeton University Press, 1993).
11   T. S. Kidd, *George Whitefield: America's Founding Spiritual Father* (Yale, University Press, 2014).
12   Ibid, p. 263.

Chapter 1

From Rebellious Youth
to Ordination

George Whitefield was born the youngest of seven children at the Bell Inn in the city of Gloucester on 16 December 1714. His father, Thomas, had previously worked for a Bristol wine merchant during which time he married Elizabeth Edwards. Then at some earlier point his parents moved to Gloucester and took over the running of the hostelry in Southgate Street. The Bell comprised of the main inn, outhouses, stables, several shops, land, and a garden worth £130 per year.[1] The city skyline, noted for its church spires, was dominated by the cathedral, which, during the eighteenth century, became a focus of choral music with soloists sometimes coming from as far away as London. The city, which had just over 1,000 houses, and a population a little over 5,000 in 1710, was a centre of corn trading. However, as larger ships were built Gloucester's port began to lose its importance to that of Bristol, which had the capacity to accommodate them. Despite this, Gloucester continued to be a growing centre of commerce which attracted many visitors. By 1720 the Saracen's Head in Eastgate Street was able to offer stables for sixty horses.[2] It is a significant fact that at this time many wealthy families in Gloucestershire kept black African slaves; this may well have impacted on Whitefield's later controversial advocacy of slavery in the American colonies.

George, it should be said, had clerical blood in his veins. His great-grandfather, Samuel Whitefield, had been rector of North Ledyard in Wiltshire and then moved on to become incumbent of the parish of Rockhampton in Gloucestershire where his son, also Samuel, succeeded him as incumbent.[3]

Very little information about Whitefield's infancy has come to light. It is known from extant records that he enrolled at a school run by the cathedral in 1726. The main source of his early years is a brief autobiographical sketch of his life entitled *A Short Account of God's Dealings with the Reverend Mr. George Whitefield*. This was supplemented by *A Further Account of God's Dealings* which covered the time from his ordination to his embarking on a ship bound for Georgia in 1737. The "Short Account" was written in 1740 at an early point in his ministry and gives some fairly detailed accounts of the misdemeanours of his youth, some of which he toned down in a later edition. At the time of writing the first account Whitefield was only at the beginning of his ministry but already he had become a celebrity preacher. He was keen that the people who hung on his every word should not cherish unreal opinions of him. At the outset he tells his readers that in most of the biographies of other men that he had read the writers "have given us the bright, but not the dark side of their character. This, I think, proceeded from a kind of fraud, lest mentioning a person's faults should encourage others to sin."[4] Whitefield justified this baring of his soul on a biblical ground recalling that the sacred writers give an account of their failings as well as their virtues. In particular he mentioned Peter who was not ashamed to confess that he had denied his Master three times with oaths and curses. Nor, he pointed out, did the Gospel writers avoid telling us that Jesus had cast out seven devils from Mary Magdalene. So, he concluded, "I have... follow[ed] their good example" and "simply told what I was by nature, as well as what I am by grace."[5]

From a young age George remembered his mother telling him that she had endured fourteen weeks of sickness after she had brought him into the world and "that she expected more comfort from me than any other of her children".[6] These expectations coupled with experience of working in the inn later stirred his desire to be a wholehearted follower of Christ. Notwithstanding these aspirations George was able to recall and recount a number of aspects of misspent youth.

> I can truly say, I was froward from my mother's womb. I was so brutish as to hate instruction, and used purposely to shun all opportunities of receiving it. I can date some very early acts of uncleanness... Lying, filthy talking, and foolish jesting I was much addicted to, even when very young. Sometimes I used to curse, if not swear. Stealing from my mother I thought was no theft at all, and I used to make no scruple of taking money out of her pocket before she was up. I have... more than once spent the money I took from the house, in buying fruits, tarts etc., to satisfy my sensual appetite. Much money have I spent in plays, and in the common entertainments of the age. Cards and reading romances were my heart's delight.[7]

In December 1724, when Whitefield was about ten years old, his mother was remarried to a Mr Capel Longdon, who was a near neighbour. It proved to be a disastrous union and Elizabeth finally left her husband in 1728. Notwithstanding this hardship George's mother always took great care over her young son's education and when he was twelve years old he was sent to the Crypt School in

Gloucester where he became an avid reader. George was clearly a bright child but his education was of short duration owing to his mother's reduced circumstances. He later wrote, "My mother was very careful of my education and always kept me in my tender years, for which I can never sufficiently thank her."[8] Whitefield recalled that during his time at school he was blessed with a retentive memory and was very good at elocution. He also became especially fond of reading plays and acting in them, skills which were later to prove highly valuable in his dramatic preaching and public speaking. It also enabled him to be confident in conversation and at ease with all sections of society from mine workers to London aristocrats and Oxford dons.

With the passing of time it became clear to the young Whitefield that his mother's circumstances were insufficient to give him a university education. He therefore left off learning Latin and began to help her run the hostelry. He wrote, "I put on my blue apron and my snuffers, washed mops, cleaned rooms, and in one word, became a professed and common drawer for nigh a year and a half."[9]

After this early period of George's "servile employment" his mother decided to leave the inn. The business was then placed in the hands of his younger brother who had recently married, with George appointed as his assistant. Unfortunately the situation became difficult with George falling out with his sister-in-law and it was eventually agreed that he should go and stay with his older brother in Bristol. There, in St John's Church, he related how "God was pleased to give me great foretastes of His love" and filled him "with such unspeakable raptures" that he "was carried out beyond [him]self." These were accompanied with "great hungerings and thirstings after the blessed Sacrament". By this he referred to his strong desire to receive Holy Communion, a practice that became his lifelong habit. In consequence of this experience he wrote many letters, including one to his mother, telling her that he would never go into public employment again. At this same time he found a "great delight" in the writings of medieval mystic, Thomas à Kempis, and must have wondered at his beautifully written *The Imitation of Christ.* He also read at this time Thomas Ken's *Manual for Winchester Scholars*, "a book which much affected me".[10]

After about two months away in Bristol George returned to Gloucester where he recalled "Alas! All my fervour went off." Much of his days reverted to "reading plays and in sauntering from place to place". In short it was, he said, "a proper season for Satan to tempt me.[11] During this time all George's efforts to obtain an apprenticeship in the city came to nothing and it struck him that God was going to provide some other way he could not comprehend. And so it proved!

Oxford bound!

A young student who had been one of Whitefield's friends at the Crypt School chanced to pay a visit to his mother. During the course of their conversations he mentioned that he was a servitor at Pembroke College, Oxford, and explained how in this position he had been able to pay his way by performing the duties of a domestic servant for his fellow wealthier students. George vividly recalled that, on hearing this, his mother cried out, "This will do for my son" and turning to him said, "Will you go to Oxford George?" His reply was, "I will with all my heart."[12]

George's mother shared the same friends who had sponsored this young undergraduate student. They promised to do their best to get him a servitor's place in the same college. In little more than a week Elizabeth Whitefield approached her son's Master at the Crypt who proved to be much in favour of this proposed move. George who at once returned to his studies had clearly not lost his Latin and surprised his master by an almost faultless translation of the first passage he was given. Now with his eyes set on Oxford George recalled that "I learned much faster than I did before."[13]

Although the young Whitefield made great strides with his studies his behaviour didn't follow suit. "All this while," he wrote, "I continued in secret sins and at length got acquainted with such a set of debauched, abandoned, atheistical youths, that if God by his free, unmerited, and especial grace, had not delivered me out of their hands, I should long since have sat in the scorner's chair and made a mock at sin."[14] Among other ills he got drunk on at least two occasions, took part in lewd conversation and struggled with "his corrupt passions"; probably a reference to his strong sexual desires. Whitefield also recalled having fallen into "abominable sin" which Kidd has suggested was likely to have been masturbation.[15]

Shocked at having been "overtaken in liquor" and finding himself at the beginning of his seventeenth year and now an "upper boy in the school", George resolved to take himself in hand. He began to study with even greater determination and was especially diligent in reading his Greek New Testament. One night, while in this new frame of mind, George was running an errand for his mother when he had "a very strong impression that I should preach". However, on his return he found his mother was less than impressed with this idea and told him to hold his tongue. George was undeterred and started to receive Communion each month and attended public worship as often as he could. One of his brothers told him he was just having another phase, which would soon pass away when he reached Oxford. George was glad of the caution which led him to start praying for perseverance against the temptations with which he was struggling.

Pembroke at last

George, however, remained steadfast in his new-found resolve and recorded in his autobiography that "Being now near eighteen years old, it was judged proper for me to go to the university God had sweetly prepared for me." He arrived in Oxford near the close of 1732. His mother's Gloucester friends had indeed paved the way, commending him to the master of Pembroke and providing him with the sum of ten pounds. At the time of his arrival Pembroke College, which had been founded in 1624, had a community of about sixty fellows and scholars. On beginning his tasks as a "servitor" in the college George soon found that the work in his mother's public house had prepared him well for his new tasks. His diligent and prompt attendance to the needs of his wealthier fellow students meant "that many who had it in their power chose me as their servitor". His income together with some "little presents made by my kind tutor" meant that he had only a small debt to repay at the time of his graduation.

Despite his brother's derisory remark that his recent habit of attending daily worship was just a phase George resisted the invitations of his fellow students "to go out amongst them". Indeed he strengthened his devotional life buying a copy of William Law's *Serious Call to a Devout Life*, through which "God worked powerfully on my soul".[16] He also began the practice of singing the psalms and praying three times a day, as well as receiving the sacrament at a parish church near the college.

The Holy Club

Twelve years before Whitefield entered the university John Wesley had studied at Christ Church. He had completed his Master of Arts degree and been elected a Fellow of Lincoln College, Oxford in 1726, being ordained deacon the following year. His younger brother Charles became a student at Christ Church in 1726, graduating with an MA in 1733 and being ordained in 1735. In the summer of 1729 the two brothers began meeting together with Robert Kirkham, William Morgan, Benjamin Ingham, and others to read pious works together. They met at set times for prayer and conversation in various college rooms and began the practice of visiting the poor and some of the prisoners in Oxford gaol. In 1732 John Wesley drew up a set of General Rules for self-examination, which other members of the group (later becoming known as the "Holy Club") began to use for themselves.

Having read William Law's *Serious Call*, Whitefield was anxious to progress in his Christian commitment when at Oxford. Once, in Pembroke College, he was keen to find out about the Holy Club and he sought them out for their company. Whitefield was particularly impressed when he chanced to see "the Methodists" as they were derisively called, go through a mocking crowd to receive Holy Communion at the University Church of St Mary the Virgin. He wrote that "his soul was a thirst for some spiritual friend to lift up my hands when they hung down, and to strengthen my feeble knees".[17]

Surprisingly it was more than twelve months before Whitefield at last had an opportunity to meet some of the Holy Club members. He sent a note to Charles Wesley concerning a poor woman in one of the workhouses who had made an unsuccessful attempt to cut her throat. In reply he received an invitation to come to breakfast the following morning. He later reflected, "I thankfully embraced the opportunity; and, blessed be God, it was one of the most profitable visits I ever made in my life."[18] Wesley loaned him Professor August Hermann Francke's *Treatise against the Fear of Man* and another book entitled *The Country Parson's Advice to His Parishioners*, a work "which was wonderfully blessed to my soul".[19] Francke's book instilled in Whitefield a strong courage which enabled him to withstand opposition and persecution for the rest of his days.[20] He noted in his manuscript diary for 8 March 1736, "Glad sweet communion in God in Frank's *Pietas Hallensis*. I hope God will enable me in some measure to follow that good man's steps."[21]

A short time later Charles put into Whitefield's hands Henry Scougal's book, *The Life of God in the Soul of Man*. Scougal had been a young and distinguished professor in the University of Aberdeen. From this volume which had first been published in 1677, Whitefield realized that what Scougal described as "falsely placed religion" precisely described his own experience of "going to church, doing hurt to no one, being constant in the duties of the closet [by which he meant private personal prayer], and now and then reaching out... to give alms to their poor neighbours". Mystified Whitefield remarked that "I never knew what true religion was, till God sent me that excellent treatise by the hands of my never-to-be-forgotten friend."[22]

As he took in Scougal's words his heart shuddered "like a poor man who is afraid to look into his ledger, lest he should find himself a bankrupt". He was pulled apart within and found himself debating whether to throw the book to one side or search further. He took the latter course and held the book in his hand and prayed out loud, "Lord, if I am not a Christian, for Jesus' sake show me what Christianity is, that I may not be damned at last." He read on a little further and found that those who knew anything about real Christianity know that it is "a vital reunion with the Son of God – Christ formed in the heart".[23] In that moment as he read those words "a ray of divine light was instantaneously darted in upon my soul, and from that moment, but not till then, did I know that I must be a new creature".[24] In the 1756 revised edition of his *A Short Account* Whitefield further reflected on this moment of his conversion and wrote:

> God was pleased… to enable me to lay hold on
> His dear Son by a living faith, and by giving me
> the Spirit of adoption, to seal me as I humbly hope,
> even to the day of everlasting redemption. But Oh!
> With what joy unspeakable – even joy that was full
> of, and big with glory, was my soul filled, when the
> weight of sin went off, and an abiding sense of the
> pardoning love of God, and full assurance of faith
> broke into my soul!… At first my joys were like a
> spring tide and, as it were, overflowed the banks;
> afterwards it became more settled – and blessed be
> God, saving a few casual intervals, has abode in
> my soul ever since.[25]

Whitefield always dated his conversion from this moment which seems to have taken place in 1735, about seven weeks after Easter. He referred to it as "a day to be had in everlasting remembrance". This was three years before John Wesley had a similar experience and "felt his heart strangely warmed" in the Moravian Chapel in Aldersgate Street in the city of London. It means that Whitefield was probably the first among the Holy Club to gain a deep experience of the "new birth". Some have wondered why it took such a length of time before the Wesleys came to share Whitefield's new-found joy for themselves. The most likely explanation was that they had left Oxford for the American colonies. Be that as it may Whitefield appears from this moment to have retained an almost physical sense of the presence of God. For him the reality of Christ was "like a Spring tide, overflowing at the banks". Twenty years on he wrote that this presence remained "and increased in my soul ever since".[26]

Following his conversion Whitefield's letters were dominated by the topic of the new birth. He wrote from Bristol on 12 June 1735 to a friend suggesting to him that "the sighs that he had experienced" on the previous Sunday were "infant strugglings after the new birth". He went on to say that "he would willingly undergo those pangs, so that you might enjoy the pleasures of the new birth".[27] In another letter penned to the same friend in the autumn of that year, Whitefield wrote, "Pray earnestly from your heart. Wrestle with God, beg him to hasten the new birth."[28]

Return to Gloucester and ordination

Whitefield spent nine terms up at Oxford working hard as a servitor, striving to live by the ideals of the Holy Club, and attending to his studies. At this time he strove to live by the strict disciplines suggested by Thomas à Kempis and William Law (1686–1761). In his journal he reflected,

> I always chose the worst sort of food. I fasted twice a week. My apparel was mean. I thought it unbecoming a penitent to have his hair powdered. I wore woollen gloves, a patched gown, and dirty shoes... I resolutely persisted in these voluntary acts of self-denial, because I found in them great promotion of the spiritual life.[29]

Having not taken a single vacation during this time he was now at the point of exhaustion. Indeed, he later wrote of "my sickness" and "the dangers to which I was exposed" and recalled that his tutor had urged him to go away into the country. In consequence, and possibly because, like many others before and after him he was lacking in money, Whitefield decided to make for Gloucester and home. He was away from the college from the end of May 1735 until March 1736. On arrival in Gloucester he found his mother needing to retire from work and his brother John, now the manager of the Bell Inn, having suffered "a variety of misfortunes". In a letter dated 11 June, Whitefield remarked, "I hope I can get him to use prayer, he will soon grow better."

On the positive side Whitefield found the friends beyond his family circle in an altogether better frame. A number of them started to pay him visits including three clergymen from Gloucester and a minister from the neighbouring town of Stonehouse and together they were able to form a small religious society. Whitefield began to devote as much time as he possibly could to the study of the Scriptures. He reflected in the later edition of his autobiography, "I got more true knowledge from reading the book of God in one month, than I could *ever* have acquired from *all* the writings of men."[30]

The time spent back in Gloucester proved to be one of spiritual and physical renewal. As he adopted the habit of claiming the promises of God in prayer, friends – even some whom he had thought were his enemies – provided for his material needs. His older brother, returning from the sea, gave him four guineas and some other necessities. Whitefield wrote of these months with positive delight.

> Oh, what sweet communion had I daily vouchsafed with God in prayer after my coming again to Gloucester! How often have I been carried out beyond myself when meditating in the fields! How assuredly have I felt that Christ dwelt in me and I in Him! and how did I daily walk in the comforts of the Holy Ghost, and was edified and refreshed in the multitude of peace![31]

As the days went by the young Whitefield found that his strength was renewed. He started to visit one or two other societies besides his own in Gloucester. He endeavoured to visit a few sick people each day and built up a small store of resources to give to the poor. Having been obedient to the Lord's command and visited the prisoners in Oxford gaol with members of the Holy Club, Whitefield started to spend time with the prisoners in Gloucester. He gained leave from the keeper to read to them and collected money for them. It was also during this period of time in his life that he came to understand Luther's doctrine that individuals are justified and made right with God by an active faith alone in Jesus. "This", he wrote, "is the good old doctrine of the Church of England." It was, he observed, what the martyrs of Queen Mary's reign sealed with their blood.[32]

This return to his home city saw Whitefield's faith in Christ enlivened and his zeal and resolve to serve God's kingdom grew stronger. It was also a period in which he "received fresh supplies to defray my expenses at the University".[33] Finally, at the end of nine months, he returned to Oxford wondering whether he was being called by God to be ordained as minister in the Church of England. He was not thoroughly convinced it was God's will, until he unexpectedly and providentially became acquainted with the Bishop of Gloucester.

Ordination in Gloucester Cathedral

The circumstances of Whitefield's chance meeting with Bishop Martin Benson and the unusual events surrounding his ordination were nothing short of remarkable, indeed providential. In an era when bishops were selected largely on account of their political views Benson stood out as a truly conscientious prelate. He was an able scholar and had been a tutor at Christ Church, Oxford. He became a royal chaplain to the Prince of Wales in 1726, a position which opened doors into the Court society where he met and became friends with John Perceval, 1st Earl of Egremont. Benson was first offered the See of Gloucester in 1734 but declined it on the grounds that he wished to live a quiet life. However the position was pressed on him a second time and he accepted and was consecrated in 1735.

Benson was a single man who was devoted to his diocese and became known for his deep pastoral concern. He was generous and remarkably hospitable. Bishop Porteous of London recalled "his strict behaviour, purity of living and his warm and outgoing nature".[34] In an age when many bishops were somewhat careless as to whom they ordained Benson was particularly thorough with his candidates. He took especial care to scrutinize their morals, learning, and age. This made it all the more remarkable that he should have consented to ordain Whitefield when he was two years below the accepted canonical age.

The manner of Whitefield's first encounter with Benson was as follows. It began with him having a dream one night in which he was talking with the bishop who then gave him some gold. This dream came into Whitefield's mind on a number of subsequent occasions and whenever he saw the bishop in church he had a strong feeling that they would meet very shortly. One afternoon the bishop walked out on his own to visit Lady Selwyn who lived close to the city. She herself had in fact partially fulfilled Whitefield's dream having given him a piece of gold. What he did not know was that she had also commended him strongly to the bishop. Shortly after this Whitefield was coming out of the cathedral at the close of a service when one of the vergers called after him and informed him that the bishop wished to speak with him. He immediately went to the palace and was greeted at the top of the stairs by the bishop who expressed his pleasure at meeting him. Whitefield later recalled their meeting in these lines.

> At his coming into the room, the bishop told me he had heard of my character, liked my behaviour in church, and enquiring my age, said, "Notwithstanding I have declared I would not ordain any one under three and twenty, yet I shall think it my duty to ordain you whenever you come for holy orders."[35]

Benson then made Whitefield a present of five guineas to buy a book, which immediately reminded him of his dream in which the bishop put gold into his hand. The only immediate concern which was now left in Whitefield's mind was where he should serve after his ordination. His friends in Oxford pressed hard that he should continue at the university. This course of action was confirmed when Sir John Philips, a great supporter of the Oxford Methodists, offered to make him an allowance of £30 a year to return. With John Wesley away in America it was clear that Whitefield would be able to bring valuable encouragement to the members of the Holy Club.

Whitefield therefore made up his mind to follow this course of action and set about studying the Church of England's Thirty-nine Articles in the light of Scripture. He also examined himself against the qualifications required of ministers in Paul's letter to Timothy.

Some two weeks before Trinity Sunday 1736, the day set for his ordination, Whitefield set out for Gloucester in order to ready himself for the occasion. He had intended to use the time preparing one or two sermons but found himself without energy or the inclination to compose anything at all. He shared the matter with a local clergyman who prayed for him and told him that he was an "enthusiast". Shortly after this rebuff Whitefield came across a quotation from the book of Ezekiel where the prophet, having been given a divine commission, was told, "You shall be dumb; but when

I speak to you, then you shall speak."[36] This put the young candidate for holy orders at rest and he spent time reading the prophets and apostles and praying that God would give him the strength to follow in their footsteps. Although he wrote in his diary for 16 June 1736, "I fear I have not taken pains enough in my preparation for orders"[37], the situation turned out well enough.

About three days before the day of the ordination Bishop Benson came to Whitefield's residence and the following evening Whitefield sent him his answers to two questions: "Do you think that you are inwardly moved by the Holy Ghost to take upon you this office and administration? And, are you called according to the will of our Lord Jesus Christ, and the laws of this land?" When they met the next morning the bishop, who was well satisfied with Whitefield's answers, graciously received him and expressed his pleasure at the allowance that Sir John Philips had given him. Bishop Benson had set aside two small parishes for Whitefield but nevertheless expressed his satisfaction at the provision that had been made for him at Oxford.

On Sunday 20 June Whitefield went to the cathedral early in the morning. He related that

> When I went up to the altar, I could think of
> nothing but Samuel standing a little child before
> the Lord with a linen Ephod. When the bishop
> laid his hands upon my head, my heart melted
> down, and I offered up my whole spirit, soul, and
> body to the service of God's sanctuary.[38]

Following this, on the bishop's instruction, Whitefield "read the Gospel with power" and then received Holy Communion. In a letter to a "dear friend" a "Mr S", he wrote,

> Let come what will – life or death – I shall
> henceforward live like one who this day, in the
> presence of men and angels, took the holy sacrament
> upon profession of being inwardly moved by
> the Holy Ghost to take that ministration in the
> Church... I have thrown myself blindfold, and I
> trust without reserve, into his almighty hands.[39]

Whitefield was not able to preach in the afternoon following his ordination but instead read prayers to the poor parishioners. He recorded in his *Short Account* that he had been restrained from giving a sermon by reading that verse from Ezekiel where God informed the young prophet he would remain dumb until God spoke to him.[40] The following Sunday, however, he recorded, "I preached to a very crowded audience, with as much freedom as though I had been a preacher for some years." The subject of his sermon, he related in a letter to a friend, a "Mr H", was "The Necessity and Benefits of Religious Society". Many of those who thronged St Mary-de-Crypt had no doubt come out of curiosity to see what this young preacher whom they had known since his childhood days had to say. Whitefield observed that he "was able to preach with some degree of Gospel authority. A few mocked, but most seemed struck." At the end of his letter he noted that "I have since heard that a complaint had been made to the bishop that I drove fifteen people mad with my first sermon."[41] Benson had apparently replied that he hoped they would not recover before next Sunday and so be spared a further homily. The truth of the matter was probably, as one who heard him speak observed, "he had preached like a lion". Even at this very early stage Whitefield's experience of acting in plays during his school days was coming to the surface. He was comfortable with words and spoke with confidence and composure.

Back to Oxford

Whitefield returned to Oxford on 30 June whereupon he was warmly welcomed by his friends. He worked a last few days as a servitor and then took his degree of Bachelor of Arts. He was disappointed to find that the enthusiasm of the Holy Club had somewhat dwindled during the time of his absence. He was however more than ready to encourage them and rekindle their faith. As before, aside from his studies, Whitefield gave time to visiting and caring for the prisoners in the city's gaol. He also went to London on 4 August for two months where he visited the soldiers each day and took the services at the Tower of London Chapel while his friend and curate, James Hervey, took a brief period away. Never one to lose opportunities for serving, Whitefield also preached in Bishopsgate Church, led prayers every evening at Wapping Chapel and preached in Ludgate Prison every Tuesday. His sermons at the Tower were crowded with numbers of his friends coming from "diverse parts of London".[42]

He was also able to visit Sir John Philips whose generous financial provision had enabled him to return to Oxford.[43] Just six weeks after returning from London an invitation came to him to take responsibility for the parish of Dummer in Hampshire for six weeks while his friend Charles Kinchin took some leave. Here he divided each day into three parts – "eight hours for study and retirement, eight hours for sleep and meals, and eight hours for reading and prayers, catechising, and visiting the parish".[44] He recalled, "The profit I reaped from these exercises, and conversing with the poor country people, was unspeakable. I frequently learnt as much by an afternoon's visit as in a week's study."[45]

Sights on Georgia

Although he was fully occupied in Oxford with his studies, prison visiting, and encouraging the Methodists Whitefield was unable to keep his mind away from focusing on the activities of John and Charles Wesley out in Georgia, America. After he had been back in Oxford for only about a month he received letters from both brothers and from their colleague, Benjamin Ingham, informing him of the need for labourers in the colony. Whitefield, however, loved the university life and was happy with his lot. Added to this, his friends persuaded him that he was needed in Oxford and that he had no definite call to venture abroad. In reply to a letter from John Wesley, Whitefield wrote that "providence had led him to continue in Oxford and superintend the affairs of the Methodists". He nevertheless recorded in his journal about the middle of November, "The thoughts of going to Georgia still crowded continually in upon me, and at length Providence seemed to point my way thither." Finally he was deeply stirred when, in December 1736, he received a further letter from John Wesley which included the following lines, cutting him to the quick, "Only Mr Delamotte is with me, till God shall stir up the hearts of some of his servants, who, putting their lives in His hands, shall come over and help us, where the harvest is great, and the labourers are so few. What if thou art the man, Mr Whitefield?"[46]

And so it proved. Whitefield finally made the decision to board the ship to America with James Oglethorpe, a British general and founder of the colony of Georgia. On his way to the port of London, he called in on the Bishop of Gloucester and reported that "His lordship received me, as he always did. Like a father, he approved of my design, wished me success, and said, he did not doubt but God would bless me, and that I should do much good."[47]

As things turned out several events delayed Oglethorpe's return to America from May 1737 until the December of that year. Understandably Whitefield immediately seized the opportunity of delaying the trip to travel and make visits to Bristol, Bath, and Stonehouse. At Bristol he preached with powerful effect on Justification and the doctrine of new birth each weekday and twice on Sundays. His time at Stonehouse was, he recalled, marked by "un-common manifestations" with some of his hearers under such conviction that they were too afraid to leave the meetings and go to their homes. Whitefield wrote in his journal that "at times I was so overpowered with a sense of God's Infinite Majesty, that I would be constrained to throw myself on the ground, and offer my soul as a blank in His hands, to write on it what He pleased."[48]

From August onwards Whitefield resolved to devote his energies to London where he was able to keep in close touch with Oglethorpe's movements. During these three months he commonly preached four times on a Sunday, often "to very large and very affected auditories" and sometimes walked as much as twelve miles backward and forward between churches. He later commented in his journal, "On Sunday mornings, long before day, you might see streets filled with people going to church with their lanterns in their hands, and hear them conversing about the things of God." During the weekdays Whitefield generally preached nine times a week and on a number of occasions assisted in the administration of the Lord's Supper.[49] He recalled "that so many came that sometimes we were obliged to consecrate fresh elements two or three times; and the stewards found it somewhat difficult to carry the offerings to the communion table".[50] This was a period when his devotional life greatly increased. On one occasion he and his fellow Methodists "spent a whole night in prayer and praise; and many a time, at midnight and one in the morning", after he had been "wearied almost to death" with "preaching, writing, and conversation, and going from place to place, God imparted new life and enabled [him] to intercede for an hour-and-a-half and two hours together".[51]

Whitefield wrote that the tide of popularity ran very high and that eventually he was compelled to travel between churches in a coach to avoid being crushed by the crowds. However, not all spoke well of him and some of the clergy complained about him to the Bishop of London. Their hostility apparently stemmed partly from his freely associating with Baptist and Congregationalist dissenters. Whitefield waited on his lordship, who was happy to endorse both his doctrine and teaching.

Finally Whitefield received notice that the soldiers and their families were ready to embark ship for Georgia and he resolved to go with them, despite the fact that Oglethorpe was still detained. Whitefield left London on board the *Whitaker* on 28 December. During the period of waiting he had preached in a good number of the City of London's churches, collecting about £1,000 for the charity schools, and receiving about £300 for the poor of Georgia. He had also raised a sufficient sum of money to provide for his own needs as a result of printing his sermon On the Nature and Necessity of Our Regeneration or New Birth in Jesus Christ.

On that winter day, it took a little while before the vessel cleared the Kent coast and took to the open seas, but clearly a new chapter in his life had begun.[52]

Providentially these early years from his youth to the time of his ordination and first departure to Georgia had given him a solid grounding for what was to follow in his life and ministry. The tough environment of living and working in the Bell Inn and his mother's desperate and caring struggles to bring him up first alone and then in a dysfunctional second marriage, made him aware of the harsh realities in many homes. His domestic service, first in the family hostelry and then as an undergraduate servitor in Oxford instilled in him the virtues of humility, practical care, and service. His early attempts at acting had enabled him to realize his natural gifts of speech and oratory. His studies at Pembroke shaped his mind and gave him a deep knowledge of the Bible and of Protestant and biblical theology. Most important of all, his experience of the new birth and his ordination had given him a deep sense of the divine presence in his life: he felt the seal of God's approval.

Chapter 1 notes

1   *A History of the County of Gloucester* (London, Victoria County History, 1988), pp. 101–12.
2   *Gloucester Journal*, 13 May 1729.
3   J. Gillies, *Memoirs of the Life of the Reverend George Whitefield* (London, Edward and Charles Dilly, 1772) pp. 1–2.
4   Whitefield, *A Short Account of God's Dealings With the Reverend Mr. George Whitefield* (London, The Banner of Truth Trust, 1965), p. 35.
5   Ibid, p. 37.
6   Ibid.
7   Ibid.
8   Ibid, p. 39.
9   Ibid, p. 40. See also Sir J. Stephen, *Essays in Ecclesiastical Biography* (London, Longmans, Green, Reader and Dyer, 1872), p. 381.
10 Whitefield, *A Short Account*, p. 39.
11 Ibid, p. 41.
12 Ibid, p. 42.
13 Ibid.
14 Ibid, p. 43.
15 T. S. Kidd, *George Whitefield* (Yale, University Press, 2014) pp. 15–16.
16 Whitefield, *A Short Account*, p. 45.
17 Ibid.
18 Ibid, p. 46.
19 Ibid.
20 D. B. Hindmarsh, *The Spirit of Early Evangelicalism* (Oxford, University Press, 2018) pp. 21–22.
21 Whitefield, *Manuscript Diary*, British Library, ADD MS 34068, p. 13.
22 R. Philip, *Life and Times*, p. 17; L. Tyerman, op. cit., Vol. 1, p. 27; Whitefield, Sermon *All Men's Place* in *Sermons on Important Subjects by the Revd George Whitefield* (London, Baynes, 1825), p. 702.
23 R. Philip, op. cit., p. 17.
24 Ibid.
25 G. Whitefield, *A Short Account*, Vol. 1, p, 25.
26 L. Tyerman, op. cit., Vol.1, p. 25.
27 Whitefield, *Letters to a Friend*, 12 June 1735.

28 *Journal*, 2 April 1736.
29 Ibid, June 1734, p. 53.
30 Ibid, 1735, p. 60.
31 Whitefield, *A Short Account*, 1756 edition in Tyerman, op. cit., Vol. 1, p. 37.
32 L. Tyerman, op. cit., Vol. 1, pp. 37–38.
33 Whitefield, *A Short Account*, Section 3, p. 64.
34 I. S. L. Ollard, G. Crosse, and M. F. Bond, *A Dictionary of English Church History* (London, A. R. Mowbray & Co, 1948) p. 251.
35 Whitefield, *A Short Account*, Section 4, p. 66; L. Tyerman, op. cit., Vol. 1, p. 42.
36 Ezekiel 24:27, cited in L. Tyerman, op. cit., Vol. 1, p. 43.
37 Whitefield, *Manuscript Diary*, 16 June 1736.
38 Ibid, p. 41. See also *Journal*, 1736, p. 69.
39 *Letter to Mr S*, 20 June 1736.
40 Whitefield, *A Short Account*, Section 4, p. 69.
41 *Letter to Mr H*, 30 June 1736; S. Drew, *A Memoir of the Rev George Whitefield* (London, Thomas Tegg, 1833) p. v.
42 *Journal*, 8 August, 1736.
43 *Letter to My Dear Friend*, 2 April 1736.
44 *Journal*, 1736, p. 79.
45 Ibid.
46 Ibid.
47 Ibid, 1 January, 1737, p. 80.
48 Ibid, p. 83.
49 Ibid, p. 88.
50 Ibid, p. 87.
51 Whitefield, *A Further Account*, p. 41.
52 *Journal*, 28 December 1737, p. 92.

Chapter 2

Georgia Missionary

The journey from London to Georgia progressed slowly for Whitefield and his four friends. It was some weeks before favourable winds finally enabled them to leave the small town of Deal and take to the open seas. During the delay Whitefield the ever-ready evangelist was able to preach to the people of the town who heard him gladly.[1]

The *Whitaker* finally departed on 2 February 1738. The young clergyman and his companions took with them a substantial cargo consisting of both spiritual resources and many very practical items for everyday living. Among the many books Whitefield had purchased were the aforementioned William Law's *A Serious Call to a Devout and Holy Life* and Thomas Broughton's *The Christian Soldier*, 150 Common Prayer books, 25 copies of Isaac Watts' *Divine Songs*, 200 copies of *The Country Parson's Advice to his Parishioners*, and 50 spelling books. There were also educational resources such as four reams of foolscap writing paper, 3,000 second quills, and a variety of pencils. On the practical side there were clothes for the poor that included twenty-six pairs of canvas breaches, twenty-four striped waistcoats, and six dozen women's caps. There were also many items of ironmongery, tools, and a large supply of food and provisions. The latter included eleven pounds of beef for the poor, two barrels of flour, three barrels of raisins, and quantities of oatmeal, oranges, potatoes, and other vegetables.

By a seemingly strange chance, while the *Whitaker* remained at anchor in the port at Deal, a disillusioned John Wesley landed on his return from the colony. Still hurt by bad experiences and opposition to his ministry, and upon hearing that Whitefield had not yet departed, he immediately wrote to him advising him to abandon his mission. Whitefield however was in no mood to change his course at this late stage and replied in a letter written onboard ship. He was adamant that he could not think of turning back "because the enemies of the Lord will so blaspheme that holy name wherever I am called". Nor could he "leave the flock now committed to his care on board" and furthermore he could see no cause for not going forwards to Georgia.[2]

The voyage

The ship was full of soldiers and there were near twenty women on board. Whitefield wrote that there was much cursing and blasphemy. However, he was patient and prudent in his attitude and began by gently reproving some of the officers. Little by little the situation began to improve. He was further encouraged when the military captain invited him to a dish of coffee. Sometime later the ship's captain met him on deck and desired that "they might have public service and expounding twice a-day in the great cabin".[3]

The ship reached Gibraltar after about two weeks, where a Major Sinclair generously, and unprovoked, offered a lodging for Whitefield; it turned out to be a stay of several weeks. The governor of Gibraltar, General Joseph Sabine (1661–1739), welcomed Whitefield to dine with him every day of the week if he so desired. It was an invitation that Whitefield frequently accepted noting that his table was "sumptuous" but that his "guests, officers and others, indulged in no excesses".[4] General Sabine and General Colombine and others were generous in their welcome and gave him invitations to preach two or three times a week. Whitefield noted in his journal for 26 February, "Preached in the morning at Gibraltar, before such a congregation of officers and soldiers as I never before saw. The church though very large was quite thronged; and God was pleased to show me that He had given extraordinary success to my sermon."[5] On the night of 2 March there were "above three hundred present" including "officers and honourable women not a few". Whitefield made other encouraging notes in subsequent entries in his journal. For 3 March he wrote, "About ten, I preached my sermon against swearing... many officers and soldiers wept sorely." On 5 March "Went to the church belonging to the garrison; preached to a most thronged audience, and received (what my soul longed after) the sacrament of Christ's most blessed body and blood. Both Generals were there, and near fifty communicants." Whitefield was given free use of the garrison church and he, together with his friend and colleague, James Habersham, met three times a day to pray, read, and sing psalms. Tyerman comments, "Like his Divine Redeemer, he 'increased in favour with God and man'. The following day his congregation reached above five hundred."[6]

Whitefield's time in Gibraltar was also significant for one particular reason. After preaching at the morning service on his last Sunday there, he "went and saw the Roman Catholics at their high Mass" and concluded that no other argument against Popery was needed than "to see the pageantry, superstition, and idolatry of their worship".[7] The experience cemented in Whitefield's mind what became a lifelong commitment to the teaching and doctrines of the great Protestant Reformers Cranmer, Ridley, and Latimer.

Also about this time extracts of Whitefield's journal began to appear in print. This was eventually to become a major aspect and vehicle of his outreach. He was one of the very first evangelists to make use of printed media to stimulate interest in his success and ministry. Whitefield had begun to send journal extracts of his travels and successful preaching to his friend the publisher James Hutton in London. By a stroke of misfortune a rival publisher, Thomas Cooper, managed to get hold of an early draft by devious means and published it in August 1738. Hutton, however, was not to be outdone and soon printed his own more detailed and official version which went through three editions by the end of the year. The circulation of large numbers of copies of his journals proved to be a powerful means of proclaiming the gospel alongside Whitefield's preaching.[8]

On course for America

Finally on Thursday 7 March the *Whitaker* set sail from Gibraltar for Savannah. The previous day numbers of the local inhabitants who had been touched by Whitefield's care and compassion for the needy and moved by his preaching had come with "tokens of their love such as cake, figs, wine, eggs and other necessaries for my voyage, and seemed to want to express their affection".[9] He added, "May the good Lord note their kindness in His book, and reward them a thousand-fold!"

Whitefield recorded, "At first the wind was fair, but afterwards blew contrary, which made both me and many others sick."[10] On 9 March he noted in his journal "the contrary wind still continuing, my sea-sickness is increased". In consequence he was obliged to omit reading prayers to the soldiers. The following day he added, "My bodily indisposition still increased: there was a great storm without, but blessed be God, a calm within."[11]

Once sufficiently recovered the young cleric was able to fulfil the role of ship's chaplain with regular services and Bible exposition. From time to time he went on board the *Lightfoot* and the *Amy*, two accompanying sister ships, and dined with their officers giving them Bibles and Testaments. On board both of these two vessels, on both Saturday 18 March and Sunday 19 March, Whitefield preached on the subject of drunkenness which he based on the text of Ephesians 5:18: "Don't get drunk with wine but be filled with the Spirit." He observed that "above two hundred men" listened to him read prayers and speak on the *Amy.* He then married a couple and found it necessary to rebuke the bridegroom on more than one occasion during the ceremony for laughing. In consequence the groom began to weep and Whitefield gave him and the bride a Bible and exhorted them to holiness of life.[12]

These hard-hitting sermons brought about a change in the habits of both the men and officers. Captain Mackay ordered a drum to be beaten each morning and evening and he himself joined with the soldiers and crew in public worship and listened to Whitefield's preaching. Indeed on one occasion after the sermon Mackay informed the soldiers that to his shame he had been a notorious swearer but now left it off prompted by Whitefield. He wished them all to follow his example. Gillies recorded that some of the women cried out, "What a change in our captain."[13] It was a change that had a positive impact on the men and enabled Whitefield to offer them Bibles and other religious books which had been given to him to disperse by the Society for Promoting Christian Knowledge in exchange for their bad books and packs of cards which he threw overboard.

This was the first of thirteen Atlantic crossings which Whitefield would eventually undertake and it proved to be perilous. From time to time Whitefield wrote of the might of the storms at sea and his voyages certainly reveal him to have been a man of courage and faith. For a lengthy period during this first voyage a fever took hold of all those on board "except three or four". Gillies wrote that "For many days and nights, he visited betwixt twenty and thirty sick persons, crawling between the decks upon his knees, administering medicines or cordials to them, and such advice as seemed suitable to their circumstances."[14] Just at the point when the voyage was nearly at an end Whitefield was himself struck with the fever. By the time the vessel reached American shores he was seriously ill and covered in blisters. He had been bled three times and dosed with an emetic. He finally reached Savannah on Sunday 7 May, more than four months after his departure from London. The day before his arrival he wrote the following to a friend:

> God has been pleased graciously to visit me with a violent fever, which he notwithstanding so sweetened by divine consolations, that I was enabled to rejoice and sing in the midst of it. I had indeed violent conflicts with the powers of darkness who did all they could to disturb and distract me; but Jesus Christ prayed for me... For a while Satan as it were had dominion over me, yet God suffered not my faith to fail; but came to my aid, rebuked the tempter, and from that moment I grew better. Surely God is preparing me for something extraordinary.[15]

Always alert to a chance to proclaim the Christian gospel, Whitefield, weak though he was, felt compelled to preach one last sermon to those he had been at sea with during the previous four months. So before disembarking, while the vessel was anchored at the mouth of the Savannah river, the young clergyman addressed the entire ship's company, first in general and then more specifically the soldiers and their wives. He began by expressing his deepest concern lest any of them to whom he had preached the gospel during their voyage "should ever have to suffer the vengeance of eternal fire". He expressed his gratitude that swearing was "in great measure abated" and that they were "all now married", a reference to those who had made their vows on board ship. He begged them to lead chaste lives and to bring up their children "in the nurture and admonition of the Lord". Turning to the soldiers in particular he prayed that God would "set his seal on their hearts" and that the good work that was begun in them would be carried on till the day of our Lord Jesus Christ.[16] So it was to prove! Whitefield had set foot on the land where he was destined to be one of the greatest spiritual influences of all time.

Georgia and Savannah

At the time of Whitefield's arrival the colony of Georgia was a mere six years old. It had been founded by James Oglethope (1696–1785), a philanthropic member of the British parliament. The first English settlers who had arrived in February 1733 consisted of a small group of 120 men and women and included a number of released debtors and small traders. Oglethorpe served as the first governor of the colony from 1732–43. The following year Oglethorpe and the trustees had invited a group of Salzburgers[17] to join them. A number of Scottish Highlanders also settled at an early point and founded New Inverness in Darien. They were to prove of great assistance to Oglethorpe in the struggles against the neighbouring Spanish colony of Florida. There were also two groups of Moravians, one of which had sailed out with John Wesley.

As soon as Whitefield set foot in the colony he made straight for Savannah where he had been given the living of the parish. There he was able to meet with Charles Delamotte whom Wesley had "providentially" left behind as schoolmaster. Weak as Whitefield was he "joined in prayer and a psalm of thanksgiving" and spent the rest of the evening in "sweet counsel".[18]

John Wesley, who had preceded him as parish priest, had been embittered by all kinds of vexations, some of which were of his own making and insistence on high church discipline. Despite Wesley's disparaging and discouraging words Whitefield found that "America is not such a horrid place as it is represented to be". He reported that "the country, mornings and evenings, is exceedingly pleasant, and there are uncommon improvements made (considering the indifference of the soil) in diverse places". He continued, "With a little the country people could do very well."[19]

Whitefield settled in the parsonage house which he found to be much better than he had expected. Here "some serious persons, the fruits of Mr Wesley's ministry were among the first who came to see him".[20] The day following he read prayers, expounded the Scriptures in the courthouse, and waited upon the magistrates. He was then confined to his new-found home for more than a week as his fever and ague returned.

Once recovered he was soon able to take in his new-found environment. He gave a lengthy account of his first impressions noting that "the people were denied the use both of rum and slaves" and that "the lands were allotted them, according to a particular plan, whether good or bad; and female heirs prohibited from inheriting". The harsh environment inevitably meant a shortness of life and children being left without parents. This paved the way for what had long been, in Whitefield's mind, a project to build an orphanage. The idea had first been proposed to him by Charles Wesley who, along with General Oglethorpe, had earlier put together an outline scheme.[21] He wrote to a Mr H, "What I have most at heart is the building of an orphan house, which I trust will be effected when I return to England."[22] The orphan house was to become a constant focus throughout the rest of his life and ministry. It took up considerable amounts of his time and emotional energy as he supervised planning and developments, the appointment and payment of staff, and was constantly begging for money and resources. In this life-long project, which ultimately ended in failure, Whitefield derived inspiration by his reading of August Hermann Francke's *Pietas Hallensis* (1705) which he had read during his time in Oxford. He was also much inspired by the orphanage which Francke had established at Halle in Germany.

Despite the opposition which Wesley had previously stirred, Whitefield found "the people receive me gladly into their homes, and seem most kindly affected towards me".[23] He enjoyed the company of those with whom he shared the parsonage and found the food supply basic and sufficient. He began visiting from house to house and held catechism classes for both young and old. He read prayers twice and expounded the two Second Lessons every day. He also read to a house full of people each week. On Sundays he expounded two lessons at five in the morning and at seven in the evening.

After his week's confinement following the return of his fever Whitefield had gained sufficient strength to go with Delamotte to visit the Native American Indian chief, Tomochichi. The entry in his journal reads, "Having by the blessing of God gotten a little strength, I went to see Tomochichi, who, I heard was near expiring at a neighbour's house."[24] He found the aging warrior lying on a blanket, frail "and little else but skin and bones". Since there was no one who could speak English Whitefield could do no more than shake his hands and leave. However, he returned the following Sunday on hearing that his nephew, Tooanoowee, who could speak English, was there. He asked the nephew to inquire if his uncle thought he was dying. The old man could not tell, whereupon Whitefield asked where he thought he would go after death. Tomochichi, "to heaven". Whitefield noted in his journal entry, "But alas, how can a drunkard enter there!" When asked further if he believed in hell, Whitefield pointing to the fire, the old man replied, "No." It left the young clergyman reflecting that "God is true and just and that as surely as the good shall go into everlasting happiness, so the wicked shall go into everlasting punishment."[25] Philip's comment on this encounter is surely right. "It is," he wrote, "highly unlikely that the man who had just been teaching soldiers and sailors the way to heaven, would have thus abruptly shut the door on a dying Indian!"[26] He warned the chief's young nephew to woo his uncle to faith.

Despite the fact there appears to have been no dramatic late conversion Whitefield's visit was important since Tomochichi and his Indians had extended friendship to Oglethorpe when he had arrived with the first group of settlers to establish the new colony. Oglethorpe had in fact found there were considerable Indian settlements or Cantons between the coast and the Allegheny Mountains. Tomochichi had his headquarters at Yamacraw, a settlement close to Savannah. Oglethorpe persuaded him to organize a conference which was attended by about fifty Indian chiefs and warriors. He explained that the English had not come to dispossess or trouble them but wanted only to live in harmony and friendship. So it proved and the happy and cordial relationship with Tomochichi came to be lifelong. In fact, when Oglethorpe had returned to England in 1734, Tomo and his wife and nephew, together with a number of Indian chiefs, had gone with him. They were given comfortable quarters at the Georgia Office in London and were impressed by the nation's power and dignity. On one occasion they were conveyed in three royal carriages to Kensington Palace and presented to George II and Queen Caroline. They were also introduced to the Prince of Wales, the Duke of Cumberland, and the princesses. During their stay they were entertained at Oglethorpe's country residence and visited all the great places in and around the capital, including Windsor Castle, St George's Chapel, and the Tower of London.

After a stay of four months they were taken in royal carriages to Gravesend and took ship to Georgia where, with a company of Salzburgers, they arrived safely. When in February 1736 Tomochichi and his nephew and heir heard that Wesley and a new group of settlers had arrived, they came to welcome them. The great chief finally died in 1739, just short of his hundredth birthday. His body was brought to Savannah where it was received by the people and magistrates. The interment took place with full military honours. Tomochichi was succeeded by his nephew Tooanoowee who remained a faithful and firm friend of the British.[27]

Even a few months' worth of entries in Whitefield's journal gives an insight into the varied aspects of his pastoral work. On 24 May he went to the nearby village of Thunderbolt which was pleasantly situated near the river, and visited just three families consisting of four men, two women, and ten servants. He was kindly received and expounded a chapter of the Scriptures and read a few collects. On Friday 2 June he parted company with his "dear friend Delamotte" who embarked for England about six o'clock in the evening. On Monday 5 June he invited a parishioner to breakfast and endeavoured to persuade him that it was not sufficient to believe in the doctrine of annihilation and that Scripture and the Creed were both clear concerning the eternity of hell. This was a doctrine which Evangelicals, and indeed high churchmen, held to with great firmness. They drew the parallel between an eternal life and an eternal hell, the same Greek word being used in both cases.[28]

On Saturday 10 June Whitefield placed one of his helpers in the village of Highgate to teach the children of the village and the neighbouring community English. On 12 June he opened a small school for girls in Savannah at which a recent settler was pleased to take on the role of teacher. On 22 June he suffered from a short but violent bout of sickness but was sufficiently well to lead prayers and preach with great power to local Freemasons. After the service he dined with them and commented, "May God make them servants of Christ and then and not till then will they be free indeed."[29] Whitefield seems to have been active in the parish until the second week in July when he paid a visit to the Salzburgers at Ebenezer and was "wonderfully pleased at their order and industry". He was particularly delighted by their orphan house, which had seventeen children and a widow who cared for them. He gave them some provisions from his poor store.[30]

On Tuesday 8 August Whitefield went by ship to Frederica, a small town about a hundred miles to the south of Savannah. The following day he began visiting from house to house and found the people "desirous of being fed with the sincere milk of the Word, and solicitous of my continuous presence among them". Evening prayers were held in the house which Mr Horton had hired for his use during the time of his stay. Whitefield was pleased to discover that timber was already being sawn ready for the construction of "a commodious place of worship".[31] Alongside these excursions to the surrounding towns and villages the work in Savannah was a continuing encouragement. Whitefield revealed himself to be a conscientious pastor. He described his Sundays as follows.

> I publicly expound the Second Lesson for Morning or Evening service as I see most suited to the people's edification; At ten I preach and read prayers; at three in the afternoon I do the same; and at seven expound part of the Church Catechism, at which numbers are usually present. I visit from house to house, read public prayers, and expound twice, and catechise (unless something

extraordinary happens), visit the sick every day, and read to as many of my parishioners as will come thrice a week.[32]

Whitefield blessed God that "they heard the word gladly and everywhere receive me with the utmost civility, and are not angry when I reprove them".[33] On Wednesday 16 August he noted in his journal that at evening prayers in Savannah "a very large congregation was present", and he "thanked them for their recent tokens of sincere affection".[34]

During this period of Whitefield's first visit to the colony, William Stephens, who was secretary of the trustees of Georgia, resided in Savannah. In later years he published in two volumes *A Journal of the Proceedings in Georgia*. In it he recounted among many other aspects the way in which the local people soon warmly accepted Whitefield's ministrations. On 21 May 1738 he noted, "Mr Whitefield officiated this day at the church, and made a sermon very engaging to the most thronged congregation I have ever seen". A week later he added a similarly fulsome comment, "Mr Whitefield manifests great ability in the ministry, and his sermons today were very moving." Whitefield soon endeared himself to the inhabitants of Savannah. In contrast to John Wesley, he was always affable and outgoing and much less formal in his churchmanship. Stephens recorded that on 18 June a child was brought to the church for baptism and that Whitefield performed the office by "sprinkling". This proved to be a source of great contentment to the people who had taken a great dislike to Wesley's rigid insistence on "dipping" infants. In consequence some parents had refused the sacrament. Later in July Stephens again observed that Whitefield was increasingly gaining the affections of the people on account of his "open and easy deportment without any show of austerity" in the performance of the Church of England services.[35]

Stephens described Whitefield as an affable, warm, and gifted preacher. He also noted that his residence in Georgia showed him to be adept in social skills and building communities. Not only did he work hard to serve the people of Savannah he also visited virtually all the large towns and many of the villages in the new colony. He had a discerning ability to assess the poor economic condition of the land and the environment. He had an eye for good business transactions and an ability to raise large sums of money for the settlers. He showed skill in organizing almost anything from supplies to his orphanage to teams of people to serve in it or in the other public concerns. Even at this early stage his ability to set up schools revealed his concern that children should be trained in Christian values and brought up in the fear and nurture of the Lord. He was a man of vision, determination, and courage.

Return to England

Just as Whitefield appeared to have become really settled and was finding favour and acceptance with the people of Savannah and the colony the entry in his journal for Sunday 27 August comes almost like a bolt out of the blue. "God having now shewn me and my friends that it was His will I should return for a while to England, this afternoon I preached my farewell sermon, to the great grief of my parishioners; for their hearts, I found, were very full as mine." Perhaps the only consolation in all of this was that he promised them solemnly before God to return as soon as possible. "May God," he wrote, "enable me to perform my promise, and prepare my way before me." The afternoon of the day following he departed. The people came from the morning to the time he left bearing gifts of wine, ale, cake, coffee, tea, and other things for the voyage.[36] Whitefield commented, "I never parted from a place with more regret; for America in my opinion is an excellent school to learn Christ in, and I have great hopes some good will come out of Savannah because the longer I continued there, the larger the congregation grew."[37]

On 28 January 1770, the year of his death, Whitefield preached a sermon to the Governor and Council, and the House of Assembly in Georgia. In it he reflected back on this his first coming to the colony.

> About this time, in the year 1737, being previously stirred up thereto by a strong impulse, which I could by no means resist, I came here, after the example of my worthy and reverend friends, Messieurs John and Charles Wesley, and Mr Ingham, who, with the most disinterested views, had come hither to serve the colony, by endeavouring to convert the Indians. I came rejoicing to serve the colony also, and to become your willing servant for Christ's sake. My friend and father, good Bishop Benson, encouraged me, though my brethren and kinsmen after the flesh, as well as religious friends opposed it. I came, and I saw (you will not be offended with me to speak the truth) the nakedness of the land. Gladly did I distribute about four hundred pounds sterling, which I had collected in England, among my poor parishioners. The necessity and propriety of erecting an Orphan-house, was mentioned and recommended before my first embarkation.[38]

There were a number of reasons why Whitefield made what appears to have been a sudden decision to leave the colony. There were certain changes in the government of the country which Whitefield wished to have amended. There were concerning issues of inheritance since the trustees of Georgia had ruled that female descendants should not inherit the estates of their ancestors. In families with only daughters this was proving to be a severe grievance. He also felt he must collect funds in order to begin the construction of an orphan house. It was also necessary for him to return to England to be ordained a priest.[39]

Whitefield's homeward passage took him via Charleston where he preached twice with much encouragement. On his arrival he was welcomed and received "in a most Christian manner" by the Bishop of London's commissary, the Revd Alexander Garden,[40] whom Whitefield warmly commended as "a good soldier of Jesus Christ". He and several others offered him hospitality. Whitefield exclaimed, "How does God raise me up friends wherever I go! Who is so good a God as our God?" He was clearly quite taken with Charleston, being much pleased with the neatness of the buildings in the town and the beauty of the church.[41]

Finally, about noon on Sunday 9 September, Whitefield boarded the *Mary* for a voyage to England which was to prove long, hard, dangerous, and demanding. The vessel did not reach the coast of Ireland until just over nine weeks later. It certainly proved Whitefield to be a man of courage and faith. He wrote of it as "a long and perilous, but profitable voyage to my soul".[42] For many days at different stages in the journey they suffered contrary winds. On 6 October the ship was hit by a violent storm for about five hours. The main sail was split in a number of places and several other sails and much of the tackle was in tatters. "In short," he wrote, "it was terror and confusion, men's hearts failing them for fear, and the wind and the sea raging horribly."[43] The voyage proved to be longer than had been anticipated and Whitefield noted, "My fresh provisions are gone, and the people are put to the allowance of a quart of water each man for a day."[44] Two weeks later he recorded, "our constant food for some time has been salt beef and water dumplings".[45] By 8 November, "Most of the great cabin now begin to be weak, and look hollow eyed," he wrote, "yet a little while, and we shall come to extremities, and then God's arm will bring us salvation."[46] Three days later, "our food [is] by no means enough... an ounce or two of salt beef, a pint of muddy water and a cake made of flour skimmings of the pot".[47] Throughout the voyage sleep was scant with Whitefield commenting on 14 November, "My clothes have not been off (except to change me) all the passage. Part of the time I lay on the open deck; part on a chest, and the remainder on a bedstead covered with my buffalo's skin."[48]

Whitefield found Captain Coe and all the crew to be "very civil". There were only a small number of passengers on board but being a conscientious clergyman Whitefield read public prayers twice each day and added a word of exhortation.[49] His fellow passengers seemed impressed by his ministry but only one, Captain Gladman, was "effectually converted".[50] He later became Whitefield's travelling companion after they landed in Ireland. Whitefield spent much of the voyage writing letters urging the need for more labourers and requesting money and resources for "my poor flock".[51] In particular he reminded the people of Savannah of the supreme importance of "the new birth in Christ Jesus – that ineffable change which must pass upon our hearts before we can see God" – and went on to specify a number of ways to make the experience of it a reality. These included self-denial, attendance at public worship, secret prayer, and reading the Scriptures.[52]

On reaching the Irish coast the captain and the mate went ashore in a small boat. They were kindly received and returned in the middle of the day loaded with provisions and fresh water. Whitefield went ashore with "my new convert" and was hospitably entertained by a Mr MacMahon who kindly provided them with horses on which they set out to Dublin. On their way Whitefield sent a hasty note to a friend announcing his safe arrival and adding, "I have tasted and known of a truth, that the Lord is gracious! *America*, infant *Georgia*, is an excellent place for Christianity."[53] Their onward journey to England passed through Limerick where Whitefield was graciously received by the bishop and invited to preach at the cathedral where a very large congregation "seemed universally affected".[54] After a brief stop in Dublin where he preached with "power" at the churches of St Werburgh and St Andrew, he finally reached London at the beginning of December. As he neared the city he was agreeably surprised by the sight of some of his Christian friends who were coming out to meet him. It put him in mind of St Paul's friends coming out to meet him at the Three Taverns on the Appian Way on his journey into Rome.[55] Whitefield arrived in the capital on 8 December 1738 and went the same evening to "a truly Christian Society" at Fetter Lane where "he perceived how greatly God had watered the seed sown by my ministry when last in London".[56] The Fetter Lane Society had been founded by a group of Moravian Christians led by Peter Böhler for the purpose of prayer, singing, and fellowship. The day following he was received by both the Archbishop of Canterbury and the Bishop of London "civilly but coldly", the latter "enquiring whether or not his published journals were not a little tinctured by enthusiasm".[57] The trustees of Georgia, however, received him more cordially and expressed their satisfaction at the accounts that had been sent from the magistrates and people of Savannah who in consequence presented him with the living of the church and granted him 500 acres of land on which to erect an orphan house.[58] The Bishop of London, Doctor Gibson, gave him letters dimissory to any other bishop.[59] Whitefield soon found that five London churches were closed to him probably for the reason that the recent published extracts from his journal had sparked accusations of enthusiasm. There had also been opposition to his emphasis on the doctrine of the new birth. Whitefield was nevertheless able to preach to large congregations in the morning at St Helen's and at Islington in the afternoon "with a great pouring out of the Spirit and with power".[60]

During the last week of December Whitefield reported that he had preached nine times and expounded the Scriptures eighteen times "with great power and enlargement".[61] He also shared in a love feast with the members of his society[62] and organized a conference at Islington with "seven true ministers of Jesus Christ" who held to the principles of Methodism.[63] These principles were the rules for holy living which Wesley and the members of the Holy Club had established. The first week was spent in much the same way with him reporting that he had preached six times and "expounded twice or thrice every night of the week".[64] Finally the day for which above all others Whitefield had returned home arrived: he was summoned to Oxford by Bishop Benson to be ordained priest. He breakfasted in the city on Friday 12 January and was kindly received by the bishop. The following day he went with other candidates for holy orders and subscribed to the Articles of Religion. Two days later he received his ordination in what he described as "a day of fat things".[65] He immediately made proof of his ministry by administering the sacrament and preaching in the afternoon to a large congregation, which included "gownsmen of all degrees" in St Alban's Church.[66]

If not able to preach in the churches of London and elsewhere the way was now set for a wider ministry proclaiming the Christian faith in the great outdoors. Before long Britain and indeed the American colonies were destined to witness preaching on a scale never before seen. Whitefield's Georgia mission was significant on several counts. He was one of the first distinctively Evangelical missionaries from England to set foot in the American colonies. His initial visit to the colony can also be considered as the starting point of the transatlantic Evangelical revival of the eighteenth century. His endeavour was a colonial government sponsored initiative.

Chapter 2 notes

1   J. Gillies, *Life of the Reverend George Whitefield*, p. 19.
2   L. Tyerman, op. cit., Vol. 1, p. 115.
3   J. Gillies, *Memoirs*, p. 20.
4   *Journal*, 22 February 1738: "We had an elegant entertainment; but my thoughts were mostly employed in pitying the unhappiness of great men who are in such a continual danger of having their table become a snare to them."
5   *Journal*, 26 February 1738.
6   L. Tyerman, op. cit., Vol. 1, p. 121. See also *Letters*, Letter xxxv, 25 February 1738: "About six o'clock I went to the church, where was assembled a number of decent soldiers praying and singing psalms to CHRIST as God."
7   L. Tyerman, op. cit., p. 121.
8   See T. S. Kidd, *George Whitefield: America's Spiritual Founding Father* (New Haven, Yale University Press, 2014), p. 52.
9   *Journal*, 6 March 1738.
10   Ibid, 7 March 1738.
11   Ibid, 10 March 1738.
12   Ibid, 19 March 1738.
13   J. Gillies, *Memoirs of the Life of the Reverend George Whitefield* (London, Edward and Charles Dilly, 1772), p. 23.
14   Ibid.
15   *Letter to Mr——*, 6 May 1738.
16   L. Tyerman, op. cit., Vol. 1, pp. 126–27.
17   The Saltszburghers or Salzburgers were a group of 20,000 Protestants who followed the teachings of Martin Luther and who had been expelled by Archbishop Firmian of Salzburg on 31 October 1731. There were 300 of their number who accepted the invitation of the trustees of Georgia to settle in the new colony. *Journal*, 7 May 1738; Whitefield, *Letter to Mr H——*, 10 June 1738.
18   *Journal*, 7 May 1738.
19   *Letter to Mr H——*, 10 June 1738.
20   J. Gillies, op cit., p. 25.
21   Ibid.
22   *Letter XL, To Mr H——*, 10 June 1738.
23   *Journal*, 10 June 1738.
24   Ibid, 16 May 1738.
25   Ibid, 20 May 1738.
26   R. Philip, *Life and Times*, p. 69.
27   See R. Philip, *Life and Times*, p. 68. See also L. Tyerman, op. cit., Vol. 1 pp. 132–35.
28   See for example G. Rowell, *Hell and the Victorians* (Oxford, University Press, 1974), pp. 127, 145 and 163.

29 *Journal*, 23 June 1738.
30 Ibid, 11 July 1738.
31 Ibid, 8 August 1738.
32 Ibid, 25 July 1738.
33 Ibid, 18 July 1738.
34 Ibid, 16 August 1738.
35 Taken from W. Stephens, *A Journal of the Proceedings in Georgia*, 2 vols cited in L. Tyerman, op. cit., Vol. 1, p. 131, footnote 1.
36 *Journal*, 28 August 1738.
37 Ibid.
38 Whitefield, *Sermon Preached before the Governor, and Council, and the House of Assembly, in Georgia on January 28, 1770*, *Works*, Vol. 6, pp. 380–81.
39 J. Gillies, op. cit., pp. 24–29.
40 Alexander Garden's attitude to Whitefield had considerably changed by the time Whitefield returned to Charleston in July 1740. See T. S. Kidd, *George Whitefield*, p. 118.
41 *Journal*, 28 August 1738.
42 Ibid, 14 November 1738.
43 Ibid, 6 October 1738.
44 Ibid, 14 October 1738.
45 Ibid, 30 October 1738.
46 Ibid, 8 November 1738.
47 Ibid, 11 November 1738.
48 Ibid, 14 November 1738.
49 Ibid, 16 September 1738.
50 J. Gillies, op. cit., pp. 30–31. See also *Journal*, Tuesday 14 November 1738.
51 Ibid, 24 September 1738.
52 L. Tyerman, op. cit., Vol. 1, p. 143.
53 *Letter to Mr—*, 16 November 1738.
54 *Journal*, 18 November 1738.
55 Ibid, 8 December 1738.
56 Ibid.
57 J. Gillies, op. cit., p. 32.
58 Ibid, p. 33.
59 *Letter to Mr H*, 30 December 1738.
60 *Journal*, 19 December 1738.
61 Ibid, 30 December 1738.
62 Ibid, 1 January 1739.
63 Ibid, 5 January 1739.
64 Ibid, 6 January 1739.
65 Ibid, 14 January 1739.
66 Ibid.

Chapter 3

The Great Outdoors

A Love Feast at Fetter Lane

Whitefield noted in his journal that 1739 began with a love feast with "our brethren at Fetter Lane". This was a society that John Wesley had formed on 1 May 1738.[1] At first it was one of many "Religious Societies attached to the Church of England"[2] but which were later to form the basis of Methodism. The love feast became a distinctively Methodist form of worship which Wesley adopted from the Moravians of Savannah.[3] The central aspect of the love feast was the sharing of a simple meal consisting of drinking water from a "loving cup" and eating a small morsel of bread or cake. The meal was interspersed with hymns, prayers, testimony, and a short address from the one presiding. A collection for the poor was also made usually between the sharing of the elements. In Methodist thinking the love feast corresponded to the *agape* meal which formed the central part of the early church Eucharist.[4] Whitefield recorded that he had "spent the whole night in close prayer, Psalms and thanksgivings" and that "God supported me without sleep".[5]

Whitefield, now an ordained priest, soon set about looking for opportunities to preach and minister in the city's churches. He naturally hoped to use such opportunities to make collections for his people in Georgia and his proposed orphan house in Savannah. Some of the London churches opened their doors to him but gradually he was to discover, as Gillies pointed out, that "some of the clergy now began to show their displeasure" so that "in two days' time, five churches were denied to [him]".[6] Whitefield noted in his journal for Monday 15 January, "Read a pamphlet written against me by a clergyman, I bless God, without any emotion; prayed most heartily for the author."[7] The incident proved to be a portent for the following day: he reported "much opposition" when he read prayers and preached to a thronged and affected audience at St Helen's in Bishopsgate.[8] Both the Archbishop of Canterbury and the Bishop of London were dismissive of him.[9] The latter, Edmund Gibson, wrote a pastoral letter which increasingly came to stir clerical opposition to Whitefield's ministry.[10] Titled *The Bishop of London's Pastoral Letter to the People of His Diocese*, it had passed through five printings by the end of 1744. The bishop began by asserting that "Lukewarmness and enthusiasm" were the bane of true Christianity. He then proceeded to caution his readers against enthusiasm of which it was clear that Whitefield was held to be the prime example. After a lengthy section on lukewarmness the bishop turned his attention to the other extreme of enthusiasm, which he defined as follows.

> The other extreme, into which some serious and well-meaning Christians are apt to be led, is *enthusiasm*, or a strong persuasion on the mind, that they are guided in an extraordinary manner, by immediate impulses and impressions of the Spirit of God. And this owing chiefly to the want of distinguishing aright the ordinary and extraordinary operations of the Holy Spirit.[11]

In this second section of his charge the bishop directed his focus sharply on Whitefield by quoting lengthy extracts from his journals. For instance, in a subsection entitled "Extraordinary communications" he cited the following entry: "This day, I intended to stay on board and write letters, but God being pleased to show me it was not his will I went on shore again."[12] In similar vein, Whitefield had written, "God having shown me it was his will I should return to England."[13] Gibson went on to present additional indications of enthusiasm illustrating them with a number of further citations from Whitefield. These included "talk in the language of those who have a special mission from God"; "those who profess to act under immediate guidance and speak of themselves in the language and power of the spirit". All these, Gibson asserted, clearly meant that Whitefield could be justly dubbed an enthusiast. He ended his pastoral letter stating that "I shall not fail to make it my earnest prayer to God... to preserve you from all error and particularly from the two dangerous extremes of *Lukewarmness* on one hand and *Enthusiasm* on the other."[14]

In a reply written on 11 August and sent to publishers two days later Whitefield[15] defended himself stoutly against the bishop's charges in a pamphlet entitled *Answer to the Bishop of London's Last Pastoral Letter* which was published in 1739. He was adamant that "I never did pretend to these extraordinary operations of working miracles, or speaking in tongues" as the bishop had intimated.[16] He pointed out that his "constant way of preaching is, first, to prove my propositions by scripture, and then to illustrate them by articles and collects of the Church of England."[17] In reply to the bishop's questioning his teaching on the presence of the Holy Spirit in the believer Whitefield countered: "Does not our church, my Lord, teach and pray that, 'God's Holy Spirit may in all things direct and rule our hearts?'" Gibson had opined that "preachers should be called upon for some reasonable evidences of a *divine Commission*". To this Whitefield replied, "But my Lord… Did I not receive letters dimissory from your Lordship's own hand to be ordained a priest?" He went on to make the point that "my Lord of Gloucester, when he ordained me priest said unto me, receive thou the Holy Ghost now committed unto thee, by the imposition of our hands, in the name of the Father, and of the Son, and of the Holy Ghost." In this forthright riposte Whitefield pressed the point, "If your Lordship in any wise disputes my acting by a divine Commission, you disclaim your own divine right and authority; nor can you possibly avoid the dilemma, of either allowing *my divine Commission*, or denying *your own*."[18]

In the last section of his *Answer to the Bishop of London* Whitefield responded to the criticism that "he ought to preach only in that congregation to which he was lawfully appointed". He made the point that all clergy who occasionally preach in other churches break this rule and he added "consequently your Lordship frequently offends, when you preach out of your diocese!"[19] This statement typifies the manner in which he made frequent defences of his subsequent ministry.

The earlier years of the eighteenth century were an age of rationalism in which fanaticism of any kind tended to be eschewed. Whitefield commenced his ministry at a time when the established church was marked by latitudinarianism. This "broad churchism" had emerged through the influence of John Tillotson (1630–94) and Thomas Tenison (1636–1715), successive Archbishops of Canterbury. Their views were further endorsed by the publication in 1695 of John Locke's volume, *Reasonableness of Christianity*. Prelates such as Edmund Gibson and Martin Benson who had pastoral responsibility for Whitefield were unsurprisingly members of an episcopal bench who were strongly of the view that reason provided all that was necessary to bring a person to Christian faith. The influence of their diocesan charges, pastoral letters, and occasional pamphleteering were inevitably going to turn the majority of clergy against the likes of Whitefield and his fellow Methodists.

For a time Whitefield managed, though with difficulty, to get a hearing in some of the London churches. Indeed he was even able to raise collections for his Georgia mission, noting in his journal for 24 January 1739 "preached at Christ Church, Spitalfields, for Orphan House". At the end of the entry he added, "God enabled me to preach with power, and £25 was collected."[20] Early in February he was still managing to find some churches that were willing to receive him: one Friday he preached at Islington where he had a great number of communicants and "collected for my Orphan House". And on the Sunday following he preached in the morning at St George's-in-the-East and collected £18 and "again at Christ Church, Spitalfields". The same evening he even managed, though not without opposition, to preach the sermon he had been invited to give at St Margaret's Westminster.[21]

When Whitefield journeyed west to Bristol toward the end of the following week, however, the situation changed rapidly and indeed dramatically. Gillies commented, "In Bristol he had the use of the churches for two or three Sundays, but soon found they would not be open for very long."[22] On Thursday 15 February he was barred from using St Mary Redcliffe by the chancellor of the diocese, and later the same day the dean of the cathedral refused to endorse his desire to preach in any of the city's churches. Thus Gillies wrote, "In about a fortnight every door was shut, except *Newgate,* where he preached, and collected for the poor prisoners, and where people thronged, and were much impressed; but this place, also, was soon shut against him, by orders from the Mayor."[23]

On 26 February Whitefield was summoned by the Chancellor of Bristol who "now told me plainly he intended to stop my proceedings". Once again Whitefield was forceful in his answers. On being told that the canons forbade clergy from preaching without a license and from speaking in private houses he replied saying that "there is also a canon forbidding all clergymen to frequent taverns and play at cards". Why he asked was this not put into execution?[24] Whitefield parted company with the chancellor plainly telling him, "If you preach anywhere in this diocese till you have a license, I will first suspend, then excommunicate, you."[25]

After this altercation, Whitefield went to St Nicholas Church where it had previously been arranged that he should preach. On his arrival he soon discovered that he had been barred from the use of the building. He therefore expounded the ninth chapter of John's Gospel in the yard outside to "a great crowd". He recorded "all were wondrously touched, and, when after my exposition, I prayed for the Chancellor, the whole company was in tears, and said most earnest Amens to all the petitions I put up for him".[26]

The very next day saw the beginning of a new and marked emphasis in Whitefield's ministry as he made his way out of the city to the village of Kingswood where it had been arranged for him to preach to the colliers. They had long been on his heart for shortly before his first embarkation for Georgia, when he talked of going abroad, many in Bristol used to reply, "What need of going abroad. Have we not Indians enough at home? If you have a mind to convert Indians, there are colliers enough in Kingswood."[27] On this day, the preacher's sermon, which lasted for nearly an hour, was on the subject of the "new birth" and taken from John 3.[28] From this day forward it was to be his delight to preach in the great outdoors. Henceforward Whitefield never hesitated to hold forth in the open air. His pulpits were to be the field, the hillside, the market crosses, the yard, the street corners, or whatever else lay to hand. Later in the same year Whitefield remarked in a letter addressed to a fellow clergyman, "The whole world is now my parish. Wherever my master calls me, I am ready to go and preach his everlasting gospel."[29]

This visit to the colliers of Kingswood was to be the first of several. Three days later Whitefield returned to be greeted by what at a moderate computation was a crowd of above 10,000. The trees and hedges were full of people. The sun was bright and the speaker was loud enough for all to hear his message.[30] The Sunday following he went to Hanam Mount, three miles from the city where almost all the colliers lived. A crowd estimated to be about 4,000 had gathered to hear him. The ground was not sufficiently high enough for Whitefield to be seen so he stood on a table and the people covered the surrounding fields. He was greatly pleased by their deep attention.[31] Other visits to the colliers followed. On Sunday 11 March he noted, "Went to Hanam Mount, where was near a third as many as last Sunday." A week later he was back again this time "to many more than were there last Sunday".[32] On 25 March he preached again to a larger congregation than ever and in the afternoon the number present "was computed to be upwards of twenty three thousand". Whitefield was afterwards told that those who stood farthest off could hear him very plainly. He was greatly pleased to have preached from the Mount for it reminded him of the Lord having preached his most famous sermon on the Mount.

The change which came over the colliers of Bristol and their community was marked. Their lifestyle was rude and uncultivated. They had no place of worship and when provoked were, in the words of Gillies, "a terror to the whole city of Bristol". Whitefield wrote that "having no righteousness of their own to renounce, they were glad to hear of a Jesus who was a friend of publicans, and came not to call the righteous, but sinners to repentance". He recalled their response to his message in the following lines.

> The first discovery of their being affected, was to see the white gutters made by their tears, which plentifully fell down their cheeks, as they came out of their coal pits. Hundreds and hundreds of them were soon brought under deep convictions, which (as the event proved) happily ended in a sound and thorough conversion. The change was visible to all, though numbers chose to impute it to any thing rather than the finger of God.[33]

The change in the colliers was quickly apparent at the beginning of April when they planned to erect a school and invited Whitefield to lay the first stone. This he did and then kneeled down and "prayed that the gates of hell might not prevail against our design".[34] Four months later he was able to collect £24 9s from his congregation at Moorfields for the building.[35]

Although many sneered at him – "a stripling in a gown", who had just begun to be an extempore preacher, Whitefield found he could confidently say, "I was never totally deserted, and frequently so assisted, that I knew by happy experience what the Lord meant by saying 'out of his belly shall flow rivers of living waters.'"[36] Indeed his spirit was often overcome by the sight of the open fields packed by vast crowds of people, with some on horseback and some in coaches. Besides the colliers and thousands of villagers, "persons of all ranks flocked out of Bristol".[37] With such huge numbers pressing in Whitefield was soon aware that more helpers were needed. He therefore sent to John Wesley and his brother Charles to come down and assist him in the work. Wesley, precise and scholarly by nature, was at first filled with doubt about this new means of proclaiming the gospel. He was disturbed by what he found and penned the following lines.

> I could scarce reconcile myself to this strange way
> of preaching in the fields, of which [Whitefield] set
> me an example on Sunday, having been all my life
> (till very lately) so tenacious of every point relating
> to decency and order, that I should have thought
> the saving of souls almost a sin, if it had not been
> done in a church... At four in the afternoon, I
> submitted to be more vile, and proclaimed in the
> highways the glad tidings of salvation.[38]

What Whitefield had begun was eventually to transform the
endeavour from a spiritual awakening among small select groups
and societies to an extensive public transatlantic movement. Field
preaching, it should be said, was not unknown in the past. The
Lollards, the Franciscans, and some of the Protestant Reformers,
including John Knox, had made use of it. What was significant in
Whitefield's case was the scale and widespread nature of it and the
way in which he so readily used it. Field preaching now became the
major means of spreading the Christian message in both England
and the American colonies. Wesley, under Whitefield's mentoring,
took to the open fields naturally and easily. In fact it was not very
long before crowds as large as had gathered to hear Whitefield came
to listen to Wesley.

Field preaching was in many ways a timely instrument for
spreading the Christian faith in the middle years of the eighteenth
century. The established church of the time was often cold and
unwelcoming toward the poor who were made to feel their lowly
place in the social hierarchy. The essence of being a Christian
was often about intellectual assent to creedal doctrines and duty.
Those at the margins of society were reminded in the words of the
catechism "to learn and labour truly to get mine own living, and

to do my duty in that state of life, unto which it shall please God to call me". The early Georgian era was sometimes dubbed the age of the hunting, shooting, and fishing clergy. Some were no doubt conscientious but many of their number were reputed to be lacking in warmth and conviction. This was also the age of pluralism and non-residence with many clergy having and drawing the income from more than one parish and not living in either of them. All this meant that the poor were much more ready to listen in the open air to preachers who came down to their level, spoke their language, gave testimony, and cared enough to go to their work places, mines, and fields. Here was an environment in which they were not made to feel unworthy and unwanted. While it was the case that missionary groups such as the Lollards and Franciscans had preached and taught in the open air, Whitefield went on to open up a new dimension which generated major public awakenings on an altogether bigger canvas.

Wales, the West, and a return to London

Shortly after this occasion Whitefield set out to preach in Wales. Here he met and shared ministry with Howell Harris, a forthright lay preacher and leading Welsh revivalist, and several other Christian friends. At Pontypool, prompted by the curate, "great numbers" had gathered to hear him. Finding the church too small to contain all the people Whitefield immediately preached in a nearby field.[39] He reflected that "I have most power when I speak in the open air. A proof this to me that God is pleased with this way of preaching."[40] At Abergavenny he preached from the cross in the churchyard. At Caerleon, the church being denied, he stood on a horse block before the inn and preached for about three quarters of an hour.[41] At Coleford he preached to about a hundred in the marketplace and then journeyed on to his native city Gloucester and the surrounding countryside.[42] On Thursday 12 April he preached in the evening "to near three thousand in a field belonging to my brother". To those who opposed his coming he replied that he had never been charged with teaching or living otherwise than as a true member of the Church of England.[43] He made brief excursions to Chalford[44] where he preached to "above three thousand",[45] Stroud,[46] and Cheltenham "to near two thousand on the Bowling Green belonging to the Plough Inn" where "some were so filled with the Holy Ghost that they were almost unable to support themselves under it".[47]

On 20 April Whitefield set out for London stopping briefly in Oxford where the vice-chancellor of the university came to the house in which he was staying and sternly rebuked him. In an angry outburst he accused the young priest of pretended inspiration and vanity and of "going about, alienating people's affections from their proper pastors".[48] Whitefield and a small group of friends left the building shortly after this confrontation and set off for London, which in the following weeks was to witness huge crowds such as had never been seen before.

London crowds

A taste of what was to come occurred soon after Whitefield's arrival in the city on Friday 27 April 1739 when he went in the morning to preach at Islington where his close friend Mr Stonehouse was the incumbent. In the midst of the prayers the church warden appeared demanding that the visitor produce his licence to preach. Whitefield reflected that he could easily have insisted on his right to use the pulpit since he had been presented with the living of Savannah which was in the Bishop of London's diocese. However, "for the sake of peace", Whitefield later recorded, "I preached in the churchyard, being assured my Master now called me out here, as well as in Bristol."[49] For good measure he returned the following morning and preached again finding that "the Word was attended with extraordinary power".[50]

It was, however, at Moorfields and Kennington Common where Whitefield suddenly began to draw crowds on a scale the like of which had not been seen before. On Sunday 29 April he preached in the morning at Moorfields to "an exceeding great multitude" and then went on in the afternoon to Kennington Common, which was about two miles from London. He recorded that "no less than thirty thousand people were supposed to be present". The wind was blowing in a favourable direction so that the preacher's voice was carried "to the extremist part of the audience". The vast crowd were quiet and attentive and joined in the psalm and the Lord's Prayer. In Whitefield's own words, "all agreed it was never seen on this wise before".[51] The day following he recorded that "my honoured friend Mr John Wesley" was now also having a similar "wonderful success" preaching out of doors in Bristol.[52] Between 29 April and 29 July Whitefield recounted in his journal nineteen occasions on which he preached to very large crowds at Kennington Common. Calculating the attendance figure which he gave in his journal, the total number of hearers was in excess of 300,000. The estimates which Whitefield gives may perhaps be overstated. That said he does record some instances in the same period where his hearers were less than 300. Significantly, his episcopal and other opponents criticized him for many things but they seem not to have disputed the numbers he gave of his hearers.[53]

One or two of the now famous preacher's journal entries enable the reader to capture a glimpse of the events at Kennington and Moorfields. Sunday 6 May: "Preached this morning in Moorfields to about twenty thousand people who were very quiet and attentive. At six, preached at Kennington. Such a sight I never saw before. I believe there were no less than fifty thousand people and near four score coaches, besides great numbers of horses. There was an awful silence amongst them."[54] Three weeks later large crowds were still eagerly attending Whitefield's preaching at these two places. On Saturday 27 May he noted, "Preached at Kennington Common to about fifteen thousand people, and we had an extraordinary presence of God among us."[55] On the following morning at Moorfields he addressed about twenty thousand, and "God manifested Himself still more and more. My discourse was near two hours long."[56]

For much of June Whitefield was in Hertfordshire, Kent, and in the West of England, but when he returned to London in July great numbers soon began to assemble at Moorfields and Kennington. On Sunday 29 July he wrote briefly, "Preached this morning in Moorfields, to a larger congregation than we had last Sunday... and preached at Kennington Common in the evening."[57]

Itinerant circuits

The focus of Whitefield's energy and preaching remained in London where he was more readily able to raise collections for his Georgia mission. He did however sometimes venture out into the surrounding countryside for just a few days in the middle of a week; sometimes it was for longer periods. As well as preaching in the open spaces and in those churches that opened their doors to him, he also visited the Methodist societies which had been formed either by himself or the Wesleys. Their purpose was to promote times for praying, worshipping, seeking the witness of God's Spirit in the lives of those who participated, and to study in a more intimate setting. More informal a context than traditional church worship, the society meetings also created a strong bond of fellowship. In these excursions it is possible to see the beginnings of what eventually under his and Wesley's organizations became Methodist circuits. Whitefield soon recognized that it was effective to leave London and travel through Buckinghamshire, Hertford, Northampton, and Bedford, and then to return to London. In later times he would start in Bristol and then travel into Chepstow, Monmouth, Caerleon, and back to Bristol through his native Gloucester. In a similar way he set out from London on 4 June and preached his way round through Blackheath, Bexley, Gravesend, Dulwich, and then back to London on 19 June.[58]

Let not your good be evil spoken of

One of the marked aspects of Whitefield's character was his courage to speak out and defend what he knew to be his calling. As well as being physically assaulted by people from the crowds who gathered to listen to him, he also had to endure hostility to his field preaching in a number of published pamphlets. In addition he had to cope with a number of stern rebukes from the ecclesiastical hierarchy. In all cases he seems to have responded with a forthright vigour.

On 20 February the chancellor of the Bristol diocese summoned Whitefield and told him that he intended to stop his proceedings and he duly sent for the registrar to come and take down his reply in writing. He questioned the evangelist's authority and right to preach in Bristol without a license. He then read over part of the Ordination Office and those canons that forbid a minister from preaching in a private house. Four days later Whitefield wrote to the bishop and informed him of the chancellor's charge that his conduct was contrary to the canons, but that he, Whitefield, had replied that the canons were not directed against the kinds of meetings which he held.[59]

While Whitefield was visiting a Christian society in Oxford the vice-chancellor of the university came to the house where they were gathered and spoke to him in private. He accused him of "vanity, pretended inspiration and alienating people from their pastors".

After the vice-chancellor had departed those who were meeting together joined in prayer for him.[60] Early in July Whitefield received a letter from Martin Benson, the Bishop of Gloucester, in which he expressed his view that "I ought to preach the Gospel only in the congregation wherein I was lawfully appointed thereunto."[61] His reply to his bishop was forthright indeed. His major point was that if clergy are obliged only to preach in the parishes to which they have been appointed then all of their number including bishops break the oath whenever they preach occasionally in other places.[62]

On 19 July Whitefield received a letter from John Abbot, a magistrate in Basingstoke seeking to dissuade him from preaching in the town in case there was a disturbance of the peace. He replied to Abbot immediately, stating that he hoped that "he had not been motivated to write from a fear of man". He also reminded Abbot that there was another meeting in town on the following day and urged him "to prevent profane cursing and swearing, and persons breaking the sixth commandment, by bruising each other's bodies by cudgelling and wrestling". He said, "If you do not this, I shall rise up against you at the great day, and be a swift witness against your partiality."[63]

Methodist societies

Throughout the spring and summer of 1739 Whitefield preached, planned, and collected money and materials for his return to Georgia. He also visited and encouraged societies wherever time and circumstances allowed. Religious societies had played their part in English Christian history long before Methodism but Whitefield and Wesley and those who had been members of the Oxford Holy Club promoted them in a much more widespread and vigorous manner. The Lollards had promoted small groups to study the Scriptures as had the Puritans in the reign of Elizabeth I who met together in what became known as "Prophesyings". On these occasions sermons were discussed, the Bible studied, and informal extempore prayers were offered. About the year 1676 Dr Andrew Horneck, the minister of Savoy Chapel in London, formed a small group of men into a society in which they aimed "to apply themselves to good discourse and to things wherein they might edify one another".[64] Other groups emerged from this beginning. Two years later a member of one of them published a book entitled *The Country Parson's Advice to His Parishioners* which became greatly valued by the Holy Club led by John Wesley. In the section entitled "Confer with Other Christians" the writer urged that "frequent conferring with serious Christians is the way by which we are more deeply affected with divine things than any other".[65] Horneck drew up rules for his society – the first and foremost of which was, "All that enter the Society shall resolve upon a holy and serious life." It was a strictly Church of England society and only those who had been confirmed by a bishop were allowed to join. The meetings consisted largely of reciting liturgical prayers and reading devotional and practical literature. Controversial doctrinal debates were to be avoided. If time permitted psalms were sung. Each member was to endeavour to pray six times a day. They were to contribute a small sum of money each week and were to love one another and speak evil of no one.[66]

Other very similar societies soon began to emerge in London,[67] Oxford, and elsewhere. In fact the Revd Samuel Wesley, the father of John and Charles, started one in Epworth in 1701. It was these gatherings which were led by clergy that had prompted the founding of the Oxford Holy Club. Both of the Wesleys and Whitefield became very active in visiting and encouraging them whenever and wherever the opportunity arose. Whitefield had a double motive for doing so since he also sought to gain praying supporters who would be able to give money or other material support for his mission in Savannah. Whitefield, and indeed the Wesleys, constantly looked for opportunities to organize those who responded to their preaching into new "Methodist" societies. Inevitably they soon became too numerous for all their meetings to be presided over by Anglican clergy and most of them adapted to the needs of the poor and those who lacked any formal education. Methodist society meetings included women as well as men and focused on testimony, singing, and extempore prayers. Love feasts and watch nights often featured. The term "society" was retained as opposed to the word "church" since the early Methodists, both Wesleyan and Calvinistic, wanted to make it clear that they were still committed members of the established church.

During the first eight months of 1739 Whitefield gave details of some twenty-six visits that he made to religious societies, most of them being in London and Bristol. Whitefield had earlier started an Oxford-style society in his native Gloucester.[68] He also formed a new society in the home of a Mr M at Beech Lane in the City of London on 3 February.[69] Once his open-air preaching took off, Whitefield seems to have left a good deal of the work of forming new societies to John and Charles Wesley. There is a hint of this when in Bristol on 11 July he recorded "my brother Wesley and I settled some affairs and united the two leading societies together".[70] Whitefield also noted that on 8 January he had spent part of the evening "with our bands, which are combinations of six or more Christians meeting together to compare their experiences". This form of organization, which was very similar to Wesley's class meetings, was probably developed from the Moravians.[71] Methodist societies were broken down into these smaller groups in order to foster a more intimate and personal faith. It became a principle that to be counted as a Methodist member a person had to attend their weekly class or band meeting regularly.

Preparations for the return to Georgia

Besides preaching and encouraging societies Whitefield also devoted considerable energy to raising funds for his parish in Savannah. He made twenty-four references in his journal to occasions when he collected money for his proposed orphan house for Savannah. In total he raised well in excess of £450.[72] This was by any standards a considerable sum of money. Some of it was sacrificially given, as for example, when he preached at Kennington on 9 May. He noted "when we came home, we found we had collected £46 amongst which were £16 in half pence".[73] A similar occurrence followed at Moorfields on Sunday 13 May when "£52.19s.6d. was collected for the orphans above £20 of which was in halfpence".[74] Gillies noted that by the time they left England "upwards of a thousand pounds had been collected for the orphan house".[75]

As well as raising money Whitefield's endeavours were also taken up with organization for the impending voyage. As early as 30 April 1739 he recorded "Declined preaching today to make preparations for my poor orphans in Georgia."[76] On Thursday 3 May he noted "was fully employed all day in making preparations for my voyage".[77] A steady stream of similar entries followed over the next few days: 7 May, "full employment in preparation for my voyage"; 9 May, "waited upon the Honourable trustees for Georgia";[78] 12 May, "Agreed today, for myself, and eleven more, to go on board the *Elizabeth*, with Captain Allen, to Pennsylvania, where I design, God willing to preach the Gospel in my way to Georgia, and buy provisions for the Orphan House."[79]

Despite this early planning Whitefield and his companions didn't finally go on board until the second week in August. Their voyage was to last nine weeks.[80] During the passage Whitefield found he experienced "unspeakable peace and tranquillity within". He held prayers morning and evening for his party and others who wished to attend and celebrated Holy Communion on a number of occasions. Toward the end of their journey the fresh livestock was gone but they had enough food for themselves and were able to give some to the ship's company. They finally reached American shores on 30 October and set out for Philadelphia where more revival preaching was destined to begin.

This short period back on home soil had been a significant time. Whitefield's preaching to the colliers of Kingswood near Bristol was the start of open-air field preaching that was to become one of the prominent features of the transatlantic revival. It was a practice quickly taken up by the Wesleys and others. Whitefield's subsequent preaching at Moorfields and Kennington Common had thrust him into the limelight. He was now a celebrity figure in high demand. However, his preaching and doctrine soon met with opposition from the bishops and Anglican hierarchy, but the young cleric stood his ground and refused to bow to what he regarded as unjustified regulations.

Chapter 3 notes

1   See J. Telford, *The Life of John Wesley* (London, Epworth, 1960), p. 99.
2   This society is now recognized to have been Moravian.
3   J. Wesley, *Journal*, 8 August 1737.
4   For love feast see F. Baker, *Methodism and the Love Feast* (London, Epworth, 1956).
5   *Journal*, 1 January 1739.
6   J. Gillies, *Memoirs of the Life*, p. 32.
7   *Journal*, 15 January 1739.
8   Ibid, 16 January 1739.
9   Ibid, 9 December 1739.
10 E. Gibson, *The Bishop of London's Pastoral Letter to the People of His Diocese: Especially Those of the Two Great Cities of London and Westminster: By Way of Caution, Against Lukewarmness on One Hand, and Enthusiasm on the Other* (London, S. Buckley, 1739).
11 Ibid, p. 32.
12 Ibid, p. 16.
13 Ibid.
14 Ibid, p. 32.

15 *Journal*, 13 August 1739.
16 Whitefield, *Answer to the Bishop of London's Last Pastoral Letter*, p. 9.
17 Ibid, p. 10.
18 Ibid, pp. 12–13.
19 Whitefield, *Answer to the Bishop of London*, p. 17.
20 *Journal*, 25 January 1739.
21 Ibid, 4 February 1739.
22 J. Gillies, *Memoirs of the Life*, p. 36.
23 Ibid.
24 *Journal*, 20 February 1739.
25 Ibid.
26 Ibid.
27 J. Gillies, op cit., p. 36.
28 *Journal*, 21 February 1739.
29 *Letter to the Rev. Mr. R. D.*, 10 November 1739.
30 *Journal*, 25 February 1739.
31 Ibid, 4 March 1739.
32 Ibid, 18 March 1739.
33 J. Gillies, op. cit., pp. 37–38.
34 *Journal*, 2 April 1739.
35 Ibid, 29 July 1739.
36 J. Gillies, op cit., p. 38.
37 Ibid, p. 39.
38 R. Davies, *Methodism* (Harmondsworth, Penguin Books, 1964), p. 69.
39 *Journal*, 4 April 1739.
40 Ibid.
41 Ibid, 6 April 1739.
42 Ibid, 9 April, 1739.
43 Ibid, 12 April 1739.
44 Ibid, 13 April, 1739.
45 Ibid, 14 April, 1739.
46 Ibid.
47 Ibid, 18 April, 1739.
48 Ibid, 24 April, 1739.
49 Ibid, 27 April, 1739.
50 Ibid, 28 April, 1739.
51 Ibid, 29 April, 1739.
52 Ibid, 30 April, 1739.
53 In his 1756 revision of his journal he added a footnote to his entry for 6 May stating that some of those present at Kennington estimated the number present to have been 30 or 40,000 as compared to his figure of 50,000.
54 *Journal*, 6 May 1739.
55 Ibid, 27 May 1739.
56 Ibid, 28 May 1739.
57 Ibid, 29 July 1739.

58   Ibid, 19 June 1739.
59   Ibid, 24 February 1739.
60   Ibid, 24 April 1739.
61   Ibid, 8 July 1739.
62   *Letter to the Bishop of Bristol*, 9 July 1739.
63   *Journal*, 19 July 1739.
64   R. E. Davies, *Methodism*, p. 35.
65   *The Country Parson's Advice to His Parishioners* (London, 1680; London, Monarch, 1998), p. 142.
66   See especially R. Davies, op. cit., p. 35.
67   H. D. Rack, *Reasonable Enthusiast* (London, Epworth Press, 2002), p. 141. See also C. J. Podmore, *The Moravian Church in England* (Oxford, Clarendon Press, 1998) pp. 38–71.
68   H. D. Rack, op. cit., p. 137.
69   *Journal*, 3 February 1739.
70   Ibid, 11 July 1739.
71   See C. J. Podmore, *"The Fetter Lane Society"*, *Proceedings of the Wesley Historical Society*, Vol. XLVI, pp. 125–53 and W. O. B. Allen and E. McClure, *Two Hundred Years: The History of the Society for Promoting Christian Knowledge 1698–1898* (London, 1898), p. 56.
72   The amounts raised which he details in his journal for the first eight months of 1739 totalled £457 11s 30d. There are however a few entries where no totals are given.
73   *Journal*, 9 May 1739.
74   Ibid, 30 May 1739.
75   J. Gillies, op. cit., p. 45.
76   *Journal*, 30 April 1739.
77   Ibid, 3 May 1739.
78   Ibid, 9 May 1739.
79   Ibid, 12 May 1739.
80   J. Gillies, op. cit., p. 46.

Chapter 4

Awakening in America

Whitefield's second visit to America began when he set sail on 14 August 1739 and ended with his arrival back in England in March 1741. Then, just after three-and-a-half years on home soil he set out once more, in August 1744, for America, for a third period which lasted four years. Whitefield and his group – consisting of eight men, one boy, two children, and his friend William Seward – reached American shores on Tuesday 30 August 1739.[1]

Whitefield and Seward went ashore immediately they arrived in order to travel over land via Philadelphia where they planned to purchase necessary provisions and supplies for the orphan house and the parish of Savannah. However, the young clergyman's reputation as a revivalist field preacher had gone before him and all along his chosen route there were invitations to stop and preach. Whitefield, who was in constant need of money to meet the demands of his projected scheme for orphans, responded to the opportunities this offered for making public collections.

Whitefield arrived in Philadelphia, the "City of Brotherly Love", on 2 November where he soon found that the popularity he had known in England had now arrived in America. He read prayers on the following Sunday and dined with Thomas, the son of William Penn, the colony's founder. He was especially pleased to find that the people preferred sermons when they were "not delivered within church walls".[2] This was fortunate because the numbers who sought to hear him preach were many times more than could have been accommodated in any of the city's churches. His main pulpit now became the court house steps. He spoke from there on the evening of Thursday 8 November "to about six thousand people".[3] On Friday he again preached in the evening to "nearly two thousand". He recorded in his journal that "even in London, I never observed so profound a silence. Before I came, all was hushed exceeding quiet. The night was clear, but not cold. Lights were on in most windows all around us for a considerable distance. The people did not seem weary of standing, nor was I of speaking."[4] Whitefield wrote that the people were "hungry for the bread of life" and that "as soon as I come home, my house is generally filled with people desirous to join in psalms and prayers."[5]

After nine days Whitefield set out for New York where he had received an invitation from Thomas Noble to preach. On his way there he was able to stop at New Brunswick, meeting with Gilbert Tennent, "an eminent dissenting minister, about forty years of age". He proved to be "a kindred spirit".[6] On arrival in New York City Whitefield made contact with the Revd William Vessey (1674–1712), the Bishop of London's commissary for New York,[7] who refused him the use of his church.[8] Whitefield therefore preached several times in the fields to "upwards of two thousand" and in local meeting houses to large numbers.[9]

After receiving gifts Whitefield set out to return to Philadelphia, passing and stopping at a number of Pennsylvanian towns on the way, including New Brunswick where he preached from a wagon to about 1,500 persons.[10] He was able to spend two days at Neshaminy in the home of the Revd William Tennent. Whitefield arrived later than expected and found his host preaching to "above three thousand people gathered together in the meeting house yard". On seeing

Whitefield appear the crowd stopped and sang a psalm, following which Whitefield spoke with "many melted down and crying much".[11]

Tennent had established a small college for training up men for the ministry. Although despised at the time it later became a large institution at Princeton in New Jersey.[12] Whitefield's time with William Tennent and his son Gilbert marked the start of his building fellowship with clergy who espoused the new birth and the doctrines of the Protestant Reformation.

Shortly before reaching Philadelphia, Whitefield stopped at German Town, which was about seven miles distance. There he preached from a balcony for "nearly two hours" to "above six thousand people". Great numbers continued weeping for a considerable time. On arriving back in the city Whitefield found that the doors of the Anglican Christ Church were now closed to him. He responded by preaching for an hour-and-a-half from a balcony "to upwards of ten thousand hearers, who were very attentive and much affected".[13] Philip noted that at Philadelphia he pleaded the cause of the orphan house and raised two collections: one of £110 and another of £80.[14]

It was at Philadelphia that Whitefield first encountered Benjamin Franklin (1706–90). Franklin was a publisher who quickly recognized the marketable value of Whitefield's sermons. He noted Whitefield's "loud and clear voice" and his ability "to articulate his words and sentences so perfectly". He was also struck by the fact that he could be heard at a "considerable distance" away from the place where he spoke. When Whitefield preached from the court house steps Franklin walked in each direction and measured the distance at which he could be heard. He then calculated the area and found that allowing two square feet per person Whitefield "might well be heard by more than thirty thousand".[15]

Whitefield's preaching in Philadelphia had a marked social effect on the community. Philip observed that after his sermons the dancing school and concert rooms were closed. It is also to be noted that Whitefield himself became deeply concerned about the plight of the African Americans.[16]

Whitefield's use of print media

Whitefield's meeting with Franklin proved to be the beginning of a lifelong friendship and working arrangement. Franklin became the chief among a number of British and American publishers who began to print and sell both Whitefield's works and accounts of his meetings. Frank Lambert in his *Pedlar in Divinity* has demonstrated that the evangelist was "a pioneer in the commercialisation of religion".[17] Lambert points out that the mid-eighteenth century was a period when literacy increased on both sides of the Atlantic and it witnessed a rapid growth in the number of newspapers and journals.[18]

Against this background Whitefield crafted his autobiography for the mass market. But this was only the beginning of what became the preacher's extensive application of the new marketing techniques that set him apart from his Evangelical contemporaries.[19] Whitefield began and continued to advertise his forthcoming meetings in a wide range of American and British newspapers.[20] His friend and colleague William Seward fed journalists and newspapers with a steady stream of material.[21] This in turn birthed a number of revivalist magazines which added to the spread of the gospel message. Lambert's researches demonstrated that Whitefield flooded the Atlantic world with his printed sermons and journal extracts as he adopted what he termed a "print and preach" strategy.[22] By way of illustrating the fact, Lambert pointed out that *The Pennsylvania Gazette* devoted 75 per cent of its coverage in 1739–40 to Whitefield.[23] In the peak year of 1740 Whitefield wrote or inspired thirty-nine titles.[24] Whitefield, Lambert asserted, "came to regard the printed word as an extension of the spoken word".[25]

Leaving Philadelphia for Savannah

On Thursday 29 November, having corrected two sermons for the press, Whitefield finally took his leave of Philadelphia and set out for Savannah. Nearly twenty gentlemen on horseback accompanied him out of the city. About seven miles along the way they were joined by another company so that they were nearly 200 in total by the time they reached the town of Chester. There the company made a brief stop for food and Whitefield preached from a balcony to about 2,000 people.[26]

The route of Whitefield's onward journey passed through countryside where there were settlements and towns and he was able to preach to some large gatherings on his way. At Christian Bridge nearly 2,000 came to hear him and about the same number listened to his message at Newcastle where there was a "gracious melting of hearts".[27] At White Clay Creek, despite the rainy weather, "upwards of ten thousand assembled to hear the word", several hundred of whom had arrived on horseback.[28] Whitefield and his party reached Williamsburg on Friday 14 December, which he described in his journal as "the metropolis of Virginia".[29] The following day he dined with the governor who gave him a courteous welcome. He also paid his respects to the Revd James Blair, the Church of England commissary for Virginia, whom he described as "the most worthy clergyman I have yet conversed with in all America". Blair, who had played a major role in the founding of a beautiful college in the town with masters from Oxford University, invited Whitefield to preach and to stay.[30]

The journey from Williamsburg to Charleston took Whitefield and his companions through largely unsettled and sometimes swampy country. On Saturday 22 December he recorded hearing wolves "howling like a kennel of hounds". A week later Whitefield recorded the dangerous conditions with bridges being out of repair and water so high that they were "obliged to swim our horses".[31] Finally, on 5 January, Whitefield and his party (whom he affectionately termed "his family") reached Charleston – the conclusion of their land-based journey. For the last stage of their itinerary to Savannah it was necessary to travel by water along the coast, a voyage which was to take a further five days.[32] The little group found the townspeople hospitable and they dined with a local merchant. Whitefield preached to a large congregation on Sunday 6 January and "expressed himself doubtful" whether the court end of London could exceed them "in affected finery, gaiety of dress and deportment".[33] Large numbers attended his address in the French church the following day, many of whom "melted to tears".[34]

Arrival at Savannah

Whitefield arrived in Savannah on 11 January and was very happy to meet with "his family" who had preceded him by three weeks, having continued their journey by sea. He found Georgia at "a lower ebb" than when he had left it. However, he immediately went with his friend James Habersham, the schoolmaster in Savannah, to inspect a tract of 500 acres of land which he had selected for the orphan house. Whitefield was of the view that being some ten miles distant from the town there would be less chance of the children following bad examples. On Thursday 24 January Whitefield took possession of the land, deciding on the name Bethesda, meaning "House of Mercy", and expressed the hope that many acts of mercy would indeed be shown there.[35]

It was clearly going to be some time before any orphan house buildings were erected on the newly acquired land so Whitefield rented "the largest house" in Savannah town, and soon had more than twenty orphans to care for. He opened an infirmary under the direction of a surgeon and supplied it with medicines he had brought with him from England. Whitefield was anxious that the children should not be idle and immediately set up a scheme for the children to be taught to spin cotton. He found that cotton grew well in Georgia and to encourage the people he purchased 300 pounds weight and agreed to take all the cotton, hemp, and flax that the colony produced in the following year. The children in his care spent five hours a day at their schoolwork and other hours spinning and carding.[36]

With the children now settled in temporary accommodation Whitefield focused his considerable energies on the construction of the permanent buildings. The main house was to be two storeys high with twenty large rooms. At the rear were two smaller buildings, one being the infirmary and the other a workhouse.[37] In all of this Whitefield demonstrated a capacity for business, organization, and an ability to get things done quickly. He wanted the Bethesda orphanage house to be self-supporting. The wood on the land would be used in the construction of the buildings. The food supply would come from raising poultry, pigs, and cattle. Income would be derived from selling cotton and the sloop which had been purchased for his use was to earn money from transporting freight.

Whitefield wrote confidently from Savannah to Howell Harris that "God, I believe, is laying a foundation for great things in Georgia. I am building a large house and taking in many children."[38] By the end of the month the situation had progressed considerably and Whitefield wrote, "The Orphan-house is in great forwardness. I feed near a hundred mouths daily, and am assured I serve a God who will supply our needs."[39] Ten days later he wrote optimistically of the progress in a letter addressed to the Hon. J. W., "I have digged [sic] low, and intend to build it high, because I have a great God to pay the charges. I have about thirty-six children which I maintain and cloath [sic], and have upwards of forty persons more who are employed in the work."[40]

Despite Whitefield's optimism as to the progress of his project, his relations with the trustees of the colony became increasingly strained. They were not happy being associated with a preacher who was regarded as an enthusiast and taunted by published episcopal tracts. They were apprehensive about the increasingly large sums of money he was raising through collections at his open-air preaching and they were also unhappy at Whitefield's proposal that he should have the sole right to manage the entire venture. However, the trustees met and agreed, doubtless with some reservations, to everything he had asked and gave "a grant of five hundred acres in trust to me and my successors for ever, for the use of the Orphan House".[41] However, when Whitefield received a copy of the agreement he was stunned to find that he was not to be allowed to bequeath the institution but instead on his death it would be taken over by the trustees. The situation was further exacerbated by the trustees insisting that the local magistrates should both inspect the house on a regular basis and exercise control over aspects of its management. Despite these unhappy circumstances Whitefield was able to see his building project make solid progress. He clearly had an inkling even at this early stage that his Bethesda orphan house was going to be a life-struggle and wrote in a letter to William S. Esq., in London, "I am almost tempted to wish I had never undertook the Orphan House."[42] It's clear from these words that Whitefield recognized that sustaining this project was going to require perseverance and hard graft.

A marriage proposal and a marriage

Whitefield had first met Elizabeth Delamotte when he was twenty-five years old and he was strongly attracted to her. He struggled to resolve his feelings for her with his love for Christ and did his best to put her out of his mind when he sailed for Georgia in 1739. However, on his arrival he found a letter from Elizabeth[43] was waiting for him and this further awakened his affections. The added burden of the strains and stresses of running the orphan house and the care of the female orphans in particular began to play on Whitefield's mind and further increased his desire for marriage. He wrote on 28 March to a fellow clergyman, Benjamin Ingham,[44] "I believe it to be God's will that I should marry. One, who may be looked upon as a superior, is absolutely necessary for the due management of affairs. However, I pray God, that I may not have a wife, till I can live as though I had none." He went on to tell his friend to feel free to share what he had written "for I would call Christ and his disciples to the marriage".[45]

Just a week after appearing to ask Ingham for advice the young priest was unable to wait for any longer. While on board ship from Georgia to Philadelphia on 4 April, he wrote at some length to Elizabeth's parents, Thomas[46] and Elizabeth Delamotte.

> It hath been much impressed on my heart, that I should marry, in order to have a help meet for me in the work whereunto our dear Lord Jesus hath called me. This comes (like Abraham's servant to Rebekah's relations) to know whether you think your daughter, Miss E—, is a proper person to engage in such an undertaking? If so; whether you will be pleased to give me leave to propose marriage unto her? You need not be afraid of sending me a refusal. For, I bless God, if I know anything of my own heart, I am free of that foolish passion, which the world calls Love. I write, only because I believe it is the will of God, that I should alter my state, but your denial will convince me, that your daughter is not the person appointed for me. He

> knows my heart; I would not marry but for him,
> and in him, for ten thousand worlds.[47]

On the same day he also wrote to Elizabeth a proposal of marriage. His letter, which began with a catalogue of the sufferings she could expect to endure as his wife, could hardly have been more off-putting. There was no mention of the deep feelings he clearly had for her or his growing desire to be intimate and share his life with her. Instead he began with a sentence which could hardly have been more gauche, "Do you think, you could undergo the fatigues, that must necessarily attend being joined to one, who is every day liable to be called out to suffer for the sake of Jesus Christ?" After further inquiring if Elizabeth could bear leaving her home and family, Whitefield then went on to offer yet more reasons why she might not want to marry him.

> Can you bear the inclemencies of the air both as
> to the cold and heat in a foreign climate? Can you,
> when you have an husband, be as though you had
> none, and willingly part with him, even for a long
> season, when the Lord and master shall call him
> forth to preach the gospel, and command him to
> leave you behind? If after seeking God's direction,
> and searching your heart, you can say, "I can do
> all those things through Christ strengthening
> me," what if you and I were joined together in
> the Lord, and you came with me on my return
> from England, to be a help meet for me in the
> management of the orphan-house.[48]

These two letters both reveal the young Whitefield to have been unable to express his desire for Elizabeth or reconcile his natural sexual feelings with his Christian faith. One cannot but feel sad that he clearly had strong feelings for Elizabeth but was seemingly unable to articulate them possibly on account of his Puritan leanings. If Thomas Kidd is correct, guilt from his teenage past over masturbation may have added to the problem.[49] Hindmarsh has helpfully drawn attention to the fact that "asceticism flourished remarkably in Oxford in the 1730s and was on display in Whitefield's diary".[50] It is therefore very possible that the rigid and strict discipline of the Holy Club and Oxford Methodism had further caused him to sublimate his feelings. There are strong suggestions of this toward the end of his lengthy letter where he wrote, "I desire to 'take you my sister to wife, not for lust, but uprightly,' therefore I hope he will mercifully ordain, if it be his blessed will we should be joined together that we may walk as Zachary and Elizabeth did, in all the ordinances of the Lord blameless." A little later he added, "The passionate expressions which carnal courtiers use, I think, ought to be avoided by those that would marry in the Lord."[51] Add to this Whitefield had begun his letter to Elizabeth's parents by informing them that one of the women he brought to Georgia had died and that two others were in a declining state. He wrote as though he was more concerned to have a manager for his orphan house than someone he could love and whose company he could enjoy. Indeed it is hard to imagine a worse way in which to make a proposal of marriage. It was destined for a refusal from the moment he put pen to paper.

Yet Dallimore's view that Whitefield "seems almost to have taken it for granted that she would be willing to marry him, and this without any attempt on his part to win her affections or declare his own", is likely to be correct. Whitefield informed Elizabeth's parents that "I have sometimes thought Miss E would be my help-mate; for she has often been impressed on my mind."[52] The reality was that no woman in her right mind, even the most dedicated of Christians, would have entertained such a prospect.

Whitefield dispatched his letters to Elizabeth and her parents from Philadelphia when he arrived there on 15 April.[53] Inevitably he now had to wait for nearly six months before receiving any replies. What he did not know was that by the time his letters reached England the Delamottes had fallen foul with the Wesleys and had joined with the Moravians. It is likely that they had begun to feel similarly toward Whitefield who shared John and Charles' opinion of the Moravians. Indeed Whitefield had himself earlier fallen out with the Moravians in Georgia.[54]

Whitefield eventually received replies from both Elizabeth and her parents but the only reference to them that survives in his correspondence is in a letter which he sent from Savannah to "Wm S, Esq", dated 26 June 1740. This was almost certainly his close friend and travelling companion William Seward, now back in London. He had, he wrote, "received many agreeable letters from England: but find from Blendon letters that 'Miss E— D— is in a seeking state only.' "Surely," he continued, "that will not do; I would have one that is full of faith and the Holy Ghost… My poor family gives me more concern than every thing else put together. I want a *gracious woman* that is dead to every thing but Jesus, and is qualified to govern children, and direct persons of her own sex. Such a woman would help, and not retard my dear Lord's work."[55] Yet again we encounter Whitefield still turned in on himself and his work with little feeling – if any – of warmth for Elizabeth. He seems almost pulled apart in a dilemma. On the one hand he appears driven with a longing for a loving and sexual union but trusts in the Lord every moment "that he will not permit me to fall by the hands of a woman".[56]

In his remark that Elizabeth is in "a state of seeking" there is a hint that she was not yet a believer. Regardless of whether this was so Elizabeth was married the following year to William Holland (1711–

61). Holland resided in London and had a large house-painting business which he sold and then became a full-time labourer with the Moravians.[57] Doubtless very disappointed Whitefield was able to take his mind off what might have been by embarking on another preaching tour which took him through Philadelphia and New York and eventually on to Northampton, where a great revival had taken place under the ministry of Jonathan Edwards. There, witnessing Edwards' loving relationship with his wife, Sarah, Whitefield once again realized how much he longed to be married.

Spring and summer tours

Whitefield's spring tour began in Savannah where he had laid the first brick for the new main building at his Bethesda orphanage.[58] He then had a short ten-day crossing by sloop to Philadelphia from where he sent the package of letters, which included those to the Delamottes. Between Monday 13 April and Thursday 5 June when he arrived back in Savannah, Whitefield visited some thirty-five towns and villages and preached sixty-eight times[59] in what can only be described as a whirlwind tour. In a number of these places Whitefield was able to raise money for the needs of the orphanage, the residents of which he often spoke of as "my family". His congregations were particularly large in Philadelphia and he recorded on 17 April, "I preached to upwards of ten thousand people, upon the woman who was cured of her bloody issue." The following Sunday, 20 April, he noted, "Preached to about ten thousand people, and collected £110 sterling for my poor orphans. The people threw in their mites willingly." The same evening Whitefield's congregation swelled to an estimated 15,000 people and "we collected £80 currency for my children in Georgia".[60]

Whitefield was much heartened by the response of both the black Africans and Quakers of Philadelphia. When he came to leave the city he was very encouraged that almost fifty of their number came and thanked him for what God had done for their souls. Whitefield for his part was touched by the way in which "those poor creatures throw in their mites for my orphans". Many of the Quakers, he recorded in his journal, "have been convinced of the righteousness of Jesus Christ and openly confess the truth as it is in Jesus".[61] On a number of these occasions Whitefield's hearers were deeply touched. At Nottingham in Pennsylvania, for example, where the hearers were reckoned to be "near twelve thousand", he had not been speaking long before "thousands cried out, so that they almost drowned my voice". Whitefield wrote, "Never did I see a more glorious sight. Oh what tears were shed and poured forth after the Lord Jesus. Some fainted; and when they had got a little strength, they would hear and faint again." Others cried out "as if they were in the sharpest agonies of death!"[62] At Faggs Manor in the same colony, "Some of the people were as pale as death; others were wringing their hands; others lying on the ground; others sinking into the arms of friends; and most lifting up their eyes to Heaven and crying for mercy."[63]

After this Whitefield recorded, "I rode at the rate of eight miles an hour to Newcastle, about twenty-four miles from Faggs Manor, preached to about four thousand, prayed with several who came many miles under violent convictions, and then went on board our sloop, the *Savannah*."[64] Whitefield now had six other persons with him who he had employed to assist in the work of his Bethesda orphanage. They arrived on 5 June to what he described as a "sweet meeting with my dear friends".[65]

Whitefield was pleased to find that "Providence seems to smile upon the Orphan-House and prosper everything I take in hand."[66] By mid-August of 1740 Whitefield felt that all his business in Savannah was well-settled and noted that the orphanage "succeeds beyond expectation".[67]

He was never one to settle anywhere for long, however, and on 18 August he duly set sail on what was to become another major, extended, and very demanding preaching tour. Whitefield's first stopping place was Charleston where many came to the wharf and welcomed him to his lodgings. He recorded in his journal that his audiences were more numerous than ever, and "it was supposed that not less than four thousand were in and about the meeting house".[68] He journeyed northward through Philadelphia, New York, and Boston before travelling further afield in New England.

He did not return to Georgia until Saturday 13 December.[69] His preaching enabled him to revisit some of the towns and cities where he had previously been instrumental in awakening many of his hearers. He drew some very large congregations, some of whom were powerfully impacted by falling, weeping, and repentant cries for mercy. Along the way he was able to receive encouragement from like-minded ministers and clergy – and in some cases governors and local people of influence. In a number of places Whitefield organized large sacramental services with Baptists, Presbyterians, and others all taking part. Such occasions with "Dissenters" participating was illegal for Church of England clergy. While these occasions strengthened Whitefield's bond of friendship with Nonconformists they exacerbated his relationships with the episcopal hierarchy. Whitefield also collected some substantial donations for his orphanage and spoke to students in colleges in both Boston and Princeton.

Boston and New England

Whitefield arrived in Boston on Thursday 18 September. On the following day he was visited by several gentlemen and ministers and went to the governor, Jonathan Belcher (1681–1757), "who received him with the utmost respect and desired me to see him as often as I could".[70] He preached that same evening to about 4,000 in Dr Colman's meeting house and exhorted and prayed with many afterwards.[71] The following morning he addressed "about six thousand hearers" and afterwards on the common gave a sermon to "about eight thousand".[72] He preached on a number of other occasions and continued to draw large numbers. His message at the Revd Samuel Checkley's meeting house proved to be a scene of tragedy when all of a sudden there was an unexpected uproar which caused large numbers to suddenly rush for the doors. In a desperate struggle to make a quick exit five people were killed and others severely injured.[73] For Whitefield, who was sensitive by nature, the tragedy was doubtless particularly disturbing.

A month later, when Whitefield was at Worcester, Governor Belcher came to meet him and listen to his preaching. Whitefield found him to be "more affectionate than ever" and noted that Belcher exhorted me to stir up the ministers because "reformation must begin at the house of God". After his sermon Belcher asked Whitefield to pray for him that he might hunger and thirst after righteousness.[74]

Boston appears to have been the pinnacle of Whitefield's time in New England. He enjoyed a particularly warm relationship with the governor who gave him hospitality and took him in his own coach to the common where he preached his farewell sermon to "near twenty thousand people". It was a sight which Whitefield had not seen since he left Blackheath in England; "a sight", he wrote, "perhaps never seen before in America".[75]

Whitefield was impressed by some of the aspects of life in Boston. It was a place of wealth "where the love of many is waxed cold", but on the positive side, he noted that there were nine Congregational meeting houses and several others belonging to various denominations. There was also a remarkable external observance of the sabbath and men in civil offices had a high regard for religion. Whitefield recorded, "I never saw so little scoffing, and never had so little opposition."[76]

Rekindling of the Northampton revival

From Boston Whitefield gradually rode his way to Hadley and Northampton, towns which had seen revival through the ministry of Jonathan Edwards. In the latter town he recorded in his journal, "No less than three hundred souls were saved about five years ago." In the same entry Whitefield described Edwards as "a solid excellent Christian, but, at present, weak in body".[77] On being invited to take the pulpit Whitefield felt drawn to speak of the privileges of being a Christian believer and reminded the congregation of the help and presence of the Spirit. The effects of the Great Awakening, which had earlier taken place, were by this time beginning to ebb, but when Whitefield reminded them of what had been and their former experiences it was "like putting fire to tinder".[78]

Despite his disappointment over Elizabeth Delamotte, Whitefield's mind was never far from hopes of being married. On 30 September he recorded in his journal that he had been entertained in the home of Revd Mr Cotton in the town of Hampton, for whom he had preached a sermon. He was impressed that Cotton's wife was "one that serveth".[79] Doubtless the rigours and loneliness he felt suddenly strengthened his desires for a wife for himself. Yet it still appeared that he was looking first and foremost for someone with whom to share his strenuous workload rather than a woman whom he could love and with whom he could share companionship.

These thoughts were further kindled when he went to stay in the Edwards' home. He was much impressed by the happiness of their marital relationship. "A sweeter couple," he noted, "I have not yet seen." He was particularly taken with Mrs Edwards' "meek and quiet spirit" and her ability to "talk solidly of the things of God".

His time with the Edwards caused him "to renew those prayers, which for some months I have put up to God" that "he would be pleased to send me a daughter of Abraham to be my wife".[80] Still, however, Whitefield seemed unable to see marriage as in any sense an affectionate and tender relationship. He went on to write in his journal, "Thou knowest my circumstances; Thou knowest I only desire to marry for Thee. Thou dist choose a Rebecca for Isaac, choose one to be helpmeet for me, in carrying on that great work which is committed to my charge."[81] Reflecting on this entry it appears as if all he really wanted or felt he needed was an efficient and Christian full-time PA.

Leaving aside Whitefield's concern to find a wife which had been stirred by his time in the Edwards' household there can be no doubt that his preaching and presence in Northampton played a significant part in rekindling the revival there and in the surrounding areas. Jonathan Edwards observed that although the revival had begun to plateau in the last few years, an upturn began in the spring of 1740. "There was," he wrote, "more serious and religious conversation of their souls, especially among the young people."[82] This improving state of affairs continued until Whitefield arrived in the town in the middle of October. Whitefield preached four sermons in the meeting house and gave several lectures including one in Edwards' house. Immediately there was a remarkable upturn in the spiritual life of the community. Edwards wrote the following lines in a lengthy letter to a fellow minister in Boston.

> The congregation was extraordinarily melted by every sermon; almost the whole assembly being in tears for a great part of sermon time. Mr Whitefield's sermons were suitable to the circumstances of the town; containing a just reproof of our

backslidings... Immediately after this, the minds
of the people in general appeared more engaged
in religion, showing a greater forwardness to make
religion the subject of conversation, and to meet
frequently for religious purposes, and to embrace
all the opportunities to hear the word preached...
In about a month or six weeks, there was a great
alteration in the town, both as to the revivals of
professors, and awakenings of others.[83]

On 29 October Whitefield began his journey south and as he did so
"gave God thanks for sending me to New England". He was of the
view that on many accounts, it "certainly excels all other provinces
in America; and for the establishment of religion, perhaps all other
parts of the world".[84] Gillies cites a report by the Revd Mr Josiah
Smith of Charleston in the *South Carolina Gazette*, to indicate
the very positive impact that Whitfield was felt to have made in
New England. Smith's account abounds with fulsome affirmations,
"Such a power and presence of God... The prejudices of many are
quite conquered... A considerable number awakened."[85]

During his time in New England Whitefield had met with, stirred,
and encouraged the faith of Gilbert Tennent and other prominent
local clergy, often sharing in Communion services with them and
their congregations. He had also taken the opportunity to challenge
and inspire students who were in training for the church's ministry.
While in Boston he visited Harvard College in Cambridge, which
he described as not quite as big as one of the Oxford colleges. He
considered the piety and discipline to be at a low ebb and reported
that bad books – Tillotson and the like – were being read by both
tutors and students. Whitefield accepted the invitation to address
the tutors and students and preached appositely on the text, "We

are not as many, who corrupt the word of God." A large number of local ministers and clergy attended his address and Whitefield reported, "the Holy Spirit melted many hearts".[86]

The following month, when he visited New Haven, he was invited by the principal, Thomas Clapp of Yale College, who later became his opponent, to preach to the students who were training for the ministry. He chose to speak on the dangers and consequences of an unconverted ministry.[87] As Dallimore pointed out, the warnings which Whitefield gave proved beneficial.[88] Dr Colman stated that Harvard was completely changed in consequence of his visit. "The students are full of God. Many of them appear truly born again. The voice of prayer and praise fills their chambers; and joy, with seriousness of heart sits visibly on their faces."[89] At Yale there were similar positive results. Jonathan Edwards reported that "the students in general became serious, many of them remarkably so, and much engaged in the concerns of their eternal welfare".[90]

This topic of unconverted ministers also featured prominently during Whitefield's time in Philadelphia and New York.[91] His hostility to those he perceived as unconverted is perhaps further understandable since it was the Latitudinarian followers of the late archbishop John Tillotson who were among his chief opponents. It was they who dubbed him an enthusiast who was guided by impressions, stirred the crowds by his dramatized heaven and hell rhetoric, and held to the doctrine of instantaneous conversion. Whitefield clearly felt the need both to defend himself and justify the revival and those who were promoting it.

To Whitefield's own reflection above must be added the fact that during his time in America in 1740 he wrote some 240 letters, many of which contained lengthy instructions about his Bethesda orphan house and affairs relating to his societies back in England.[92] In addition he delivered a number of attacks on the ways in which slaves were being treated in the colonies and debated with Wesley and others the doctrines of election and final perseverance, as well as worrying about divisions among the people in his societies back in England.[93]

Whitefield's next move was to leave New England, crossing over into the province of New York and into New York City, where he stayed for four days. On Sunday 2 November he recorded that as he preached the Spirit of the Lord "came down like a mighty rushing wind, and carried all before it". The whole congregation was alarmed and "weeping and wailing were to be heard in every corner".[94] After this Whitefield journeyed back to Georgia via Philadelphia, finally reaching Savannah at midnight on 14 December.

One cannot but be amazed at Whitefield's sheer energy and stamina. He reflected,

> I have been enabled to preach, I think, an hundred and seventy-five times in public, besides exhorting frequently in private. I have travelled upwards of eight hundred miles, gotten upwards of seven hundred pounds sterling,[95] in goods, provisions, and money, for the Georgia orphans. Never did I perform my journeys with so little fatigue, or see such a continuance of the divine presence in the congregations to whom I preached.[96]

Upon his arrival in Savannah, he preached in the parish church, and then went on to Bethesda where he found the house well-settled. After spending a comfortable Christmas with "his family" he felt he had a clear call to return to England.[97] On 29 December 1740 he left Savannah on the start of his homeward journey, leaving Charleston on board the *Minerva* on 18 January. He arrived back in England, at Falmouth, on 11 March.

In this period Whitefield established himself as a celebrity preacher who attracted huge crowds in Boston, Philadelphia, and New York. He visited Jonathan Edwards in Northampton, Massachusetts and was instrumental in rekindling the revival. He also established a friendship with Benjamin Franklin in Philadelphia. This proved to be vitally important since Franklin was to become both his publisher and his advocate.

Chapter 4 notes

1   See J. Gillies, *Memoirs of the Life*, p. 46.
2   R. Philip, *Life and Times,* p. 165.
3   *Journal,* 8 November 1739.
4   Ibid, 9 November 1739.
5   Ibid, 11 November 1739.
6   Ibid, 13 November 1739.
7   The Church of England at this point in time had no bishops in the American colonies. The responsibility for them rested with the Bishop of London. He appointed commissaries in each ecclesiastical area who were responsible for the clergy and for maintaining Church of England canon law.
8   *Journal,* 15 November 1739.
9   Ibid.
10 Ibid, 20 November 1739.
11 Ibid, 22 November 1739.
12 See J. Gillies, op. cit., p. 47.
13 Ibid, 28 November 1739.
14 R. Philip, op. cit., p. 173.
15 B. Franklin, *Works,* in A. Dallimore, *George Whitefield,* Vol. 1, pp. 438–39.
16 R. Philip, op. cit., pp. 173–74.
17 F. Lambert, *Pedlar in Divinity George Whitefield and the Transatlantic Revivals, 1737–1770* (New Jersey, Princeton University Press, 1993), p. 8.
18 Ibid, pp. 13 and 35.
19 Ibid, p. 54.
20 Ibid, p. 60.
21 Ibid, p. 57.
22 Ibid, pp. 75 and 77.
23 Ibid, p. 106.
24 Ibid, p. 128.
25 Ibid, p. 111.
26 *Journal,* 29 November 1739.
27 Ibid, 1 December 1739.
28 Ibid, 2 December 1739.

29   Ibid, 15 December 1739.
30   Ibid.
31   Ibid, 31 December 1739.
32   Ibid, 5 January 1740.
33   Ibid, 6 January 1740.
34   Ibid, 7 January 1740.
35   Ibid, 24 January 1740.
36   Ibid, 29 January 1740.
37   Ibid, 30 January 1740.
38   *Letter to Mr H. H.*, 4 February 1740.
39   *Letter to the Rev Mr J.*, 29 February 1740.
40   *Letter to Hon. J. W.*, 10 March 1740.
41   *Colonial Records of Georgia*, Vol. 5, p. 166 in Dallimore, A., *George Whitefield*, Vol. 1, p. 456.
42   *Letter to Wm S. Esq.*, 26 June 1740.
43   A. Dallimore, *Whitefield*, p. 467.
44   Benjamin Ingham (1712–72) a fellow Methodist itinerant preacher who established, pastored, and married Lady Hastings on 12 November 1741. She was instrumental in the conversion of her sister-in-law, Selina, Countess of Huntingdon. Ingham later joined the Moravians and his Yorkshire societies became part of the Moravian connection.
45   *Letter to the Rev. Mr B. I.*, 28 March 1740, *Works*, Vol. 1, p. 158.
46   1714–90.
47   *Letter to Mr and Mrs D.*, 4 April 1740.
48   Ibid.
49   T. S. Kidd, *George Whitefield*, p. 18.
50   D. B. Hindmarsh, *The Spirit of Early Evangelicalism* (Oxford, University Press, 2018), p. 20.
51   *Letter to Miss E.*, 4 April 1740.
52   A. Dallimore, *George Whitefield*, Vol. 2, p. 470.
53   *Journal*, 14 April 1740.
54   See R. S. Grumet, *The Munsee Indians: A History* (Norman, University of Oklahoma, 2009). "The Moravians settled in Georgia in 1739 at Whitefield's invite on some land he had purchased and Christened the Barony of Nazareth. Quickly falling out with Whitefield the Moravians bought five thousand acres themselves at Nazareth where they began building a city they named Bethlehem in 1740" p. 249.
55   *Letter to Wm S——*, 26 June 1740, *Works*, Vol. 1, p. 194.
56   Ibid.
57   For details of the Delamottes and their links with the Moravians see William Holland, *A Short Account of some matters relating to the Work of the Lord in England* (1845). This work is cited at length by K. Hylson Smith, *Studies in Revivalism as a Social and Religious Phenomenon, with special reference to the London Revival of 1736–1750* (Leicester University, 1973).
58   *Journal*, 21 March 1740.

59 Ibid, 25 May 1740.
60 Ibid, 20 April 1740.
61 Ibid, 11 May 1740.
62 Ibid, 14 May 1740.
63 Ibid, 15 May 1740.
64 Ibid.
65 Ibid, 5 June 1740.
66 Ibid, 30 June 1740.
67 Ibid, 18 August 1740.
68 Ibid, 22 August 1740.
69 Ibid, 14 December 1740.
70 Ibid, 19 September 1740.
71 Ibid, 20 September 1740.
72 Ibid.
73 Ibid, 22 September 1740.
74 Ibid, 15 October 1740.
75 Ibid, 12 October 1740.
76 Ibid.
77 Ibid, 17 October 1740.
78 R. Philip, op. cit., p. 188.
79 *Journal,* 30 September 1740.
80 Ibid, 19 October 1740.
81 Ibid.
82 J. Edwards, *An Account of the Revival,* p. 149.
83 Ibid.
84 *Journal,* 29 October 1740.
85 J. Gillies, op. cit., pp. 64–66.
86 *Journal,* 24 September 1740.
87 Ibid, 25 October 1740 and R. Philip, *Life and Times,* pp. 188–89.
88 A. Dallimore, *George Whitefield,* Vol. 1, p. 553.
89 J. Belcher, *George Whitefield: A Biography* (New York, Tract Society, 1857) p. 213, Tyerman, op. cit., Vol. 1, p. 418.
90 J. Edwards, *Memoirs of David Brainerd* (Edition of J. M. Sherwood, Funk and Wagnalls, 1884), p. 16, cited A. Dallimore, *George Whitefield,* Vol. 1, p. 553.
91 See A. Dallimore, *George Whitefield,* Vol. 1, p. 549.
92 *Letters,* Vol. 1, pp. 139–229.
93 See for example A. Dallimore, *George Whitefield,* Vol. 1, p. 431.
94 *Journal,* 2 November 1740.
95 As we have seen earlier, Whitefield used the opportunity of his large gatherings to collect money for his orphanage house. See his *Journal* as follows. At Roxbury on Sunday 28 September he preached to a very large crowd and collected £555. At Hampstead he preached to several thousands "with a great deal of power" and collected £41 for the orphan children. At Marble Head near Boston on October 6 two ministers

presented him with £70 from their respective congregations for the orphan house. On Friday 10 October Whitefield preached "with much freedom of spirit" at Charleston and collected £156 for the orphans. Later the same day, twelve miles distant at Redding, he preached to "many thousands and collected £51 5s for the orphans. On Sunday 26 October at New Haven in the evening, "I expounded to a great number of people at my lodgings, and collected upwards of £35 for the orphans."

96 J. Gillies, op. cit., pp. 66–67.
97 *Journal,* 29 December 1740.

Chapter 5

Catalyst of Revival in Scotland

During the course of his second visit to the American colonies Whitefield received a number of letters from two brothers, Ebenezer (1680–1754) and Ralph Erskine (1685–1752). Both were ordained ministers in the Church of Scotland although no longer in good standing. They were clearly interested in the reports of the successes which followed in the wake of Whitefield's preaching. They both therefore eagerly sought to persuade him to come to Scotland in the hopes of experiencing similar awakenings in their parishes and beyond. However it soon became apparent to Whitefield that in urging his coming they had a second underlying agenda, the background of which was a disagreement regarding the way in which ministers were appointed to their parishes.

In 1690 patronage, which gave congregations the right to appoint their ministers, had been abolished by the Scottish parliament. However, in 1712 the Tory government passed a further *Patronage Act* which restored the sole rights of landowners to appoint ministers. This was an act that which led to the first break in the established Church of Scotland. In fact it caused a disruption in the Scottish church which lasted for the next 150 years. It first began in 1732 and was led by Ebenezer Erskine.

Erskine was a celebrated preacher who strongly objected to the patronage system that allowed a landowner to choose a parish minster without the approval of the people of the parish. In December 1733 Erskine and other ministers met together near Kinross and formed the Associate Presbytery. By 1736 the Secession Church was seen as a separate entity and by 1740 the number of seceding congregations had reached twenty. Erskine was eventually excluded from his ministry at the parish church of Stirling in1740 following which he had a new church built for his expanding congregation.[1]

Initially, in the late 1730s, a warm and amicable correspondence developed between the Erskines and Whitefield but it eventually resulted in a major rift between them. This ultimately led to the Associate Presbytery opposing Whitefield's work and his ministry at Cambuslang and elsewhere in Scotland with considerable hostility.

Whitefield first became fully aware of the Erskines' agenda to gain his support for the Associate Presbytery in May, 1741 when he received a letter from Ebenezer Erskine's younger brother, Ralph. Whitefield stated that he had been advised "that it would be best for me to join the associate presbytery, if it should please God to send me to Scotland".[2] Whitefield for his part had replied from Bristol that he would come only "as an occasional preacher, to preach the simple gospel to all that are willing to hear me".[3]

By this statement Whitefield made it abundantly clear that he was not going to allow himself to get trapped in disputes over church government. He was totally focused on what he believed to be his calling as an evangelist. While he could write, "I love and honour the Associate Presbytery in the bowels of Jesus Christ",[4] he clearly had no intention of becoming embroiled in their dispute. To have done so would not only have added to the rift in the Scottish church but also removed wider opportunities in other parts and among other denominations. The situation demonstrated that while Whitefield was rigidly and firmly attached to the Calvinist doctrines of election and final perseverance he was much more flexible when it came to secondary issues of ecclesiology. Indeed he was more than ready to defend the Anglican system of government. In a letter penned on 10 August 1741 to John Willison (1680–1750), the parish minister of Dundee, Whitefield urged him not to cause trouble "by writing about the corruptions of the Church of England". He went on to write that he believed that there was no perfect church under heaven and that there was no need for him to separate from the English establishment.[5] He wrote similarly to James Ogilvie (1695–1776), the parish minister of West St Nicholas, Aberdeen that the divisions in the Church of Scotland "were a sore" and that he found it best to preach the pure gospel, and not to meddle at all with controversy.[6]

Whitefield's arrival in Scotland

Soon after Whitefield arrived back on English soil in March 1741 he received letters from William Wishart[7] and Ebenezer Erskine[8] both urging him to come to Scotland. He felt unable to make any immediate commitments in response because he had pressing business and preaching commitments in London. However he finally boarded the *Mary Ann* at Gravesend on 24 July and set sail for Leith arriving in Edinburgh on 1 August.[9]

At first, things appeared to bode well with Whitefield. In a letter sent from Edinburgh on his day of arrival, he wrote that as "the Messrs Erskines gave me the first invitation to Scotland, and hath been praying for me in the most public, explicit, I could almost say extravagant manner, for near two years past, I was determined to give them the first offer of my poor ministrations".[10] Whitefield therefore made his way to Dunfermline where on 31 July[11] he preached in Ralph Erskine's substantial "seceding meeting-house" to a very large assembly crowd. He was particularly impressed by the large number of those present who all opened their own Bibles with a great rustling noise when he gave out his text.

After the meeting was over Erskine and his friends did their best to entertain Whitefield with various accounts of the successes of the seceding congregations. They pressed him to subscribe immediately to the Solemn League and Covenant and to preach only for them. He responded by asking "whether there were no other Lord's people but themselves?" Whitefield's position was that he was "more and more determined to go out into the highways and hedges; and that if the Pope himself would lend me his pulpit, I would gladly proclaim the righteousness of Jesus Christ therein".[12] They urged him to stay longer but he had already given notice of preaching at Edinburgh.[13] After this meeting Whitefield joined them for worship in the meeting house where one of their number preached on the words, "Watchman what of the night?" (Isaiah 21:11). The good man spent the first part of his address denouncing prelacy, the Book of Common Prayer (of which Whitefield was a strong advocate), and the surplice with the result that he had hardly enough voice to invite his hearers to come to Christ. After preaching in the fields Whitefield dined with them and went on his way to Edinburgh.

Preaching in Edinburgh and other towns and cities

From the second week in August till the end of October Whitefield based himself in and around Edinburgh. Yet again he proved himself an inveterate traveller and preacher by leaving the city and riding up the east coast as far as Aberdeen and visiting Brechin, Dundee, and other smaller towns on the way. At Aberdeen, as a mark of their respect, the magistrates gave Whitefield the freedom of the city.[14] He spent the greater part of August in the capital city preaching twice a day either in churches or in the fields. Notwithstanding growing hostility from the Associate Presbytery he received many approving letters from those who had responded to his preaching. He was in buoyant mood writing that "every day fresh seals are given of my ministry".[15] He wrote to his friend Howell Harris that he would have leapt for joy if he had been with him in the city where there were upwards of 300 seeking after Jesus and where God's power was continually present.[16] His congregations consisted of many thousands and Whitefield recalled that he had never seen so many people following his preaching with open Bibles in their hands. In between preaching he spoke with people in private homes and counselled those who were in distress over their souls. He preached in Glasgow ten times to very large congregations[17] and met with great success in Aberdeen where he preached with "much freedom and power to very large congregations".[18] He found the people there and elsewhere very generous to the needs of his poor orphans and he described his time in Dundee as being "very extraordinary". On the sabbath he preached four times and lectured in the evening. On another day he preached seven times with the power of God coming with great effects.[19] As he left Edinburgh to journey by road back to England via Wales he wrote in a letter, "I scarce know how to leave Scotland. I believe I shall think it my duty to pay the inhabitants another visit as soon as possible."[20] It was to be another ten months before he was to return and play a significant role in the great revivals in Cambuslang and Kilsyth.

Prelude to revival in Cambuslang and Kilsyth

Although Whitefield proved to be the instrument which opened the flood tide of revival in Cambuslang, Kilsyth and beyond it is clear that there was a quickening of the Spirit's presence for some months before his arrival in Scotland. William McCulloch (1691–1771), the parish minister of Cambuslang, had for some time been downcast but had begun to be inspired by reports of the revival in New England which were reaching Scottish shores. On Sunday evenings after the sermon he started the practice of reading to his congregation accounts of the revival under Whitefield's preaching. Soon after, in February 1741, he began a course of sermons on the subject of regeneration and his parishioners began to feel an increased sense of hope and expectancy.[21] This soon led to numbers of them praying for a revival of religion.[22] Philip noted that McCulloch's sermons had begun to impact his hearers in considerable numbers well before Whitefield had arrived on the scene. Indeed "some were so violently agitated... as to fall down under visible paroxysms of bodily agony".[23]

Similarly to McCulloch's ministry in Cambuslang, James Robe (1688–1753), the parish minister at Kilsyth, found his work hardgoing. He had been appointed to Kilsyth in 1713 and continued his ministry there until his death in May 1753. In the summer of 1740 he was particularly troubled by the plight of the poor resulting from the extraordinary drought which threatened both man and beast. Like McCulloch he had also begun a series of sermons on the subject of regeneration in the later months of 1740, but for all his endeavours no visible change was to be seen in the lives of his hearers.[24]

Whitefield's coming

Whitefield had embarked for Scotland once more on the *Mary Ann* on 29 May and arrived on 3 June. On board ship he wrote, "I spent most of my time in secret prayer."[25] Unsurprisingly, as soon as he went on shore he felt the Holy Spirit filling his soul. Many people came to him weeping and blessing him and great numbers followed his coach as he travelled to Edinburgh.[26] He spent the next four weeks ministering in and around Edinburgh and Glasgow. Looking back on what had taken place he wrote to a friend in London:

In every place there was the greatest commotion among the people as was ever known. Their mourning in most places, was like the mourning for a first born. The auditories were very large, and the work of God seems to be spreading more and more. Last Sabbath-day I preached twice in the Park, and once in the church, and twice every day since.[27]

Word continued to reach Whitefield about the awakening in Cambuslang from the moment he had set foot on Scottish soil. On 8 June he wrote encouragingly to McCulloch, "I believe you will both see and hear of far greater things than these. I trust that not one corner of poor Scotland will be left unwatered by the dew of God's heavenly blessing."[28] A month later, on 6 July Whitefield left Glasgow for Cambuslang arriving at noon the same day.[29] His intention was both to be a part of the move of God that was taking place but more specifically he had been invited by McCulloch to assist in serving Communion at the tables.

The revival which took place in both Cambuslang and Kilysth was notable for several reasons. First, as has been noted, for some months there had been a quickening of spiritual life in both of these towns and parishes with gatherings for earnest prayer and a reviving of personal religion. Second, in both parishes the central focus of the move of God was the gathering for corporate Communion. Third, the revival was marked by the preaching of a literal hell often with depictions of punishment.[30] That said, there were, as Fawcett noted, "many who were melted down by the love of Christ".[31] Fourth, the revival proved to be portable. The gatherings in both Cambuslang and Kilsyth were attended by ministers and clergy from many places across the country. They then travelled home and carried the Spirit of God with them to their parishes and meeting houses much in the way that the Old Testament prophet Elisha had carried away the mantle of his master Elijah.

Some of those who participated in the revival saw it as the Spirit of God being poured out in the Last Days and began in consequence to think in terms of the imminent return of Christ. John Erskine (1721–1803), who was later to become the minister of Old Greyfriars Church, Edinburgh, was so taken by what he had witnessed and experienced that he published a small treatise entitled *THE SIGNS OF THE TIMES CONSIDERED, or the high PROBABILITY that the present APPEARANCES in New England, and the West of Scotland, are a PRELUDE of the Glorious THINGS promised to the CHURCH in the latter ages*.[32] Avoiding the trap of speculating about dates or times Erskine gave it as his view that the work of God now carrying on would in all probability spread and increase. "Blessed be God," he wrote, "our eyes see and ears hear such glorious things as these. The Lord has indeed done marvellous things."[33]

Whitefield's arrival in Cambuslang

On his arrival in the town Whitefield preached "to a vast body of people, and at six in the evening, and again at night". "Such a commotion," he wrote, "surely was never heard of, especially at eleven at night. It far out-did all that I ever saw in America."[34] For about an hour and a half there was "such weeping", with uttering agonized cries, many falling into deep distress and the people slain by scores. Many were carried to shelter like wounded soldiers taken off the battlefield. After Whitefield had finished speaking McCulloch preached till past one o'clock in the morning. Even then he found it an uphill task to persuade the people to depart to their homes. Throughout the night the voice of praise and prayer could be heard in the fields.[35] On the day following, 7 July, he preached several times and the level of the commotions increased.[36]

On Friday 9 July he preached to more than 20,000 people and then on the sabbath he assisted with the sacrament and wrote that "there were undoubtedly twenty thousand people present". Two tents had been set up and the Lord's Supper was administered in the fields. When Whitefield began to serve at one of the tables the presence of God came on him in a powerful way and the people began to press in on him. In consequence, he was compelled to go and preach in one of the tents while other ministers continued to serve the remainder of the communicants. Preaching continued throughout the day and those who had received the sacrament were able to go and listen. In the evening, when the sacrament was over, Whitefield preached at the request of the ministers to the entire gathering. He did so for an hour and a half and many of those who listened either cried out, wept or wrung their hands.[37] On the Monday following Whitefield preached again to nearly as many and wrote to John Cennick that "such an universal stir I never saw before".[38]

The fact that the Cambuslang revival had its central focus at a sacramental meeting may well have been due at least in part to the Presbyterian practice. Their custom of sharing the Lord's Supper annually meant that communicants treated the matter with great seriousness. They came to the Lord's Table with reverence and awe having carefully prepared themselves. In order to be admitted as participants they were required to obtain a small metal token from their minister and these were not readily given out.[39] Many of those who took part at Cambuslang travelled considerable distances and arrived with great expectancy. A gentleman from Kilmarnock who was present recorded his impressions in the following lines.

> Persons from all parts flocked to see, and many
> from many parts went home convinced, and
> converted to God. A brae, or hill, near the

manse at Cambuslang, seemed to be formed by
Providence, for containing a large congregation.
People sat unwearied till two in the morning,
to hear sermons, disregarding the weather. You
could scarce walk a yard, but must tread on some,
either rejoicing in God for mercies received, or
crying out for more... The communion-table was
in the field; three tents, at a proper distance, all
surrounded with a multitude of hearers; above
twenty ministers (among whom was good old
Mr Bonner) attending to preach and assist, all
enlivened by one another.[40]

William McCulloch wrote, "It is not quite five months since the
work began, and during that time, I have reason to believe that
upwards of five hundred souls have been awakened" and "brought
under deep conviction". "Most of these," he continued, "I trust,
have been savingly brought home to God."[41] McCulloch estimated
that there could not have been less that 30,000 present on the day
of the sabbath sacrament. Whitefield himself put it at 20,000.[42]

Such was the joy and the overwhelming presence of God in the
sacrament that both the ministers and the people resolved to have
another in imitation of Hezekiah's Passover.[43] The proposal to do
this was made by Alexander Webster of Edinburgh and supported
by McCulloch. Whitefield readily agreed and wrote in a letter, "In
less than a month, we are to have another sacrament at Cambuslang,
a thing not practised before in Scotland."[44] James Robe observed
that it had not been known for the Lord's Supper to be held twice
in a summer anywhere in Scotland before the revival.[45] Whitefield,
however, had from the time of his conversion and membership in
the Oxford Holy Club greatly valued the sacrament which he took

whenever the opportunity arose. He immediately seconded the proposal for another sacrament at Cambuslang. There is no doubt that his encouragement contributed to the decision to hold it.[46]

The day chosen for the second Lord's Supper was 15 August. Whitefield reported that he found himself opposed on every side and that the Erskines and the Associate Presbytery were holding a fast against him and denouncing his preaching as an instrument of delusion and an agent of the devil.[47] They had evidently reached the conclusion that their stance against the Church of Scotland was right and were therefore of the view that any blessing that appeared to come upon it could not be of God. Whitefield was of course undeterred by these arrows from their bows and remained in Cambuslang and the vicinity until the end of August when he moved on to Glasgow and Edinburgh.

He wrote of the moving scenes of the second gathering for the Lord's Supper stating that "the voice of prayer and praise could be heard all night" and that it was supposed that between 30,000 and 40,000 people were assembled, of whom 3,000 communicated. Significantly the *Glasgow Weekly History* estimated the crowd to have been "upwards of 30,000".[48] The very large collections which were taken would also seem to endorse the estimated numbers present. The first Communion brought in £117 12s and the second £194 2s which can be compared with the normal sabbath day offerings of between £3 and £12.[49] Numbers of people to whom Whitefield served the bread and wine had an overwhelming sense of God's presence. James Robe recorded the testimony of Mr L. M. a twenty-eight-year-old man who attended the sacrament at Cambuslang.

> I went to the sacrament at Cambuslang, and being at the table, the Rev. Mr. Whitefield expressed these words, "O dear Redeemer, seal these lambs

of thine to the day of redemption." At which words my breath was near stopping, and the blood gushed at my nose. He said, "Be not afraid, for God shall put up thy tears in his bottle. These words were put into my heart, 'A new heart I will give you, and a right spirit will I put within you...'" I sat afterwards at the table overjoyed with the love of my dear Redeemer.[50]

He also stated that there were three tents and that "the ministers were enlarged, and great grace was among the people". He himself preached on the Lord's Day morning, served five tables, and preached at about ten at night to a great company in the churchyard. Though it was raining there was a considerable awakening.[51] Another communicant informed James Robe that while Whitefield was serving the tables at the second sacrament "he appeared to be so filled with the love of God as to be in a kind of ecstasy or transport".[52] McCulloch reported that Whitefield's sermons were attended with "much power" and that there was "a very great but decent weeping". He also stated that "the lowest estimate I hear... has been upwards of thirty thousand".[53]

Many ministers and clergy came to Cambuslang from across Scotland and others were present from England and Ireland. Prominent among them were Alexander Webster from Edinburgh, John Gillies from Glasgow and James Robe from Kilsyth where an awakening similar to that at Cambuslang took place in its wake. Also present were a number of people of rank and distinction. Many of these individuals carried the presence of God's Spirit with them to the places from which they had come. In this way Whitefield's seemingly prophetic words to McCulloch that the revival would spread across the land were more than fulfilled. The second Communion at Cambuslang is generally taken to be the high point of the revival in Scotland. Indeed Whitefield wrote that "such a Passover has not been heard of ".[54]

In 1752, nine years after the revival, McCulloch published an account of the fruits of the revival in Cambuslang. In addition to the transformation of the worshipping life of many parishes there were dozens of towns and villages where there was a social impact. McCulloch noted that "Such as were given to cursing and swearing have laid aside the practice, learning to speak the language of heaven... such were accustomed to frequent taverns, to drink and play cards, & co, till late, or it may be morning hours, have for these nine years past, avoided all occasions of the kind, and kept at home, spending their evenings in Christian conference, in matters profitable to their families, and in secret devotion."[55]

Revival in Kilsyth and beyond

James Robe (1688–1753), the parish minister at Kilsyth, was a frequent attender and helper in the ministry at Cambuslang. He did his best to encourage his people to attend the meetings but with little success. However on Sunday 16 May he preached with unusual power and "some strong and stout men cried out in distress".[56] So it is clear that as at Cambuslang there were tokens of revival at Kilsyth before Whitefield arrived on the scene. That said, he once again proved to be the catalyst which God used to kindle the flames. On Tuesday 15 June, Whitefield preached there to 10,000 and wrote, "such commotion, I believe you never saw. O what cries of agony were there!"[57] The first sacrament of the Lord's Supper was held on 11 July, the same day as that which took place at Cambuslang. Robe attended the second Communion there on 15 August and McCulloch suggested to him that he consider a second occasion at Kilsyth. Initially he was apprehensive but was eventually persuaded by one of his elders for whom he had great respect. The date was set for Sunday 3 October. Although the days were shortening large crowds came across, many having travelled a considerable distance. There were twenty-two servings and about 1,500 communicants.

Whitefield was an enthusiastic participant and wrote in a letter dated 6 October that "we have seen Jesus exalted to the glory of his name in Scotland". He went on to relate that "last Sabbath-day and Monday, very great things, greater than ever, were seen in Kilsyth".[58] During this period Whitefield preached twice every day with great power. The following week he wrote again that "the work is still increasing in Scotland, especially at Kilsyth" and that in consequence he would be spending a further three weeks in the country before setting out to London.[59]

The revival spread beyond Kilsyth to Dundee and southern Perthshire where it centred on Muthil a few miles from the town of Auchterarder.[60] William Halley, the parish minister at Muthil, reported fifty people had been awakened in his parish in just three months between March and the beginning of July 1842.[61] The Lord's Supper was administered on the third Sunday in July and many were brought to Christ. From that time onward "unusual power" attended Halley's preaching. Each week crowds came to the manse for spiritual counsel after evening worship was concluded. Formerly there had been two praying societies in the parish but within a year there were eighteen.

Whitefield remained in the vicinity of Cambuslang until the end of September. Then for the most part he based himself in Edinburgh until his departure for London at the end of October. He preached twice and sometimes three or four times a day in the city and found the people more eager than ever to listen to his message.[62] He was also able to collect considerable amounts of money at these gatherings. At Edinburgh he received £128, at

Glasgow a comparable sum, and in all about £300. Before he left Scotland he was able to say, "Blessed be God, I owe nothing now in England on the orphan house account."[63]

The revival assessed

Stirred by sacramental meetings

First, it is clear that the revivals in Cambuslang and Kilsyth were both intensified by the sacramental meetings. They were occasions of great solemnity which was added to by their infrequency and by the serious preparation of the clergy. The majority of those who sat at the tables to receive the bread and wine did so with great expectancy of experiencing the presence of God. James Robe, for example, noted that "some people came to the Lord's table at Kilsyth under much terror".[64] The revival which took place at the same time at Muthil appears to have broken out following the administration of the Lord's Supper. Halley, the parish minister, reported that "many were brought to the Conqueror's Feet".[65]

Second, many ministers from other places took part both in preaching and in serving at the sacramental meetings. In some cases preaching went on continuously throughout the course of an entire day. Much of the preaching was done in the open air and in the fields in particular. At the time of the second Lord's Supper at Kilsyth on 3 October Robe was assisted by John McLaurin of Glasgow, Thomas Gillespie of Carnock and William McCulloch from Cambuslang.

Third, the revival spread by writing and publicity. McCulloch and Robe, much like Whitefield, were constant correspondents writing letters to ministers and people in many parts of Scotland, the British Isles and overseas. This played a major part in widening the revival and its impact. There was also a growing correspondence with ministers in the New England colonies. Robe's publication at Glasgow in 1742 of his *A Faithful Narrative of the Extraordinary Work of the Spirit of God* also played a part in spreading news of the awakening in Cambuslang and Kilsyth. In his preface to the pamphlet he stated that it was his hope that his narrative would awaken the godly and allay prejudice and fear in others. Many of those who came to the meetings carried the Lord's presence away with them to other places.

Fourth, the revival in both Cambuslang and Kilsyth had many positive outcomes. The evidence suggests that most of those who professed conversion remained steadfast in the faith. McCulloch writing in April 1751 stated that he had a list before him of about 400 people who had been awakened at Cambuslang and who were still living as "becometh the gospel".[66] A similar endorsement was found at Kilsyth in the same year with more than a hundred who had come to faith in Christ in 1742 still continuing in the faith. Again at Kilsyth Robe observed that many former feuds and animosities in his parish had now been "in great measure laid aside". He noted also that the summer of 1742 was "the most peaceable among neighbours that could ever be remembered".[67] Similar benefits were witnessed at Cambuslang where there were many instances of injuries being forgiven and "evidences of love to one another".[68] In general the defenders of revival were quick to point out the ways in which it had changed the quality of people's lives. Drunkards, swearers, whoremongers, and liars had put away their past and were demonstrating their Christian commitment in transformed living.

Fifth, the revival was, Dallimore contended, a revival in the way that Jonathan Edwards understood the term. It was not he argued humanly planned although the sacramental meetings took a good measure of negotiating, organization, and discussion. It was however born of much prayer and there was no attempt at sensationalism or showmanship. Those who professed conversion were examined by one or more of the ministers.[69]

Whitefield a catalyst for revival

While it is the case that the revivals in these two towns had begun before Whitefield arrived, there is no doubt that his presence acted as a catalyst in a number of ways. The faith of McCulloch and others had been stirred by their reading reports of Whitefield's ministry in America and the huge numbers who attended his preaching and gave their lives to Christ. Whitefield's celebrity status and his acceptance of the invitations to come to Scotland created considerable expectancy among the faithful. His ability to dramatize his sermons could pull in the curious and those who needed entertainment. There is a tendency to overlook the fact that the range of attractions in the mid-eighteenth century was very limited compared to what became available in the following centuries. People therefore often travelled long distances to listen to powerful preaching as was seen for instance when twenty-seven members of Halley's parish walked nearly thirty miles from Muthil to the second Communion at Kilsyth.[70] The role and impact of Whitefield as a preacher in Scotland and at Cambuslang and Kilsyth were well assessed by one of the ministers in the city of Aberdeen.

> I shall acquaint you freely of what I think of the Rev. Mr. Whitefield... He is, I believe, justly esteemed by all who are personally acquainted with him, an eminent instrument of reviving, in these declining times, a just sense and concern for the great things of religion... the Lord has raised up this eminent instrument, from a quarter, whence we could not have expected it, to call us to return to him, from whom, it is plain, we have deeply revolted.[71]

Role in the sacramental services

Whitefield played a significant role in encouraging the church leaders in Cambuslang and Kilsyth to break with Presbyterian practice and hold second sacramental meetings within just weeks of the previous ones. Although the general custom of the Church of England was to hold Communion services four times a year Whitefield attended or administered the sacrament whenever an opportunity arose. He wrote to a friend, "I purpose going to Cambuslang tomorrow, in order to assist at the Communion; and shall preach at various places westward before I return."[72] It's almost as if the foremost reason for his first visit was the sacramental meeting followed by the prospect of preaching. Significantly Whitefield's name is first in McCulloch's list of those who assisted him in administering Communion.[73]

It was because of his central role at this occasion that McCulloch urged him to come for another Communion a month later. One result of the revival and Whitefield's part in it was a growing desire to have more frequent Communion services. This was made plain in 1749 when John Erskine (1721–1803) published *An Attempt to Promote the Frequent Dispensing of the Lord's Supper* in which he argued that four times a year would have much greater spiritual benefit than the church's annual sacramental service.[74]

Healer of divisions

It has often been said that Whitefield promoted discord and division and clearly his preaching evoked a good deal of hostility. However, by not aligning himself with any one section of the Scottish church Whitefield did a great deal to heal what had been a growing rift. His determination and resolve to preach the gospel wherever the opportunity arose set a pattern which many later revivalists came to adopt.[75] The awakenings were far less divisive than the opponents of Whitefield and the revival had tried to portray them in their tracts and pamphlets. At first the seceders appeared free of sectarianism and Ralph Erskine went with Whitefield to Edinburgh, sharing the pulpit with him in Canongate Church. Indeed, Whitefield went further and preached to Ralph Erskine's meeting house in Dunfermline. He was, however, clear from the very outset that he had come to Scotland solely in the role of an evangelist and insisted on having the freedom to go to all denominational churches. And if people were of the devil, as Erskine and those of the Associated Presbytery later came to suggest, he would preach to them nonetheless for the devil's people need him the most!

Man of peace

Whitefield was of the view that no system of church government was perfect. They all had virtues and defects. In contrast the Erskine brothers and those with them were wedded to the *Solemn League and Covenant* by which parliament had given legal guarantee to the Presbyterian form of government. They were adamant that God could not bless a minister from an un-covenanted church. They had no doubt that Whitefield who had been ordained by a church which recognized bishops and unreformed practices must be regarded as the enemy from within. Whitefield, according to Philip, "was far ahead of both parties on the subject of religious liberty".[76]

The most vehement attack on him came from the pen of Adam Gib (1714–88) a leading secession theologian and minister in Edinburgh. On 6 June, the very first sabbath of Whitefield's ministry in Edinburgh, he published a pamphlet entitled, *A WARNING against Countenancing the Ministrations of Mr George Whitefield.*[77] Its vicious nature can immediately be seen from the introduction to the Appendix, "Wherein are shewn that Mr Whitefield is no Minister of *Jesus Christ*; that his Call and *Coming* to *Scotland* are *scandalous*; that his Practice is *disorderly* and *fertile* of Disorder... so that People ought to *avoid* him from *Duty* to God, to the Church, to themselves, to Fellow-Men, to Posterity, and to *him*."[78] Toward the end of this pernicious document Gib concluded "that all Mr Whitefield's hearers are exposing themselves to satanic influences".[79]

Just over a month later on 15 July the Associate Presbytery became so convinced that Whitefield's widespread reception was an expression of the Lord's anger that they called for a public fast on account of the "awful work upon the bodies and spirits of men going on at Cambuslang". Ralph Erskine opined, "We have seen convulsions instead of convictions", but Robe responded that "they are greatly mistaken who imagine that all those who have been observably awakened, have come under faintings, temblings, and other bodily distresses. These have been by far the fewest number."[80] Robe made a further observation that in 1742 "conversion carried on in a calm, silent and quiet manner are the more numerous".[81] In response John Currie of Kinglassie pointed out to the Associate brethren that "he himself had heard such loud outcryings in the seceding meeting house in Dunfermline that the sermon could not be heard".[82]

It wasn't only the seceders who attacked Whitefield. The Reverend John Bissett, a minister of the established Church of Scotland in Aberdeen denounced him as "the strolling Priest" and "a strolling Imposter, whose Cheats in due Time, I hope will be discovered".[83] John Willison (1680–1750), the minister at Dundee, wrote that Whitefield "is heard, and spoken against, by all the episcopal party, and even most of our clergy do labour to diminish him".[84]

Despite having to suffer numerous attacks for his role in the revivals at Cambuslang and Kilsyth Whitefield wisely left the work to vindicate itself. Although he did often respond to his critics there were times when he was happy to leave the task of defending the cause to others. He was thus able to conserve what little energy he had left. Gillies observed that "he was calm and serene under all he meets with, yea his joy in tribulation, is to me surprising".[85] Indeed he did his best to keep the doors of friendship open with the Associate Presbytery. He wrote to Ebenezer Erskine in June 1742 assuring him that he loved and respected them and applauded their zeal for God. He went on to say that he felt no resentment in his heart toward them and "would gladly sit down and hear you or your brethren preach".[86]

By extending the hand of friendship across the denominational spectrum and working with ministers from the Church of Scotland Whitefield strengthened the hand of Scottish Evangelicals. Whitefield's visits north of the border revealed his remarkably wide sympathies. Thomas Somerville (1740–1830), minister of Jedburgh, paid great tribute to his conversation and preaching contending that he was a major cause in ending "narrow prejudices… and the more rapid progress of a catholic spirit".[87]

Denouement

One abiding and particularly positive note was the way in which those who professed conversion during the revival continued in the faith. When Whitefield returned to Scotland in 1748 and revisited Cambuslang and other places, vast crowds came out to meet him. Writing in September, 1748 Whitefield stated, "very great multitudes have flocked to hear: and in Glasgow the prospect of doing good is rather more promising than in Edinburgh".[88] In a letter penned on 28 September Whitefield reported, "Some of my spiritual children, I hear, are gone to heaven, and other come to me telling what God did for their souls when I was here last. I desire to cast my crown before the Lamb; I desire always to be crying out, 'Why me, Lord, why me?'"[89]

In total Whitefield made fifteen excursions to Scotland.[90] In those that followed Cambuslang Whitefield continued to be hugely popular. In March 1745 we find him sending published pamphlets ahead of him.[91] In September to October 1748 we have a record of him preaching "to thronged congregations in Glasgow and Edinburgh".[92] In 1751 we find him preaching twice a day in Edinburgh and large crowds assembling to hear the word, by three or four in the morning.[93] In a letter written in July 1753 he noted that he had been preaching very day to many thousands in Edinburgh.[94] His working in partnership with William McCulloch and James Robe at Cambuslang and Kilsyth was the pinnacle of the revivals in Scotland of which he was certainly a catalyst. Small wonder that he wrote in a letter from Edinburgh to his wife, addressing her unusually as "my dear love", that "it far out-did all that I ever saw in America".[95]

Chapter 5 notes

1   See A. T. N. Muirhead, "Erskine", *Biographical Dictionary of Evangelicals* (Leicester, IVP, 2003, pp. 211–12.
2   *Letter to Mr E— E—*, 16 May 1741, *Works*, Vol. 1, p. 262.
3   Ibid.
4   Ibid.
5   *Letter to John Willison*, 10 August 1741, *Works*, Vol. 1, p. 309.
6   *Letter to James Ogilvie*, 10 August 1741, *Works*, Vol. 1, p. 310.
7   *Letter to William Wishart*, 16 May 1741, *Works*, Vol. 1, p. 261.
8   *Letter to Ebenezer Erskine*, 16 May 1741, *Works*, Vol. 1, p. 262.
9   *Letter to Mr J—C—*, 1 August 1741, *Works*, Vol. 1, p. 304.
10 Ibid.
11 Ibid, p. 301.
12 *Letter to Thomas N—*, New York, 8 August 1742, *Works*, Vol. 1, p. 307.
13 *Letter to Mr J—C—*, 1 August 1741, *Works*, Vol. 1, pp. 304–305.
14 D. Macfarlan, *The Revivals of the Eighteenth Century with Three Sermons by the Rev George Whitefield* (Edinburgh, Johnstone, 1800), p. 112.
15 *Letter to Howell Harris*, 13 August 1741, *Works*, Vol. 1, p. 313.
16 Ibid, 15 August 1741, *Works*, Vol. 1, p. 315.
17 *Letter to Mr W—*, 19 September 1741, *Works*, Vol. 1, p. 319.
18 Ibid.
19 *Letter to Mr J—C —*, 27 October 1741, *Works*, Vol. 1, p. 337.
20 Ibid.
21 A. Fawcett, *The Cambuslang Revival* (London, The Banner of Truth Trust, 1971) p. 98.
22 Ibid, p. 104.
23 R. Philip, *The Life and Times*, p. 294.

24 A. Fawcett, op. cit., p. 128.
25 *Letter to Mr A—*, 4 June 1742, *Works*, Vol. 1, p. 399.
26 Ibid.
27 *Letter to Mr D—A—*, 7 July 1742, *Works,* Vol. 1, p. 403.
28 *Letter to Mr McCulloch,* 7 July 1742, *Works*, Vol. 1, p. 403.
29 *Letter to Mrs Whitefield,* 7 July 1742, *Works*, Vol. 1, p. 405.
30 See A. Fawcett, op. cit., p. 154.
31 Ibid.
32 J. Erskine, *The Signs of the Times Considered* (Edinburgh, T. Lumisden and J. Robertson, 1742) p. 34.
33 Ibid, p. 33.
34 D. Macfarlan, *The Revivals of the Eighteenth Century,* p 63. Duncan Macfarlan (1771–1857) copied this from William McCulloch's original accounts of the revival.
35 Information and quotations in this paragraph are taken from Whitefield, *Letter to Mrs Whitefield,* 7 July 1742, *Works*, Vol. 1, p. 405.
36 Ibid.
37 *Letter to Mr John Cennick,* 15 July 1742, *Works*, Vol. 1, p. 409.
38 Ibid.
39 A. Fawcett, op. cit., p. 118.
40 Report by a Gentleman from Kilmarnock, cited in J. Gillies, op. cit., p. 124.
41 D. Macfarlan, *Revivals of the Eighteenth Century,* p. 64.
42 Ibid, p. 65.
43 J. Gillies, op. cit., p. 124.
44 *Christian Monthly History*, November 1743, p. 28, cited in A. Fawcett, *The Cambuslang Revival* p. 118.
45 Ibid.
46 J. Robe, *A Faithful Narrative of the Extraordinary Work of the Spirit of God* (London, S. Mason, 1742–1743), p. 222.
47 *Letter to Howell Harris,* 26 August 1742, *Works*, Vol. 1, p. 426.
48 *Glasgow Weekly History,* No 39 pp. 1–2, cited in A. Fawcett, *The Cambuslang Revival,* p. 119.
49 A. Fawcett, op. cit., p. 119.
50 J. Robe, *Faithful Narrative,* pp. 85–86.
51 *Letter to Mr A—,* 27 August 1742, *Works*, Vol. 1, p. 429.
52 J. Robe, op. cit., p. 225.
53 D. Macfarlan, *Revivals of the Eighteenth Century,* p. 73.
54 *Letter to Mr A—,* 27 August 1742, *Works*, Vol. 1, p. 429.
55 Attributed to J. Robe, *Faithful Narrative*, in D. Macfarlan, *Revivals of the Eighteenth Century*, pp. 99–100.
56 A. Fawcett, op. cit., p. 129.
57 L. Tyerman, *Life*, Vol. 2, p. 5.
58 *Letter to Mr E—C—,* 6 October 1742, *Works*, Vol. 1, p. 446.
59 *Letter to John Wesley,* 11 October 1742, *Works*, Vol. 1, p. 449.
60 A. Fawcett, op .cit., p. 132. Fawcett details many of the places to which

the revival extended. See pp. 124–25 and 136–42.

61   A. Fawcett, op. cit., p. 133.

62   *Letter to Mrs Ann D*, 13 October 1742, *Works*, Vol. 1 p. 449.

63   R. Philip, op. cit., p. 299.

64   J. Robe, *Faithful Narrative,* p. 104.

65   A. Fawcett, op. cit., p. 133.

66   W. McCulloch, *Sermons*, preface, p. 8, cited in A. Fawcett, op. cit., p. 168.

67   J. Robe, op. cit., p. 15.

68   Ibid, p. 16.

69   A. Dallimore, *George Whitefield*, pp. 135–36.

70   A. Fawcett, op. cit., p. 134.

71   J. Gillies, op. cit., pp. 88 and 90.

72   *Letter to Mr D—A—*, 7 July 1742, *Works*, Vol. 1, p. 403.

73   J. Robe, *Faithful Narrative*, p. 244.

74   J. Erskine, *An Attempt to Promote the Frequent Dispensing of the Lord's Supper* (Kilmarnock, 1749) p. 4.

75   Charles Finney, for example, always tried to preach in several different churches when he held revival campaigns in particular towns. D. L. Moody attempted wherever possible to locate his meetings in secular buildings rather than church premises, which might be construed as his being aligned with one particular denomination.

76   R. Philip, op. cit., p. 304.

77   A. Gib, *Warning Against the Ministrations of Mr George Whitefield* (Edinburgh, David Duncan, 1742).

78   Ibid, p. i.

79   Ibid, p. 61.

80   R. Philip, op. cit., p. 304.

81   Ibid.

82   J. Currie, *New Testimony and Vindication* of the *Extraordinary Work of God at Cambuslang, Kilsyth and other places in the West of Scotland* (Robert Smith and Alexander Hutchinson in Company, 1743), p. 15.

83   A. Fawcett, op. cit., p. 187.

84   J. Gillies, op. cit., p. 92.

85   J. Gillies, op. cit., p. 90.

86   *Letter to Ebenezer Erskine*, 10 June 1742, *Works*, Vol. 1, p. 402.

87   A. Fawcett, op. cit., p. 218.

88   *Letter to Mr S—*, 28 September 1748.

89   *Letter to Mrs E—*, 28 September 1748.

90   See A. Dallimore, op. cit., Vol. 2, p. 472.

91   Letter to Mr J—S—, 12 March 1745.

92   L. Tyerman, op. cit., Vol. 2, p. 200.

93   *Letter to the Countess of Huntingdon*, 30 July 1751.

94   *Letter to Mr B—S—*, 25 July 1753.

95   *Letter to Mrs Whitefield*, 7 July 1742.

Chapter 6

Howell Harris and the Countess

In his travels and preaching across the British Isles Whitefield found his two greatest allies and supporters to be the Welsh evangelist Howell Harris and Lady Selina, the Countess of Huntingdon. Both Harris and the countess shared his passion for evangelism, his care for the poor and disadvantaged, his vision to establish societies, and his belief in predestination and the final perseverance of the saints.

Howell Harris

Calvinistic Methodism initially grew out of the ministry of the Revd Griffith Jones (1684–1761) of Llanddowror in Carmarthenshire, who set up a system of charity schools for the poor and also engaged in a powerful preaching ministry. Among his hearers Daniel Rowland (1713–90), the curate of Llangeitho in Caeredigion, was deeply moved and became a fervent apostle of the new movement. About the same time Howell Harris (1714–73) was converted at a Communion service in Talgarth on Whitsunday in 1735.[1]

Harris immediately began to organize meetings in his own home, urging those who came to share the assurance of Christ's forgiveness that he had received. This was a religion of the heart. Harris opened a school and began to organize those who were converted through his preaching into societies. He twice failed to be accepted for ordination in the Church of England because his views were regarded by the bishops as suspect and "Methodist". Undeterred, he became a self-appointed lay preacher and travelled throughout Wales. Because he was not an ordained minister Harris styled himself an *exhorter* and he avoided preaching structured homilies after the fashion of the parish clergy. He spent long hours in prayer, walked many hundreds of miles, and spoke like Whitefield in a strong voice with power and passion. Because of his vehement in-your-face manner Harris became known as "the hammer and the axe". Hugh Hughes observed that his preaching and those of his associates frequently evoked "loud cries and ejaculations, such rejoicing and ecstasy, as to give offence".[2] The first society he formed was in 1736. These societies would have been small groups, usually with less than twelve members, who would meet to pray and mutually encourage one another in their faith. According to Whitefield, by 1738 there were "nearly thirty",[3] and they came to form the basis of Welsh Calvinistic Methodism. Harris proved to be a significant role model for Whitefield and it was his example which must have encouraged him to try his hand at open-air preaching. He wrote in a letter from London, "Mr Howell Harris, and I, are correspondents, blessed be God! May I follow him, as he does Jesus Christ. How he outstrips me!"[4]

Although Whitefield and Harris had written to one another on several occasions it was not until 7 March 1739 that they first met face to face in Cardiff.[5] It was soon clear that they were kindred spirits who shared the same Calvinist convictions and a strategy to establish societies. Both men held the same views about the doctrines of election and reprobation: neither of the two were "supralapsarian", that is double predestinarians who asserted that some were chosen to eternal life and some to eternal death even before the foundation of the world.[6] Whitefield's Calvinism was altogether more moderate in tone reflecting Article 17 of the Church of England, which counsels against overstating the doctrine of double decrees.[7] Harris openly professed in 1737 to having rejected a belief in reprobation. From that time he spoke and taught only of the Lord's positive election of grace.[8] The two men worked together preaching widely in both England and Wales Whitefield's endorsement of Howell's ministry greatly encouraged him in the work. Harris travelled the length and breadth of Wales and preached wherever any would listen. Whitefield longed to experience his dynamism and wrote in his journal, "When I first saw him, my heart was knit closely to him. I wanted to catch some of his fire."[9] The two men left Cardiff together on Friday 9 March, stopping at Newport, where Whitefield preached to "about a thousand people".[10] Over the years they preached together at a number of places with Howell addressing the people in Welsh and Whitefield following in English.

Whitefield's societies

Whitefield's powerful preaching produced a trail of converts and following Howell's Methodist practice he organized them into societies. The very first society he formed was in his native city of Gloucester in 1735.[11] Those that followed he organized into four "associations" with a quarterly meeting held in turn at each of the four main centres of London, Bristol, Wiltshire, and Gloucester.

After 1741 Whitefield's Calvinistic Methodist societies developed around his four main centres of activity: London, Bristol, Gloucester, and Wales. These places acted as resource centres for a patchwork of societies, mostly scattered over the West of England, which had reached thirty in number by 1747.[12] By the end of the decade he had established more than sixty societies and preaching places with over fifty preachers and exhorters. Whitefield's connexion spread still further in the years that followed in these areas, and his Moorfields

Tabernacle became the centre of a London area network of societies organized by his assistant Joseph Humphries.[13] Recent research has indicated that the majority of Calvinistic Methodists were of "the middling orders" such as merchants, shopkeepers, booksellers, small farmers, and industrious labourers. In some societies women made up more than half of the membership.[14]

The first conference of Calvinistic Methodists was held at Waterford in South Wales in January 1743. Shortly after this Whitefield returned to London, perhaps because the birth of his son was imminent. His wife Elizabeth was a godly woman who did much to support her husband in his ministry.[15]

Despite his absence the work in Wales developed apace. Daniel Rowland wrote a month later, "We met today, according to appointment, and had a most heavenly Association."[16] Ten days later Harris reported, "With us, the work goes on more and more sweetly. I trust we shall have good order."[17] A fortnight later Harris wrote to Whitefield:

> My dearest brother Whitefield, last Sunday, I was with brother Rowland at the ordinance, where I saw and heard, and felt such things as I cannot communicate on paper. I never before witnessed such crying, heart-breaking groans, silent weeping, holy mourning, and shouts of joy and rejoicing. Their "Amens" and crying "glory to God in the highest!" would have inflamed your soul, had you been there.[18]

During this early period of Methodism Whitefield and the Wesleys worked in tandem but with the passing of time they gradually drew apart over their differences concerning the doctrines of election and reprobation. Much later, however, all three became less rigid and were to some extent reconciled. Many of the societies which Whitefield had founded either remained independent of the Wesleys or else joined themselves to the Countess of Huntingdon's Connexion in which Whitefield came to play a significant role. John Cennick (1718–75) was another early Methodist leader who also established societies from among those who responded to his preaching. His sympathies lay with Whitefield and his Calvinist doctrines, and for a time he shared in the preaching at the London Tabernacle. However, he left the Calvinistic Methodists in December 1745 and joined the Moravians, taking 400 members of the Tabernacle congregation with him as he did so.[19]

In a few of the prominent centres of Whitefield's activities Tabernacles were built. Details of some of them are given in *Christian History*, a journal that was sold by J. Lewis of Bartholomew's Close in the city of London, which, in reality was under Whitefield's editorial control. It was also printed in America and published by Thomas Prince in Boston. An advert attached to No 3 Volume VI stated that the publication "contains a general account of the progress of the gospel, under the ministry of the Rev. Mr George Whitefield, his fellow labourers and assistants". Although it was originally printed in folio size, Whitefield, ever one with an eye for publicity, ordered it to be printed in a "pocket volume" which would be easier to handle and therefore much more accessible to the general public.[20]

The 16 November 1744 issue typifies the publicity information carried by the journal. It gave details sent in by Herbert Jenkins who reported that "the hall in Bristol is commonly full" and that Jenkins generally preached morning and evening "with freedom and great delight". He also reported that he had walked out to Kingswood, where Whitefield had preached with such great success to the miners.

James Ingham, a society leader in the Ludlow and Leominster area, sent in a letter dated 12 December 1744 stating that he had preached "to a serious auditory" and that the loving people would not willingly part with him. A Mr E. Godwin reported, "Wiltshire is surely a garden of the Lord" and that "I went to Blunsdon and preached out of doors, and great power seemed to attend the word, some crying, who had hardly wept since they were children."[21]

Some of these early societies encountered a good deal of opposition. During a society meeting at Wickwar in Gloucestershire a mob interrupted George Cook as he was leading the gathering. They had sheep bells tied to sticks, banged frying pans, horse-bugles, and a post horn. Some put their mouths to the windows and made noises like a dog.[22] John Edwards of Avebury was summoned by the local clergyman who called him "an ignorant unlearned fool". That same evening a group entered the building during his discourse and threw stones at him, one of which struck him on the breast, while those outside rang bells and blew horns. They then broke the windows with clubs and some of the people's faces were cut by flying glass.[23] The journal provided many similar accounts of society meetings from a variety of other societies attached to Whitefield, including Birmingham, Essex, Buckinghamshire, Northamptonshire, and Devonshire.

From these reports it is clear that Whitefield played a substantial role in laying the basis of Methodism in England. Then through his friendship with Harris he became closely involved in setting up societies in the principality of Wales, with the pair travelling considerable distances together. Whitefield was both impressed and supportive of the ways in which both churchmen and Dissenters worked together in the Welsh revival, remarking that "Wales was a noble soil for Christianity" and that its inhabitants were much readier to receive the Gospel than the people of England.[24]

Organization and leadership

Whitefield's skills as an organizer and leader were called upon when a dispute arose among the Welsh Calvinistic Methodist leaders, four of whom were ordained and four who were not in holy orders. The issue was largely a matter of status between the eight. They unanimously agreed to invite Whitefield to be their arbiter. Eventually it was agreed that the ordained ministers were to be "overseers", each with a district under their leadership, while the exhorters were to be appointed by them to share in preaching and pastoral responsibilities.[25] A second meeting held soon afterwards, also in Waterford, brought the English and Welsh Methodists together in what came to be known as "The Calvinistic Methodist Association". Whitefield was appointed moderator with Harris given responsibility to act during his absence.[26]

The meeting sought to divide the lay preachers into two classes – superintendents and exhorters – with Howell Harris as their general overseer. Each superintendent was to have a certain district or circuit in which to labour. Ordained clergy were to be visitors to areas across districts insofar as they were able. Exhorters were divided into two categories – public and private. Private exhorters would have their labours confined to one or two societies. Public exhorters could travel within a specified circuit. So as a result of this assembly the Calvinistic Methodist Connexion was formed with Whitefield as its head and the London Tabernacle as its administrative base.

It is significant that Whitefield's Calvinistic Methodist Association was formed eighteen months before Wesley held his first Methodist Conference. Perhaps in the light of this, as some have argued, Whitefield deserves the accolade of being "the founder of Methodism". Studies of Methodism speak of Wesley as being the great organizer and Whitefield as the great revivalist preacher. Yet perhaps we do Whitefield an injustice on this score. He, like,

Wesley had skills in preaching as well as business dealings and organizational ability.[27] It is significant that Wesley's conference structure when it emerged was very similar to that of the Calvinistic Methodists. Howell Harris, it should be added, was the general overseer of the Calvinistic Methodists in Wales while Whitefield supervised those in England.

Harris and Whitefield

The closeness of feeling which Whitefield and Harris had for one another was apparent in the somewhat bizarre circumstances between them which led to Whitefield's marriage to Elizabeth James (1704–68) on 14 November 1741. Elizabeth was a widow living at Abergavenny who had been converted during the revival in 1738. She became a dedicated Christian woman and assisted Howell Harris in his work. They both developed strong feelings for one another and there is little doubt that Elizabeth would immediately have accepted a proposal of marriage had one been put forward, but Harris held back, being uncertain that it was the will of God. In the middle of his dilemma a way out presented itself. He learned that Whitefield who, in 1741, was back in America had publicly made known that he was praying for a wife who would manage his orphan house and work alongside him. When Whitefield returned to England Harris sent him a letter recommending Elizabeth James as the ideal wife to meet his needs.

A short time later, when Whitefield was preaching in the west of England, he journeyed into Wales and met with Mrs James. He was soon attracted by her deep commitment to the Lord and her Calvinist convictions. He subsequently met with Harris and declared his intention to correspond with her with a view to proposing marriage. Matters took an even stranger turn since both Harris and Elizabeth remained deeply attached to each other and neither seemingly able to end their relationship. Eventually the three of them met together and Whitefield, believing she was the wife God had planned for him, made his proposal of marriage in tenderness and love. After four days' thought she decided for Whitefield and they were duly married by the Reverend John Smith in St Martin's Chapel near Caerphilly, in the parish of Ilan.[28] However, as had been the case in his marriage proposal to Elizabeth Delamotte, Whitefield seemed unable to openly express any loving affection toward his new wife. Just five days later he wrote in a somewhat matter of fact way to Gilbert Tennent, "On Saturday I was married, in the fear of God, to one who, I hope, will be a help meet to me... Be pleased to direct your next to London. I hope to be there in about three weeks. My wife I shall leave in the country for some time."[29] At the end of December he wrote to a fellow cleric in Aberdeen,

> The Lord has blessed my ministry in England, and
> in Wales, where I trust I was married in the Lord;
> and as I married for him, I trust I shall not be
> hindered, but rather forwarded in my work. O for
> that blessed time when we shall neither marry nor
> be given in marriage, but be as the angels of God!
> My soul longs for that glorious season.[30]

In this reflection Whitefield gives a hint of uncertainty as to whether he had done the right thing by his marriage. Perhaps because of his deep-seated Puritanism Whitefield was inhibited from expressing his feelings for his wife. Nevertheless, his marriage, as Harry Stout has reminded us, continued to be consummated since Elizabeth suffered four miscarriages.[31] But she became weak in health after the last of them in 1746 and was no longer able to travel with her husband on his extended preaching tours.

It is difficult to know whether Whitefield's marriage to Elizabeth was a happy one. Clearly there were long periods when they were away from each other. On 22 November he penned a letter to Lady Dartmouth in which he wrote: "I have altered my state: I trust for the better; for I think my soul is more intimately united to Jesus Christ than ever."[32] On another occasion they were separated for eighteen months when Whitefield journeyed to the West Indies in February 1747 and then decided to sail from there direct to England leaving his wife in America to cross the Atlantic on her own. Soon after her arrival back on home soil Whitefield wrote to a friend that he planned to persuade her to stay in England while he went back to America once again in the hope of turning his orphan house into "a seminary of learning".[33] In March 1754 he wrote from Lisbon en route to America to a "Mr C" and urged him "not to forget my widow wife".[34] That said, on the occasions when Elizabeth was preparing to give birth, Whitefield laid aside his preaching to spend time with her.

Significantly there are relatively few references to Elizabeth in more than 1,500 of his published letters. In several of that small number Whitefield nevertheless spoke both warmly and lovingly referring to Elizabeth as "my dear wife", "my help meet", and "my dear yoke fellow".[35] Writing, for example, to a close friend in Edinburgh, he referred to Elizabeth as my "dear companion" with whom he had enjoyed much of "the divine presence".[36] Shortly after Whitefield returned to London Elizabeth was taken with an inflammatory fever. She had been in a weak state of health for some months and passed away on 9 August 1768. Whitefield led the funeral service and gave a sermon based on Romans 8:20 in which he recounted her virtues. She was buried in a vault at Tottenham Court Road chapel.

Harris in temporary charge of Whitefield's societies

Whitefield and Harris's friendship continued to grow and their leadership of the Calvinistic Methodists became stronger and more significant following the split with the Wesleys over predestination in 1740.[37] From this point Wesley quickly began to organize his own separate Methodist Connexion and purchased a large piece of land in Bristol's Horsefair Street where he built a substantial room for his followers. Whitefield also erected a new tabernacle in the city and in the spring of 1741 found it necessary on account of his growing number of followers to have a society room built alongside it.[38]

The increase in numbers was accompanied by a significant issue of pastoral concern. He wrote to a friend in Worcester on 16 May that "sad tares have been sown here". He was referring to the doctrine of sinless perfection which Wesley was teaching his followers. He wrote in a letter to Howell Harris on 28 April, "We shall never have such dominion over indwelling sin, as entirely to be delivered from the stirring of it."[39] Despite his endeavours Whitefield began to lose a number of his followers in the city who joined with the Wesleyans. He was also to suffer further defections in the periods of his absence overseas. During those times he entrusted Harris with the pastoral oversight of his London Tabernacle and societies. This was particularly important during his lengthy time in the colonies between 1744 and 1748.[40] In these years the Tabernacle became severely tarnished by antinomianism – the belief that Christians were under grace and so freed from the obligation to keep the moral law. Harris was denounced for failing to clamp down on unacceptable behaviour which included accusations of adultery, fornication, and sodomy.[41]

The problem for Harris was that his time in London was inevitably limited since he was both married and also carrying the responsibility for the societies in Wales. During the times when he was away from the capital and back in Wales younger preachers took his place at the Tabernacle which further diminished attendances. Harris wrote to Whitefield on 17 December 1747, "On Sabbath days the Tabernacle is quite crowded, and on week-days morning and evening there is a goodly company. A spirit of love runs through the whole body."[42] Before Whitefield returned once more from America in the summer of 1748 he persuaded the reluctant Harris to assume the full leadership of both the Tabernacle and his societies. This appointment took place at a meeting held in London on 27 April 1749.[43] Despite his willingness Harris was by this time suffering from total exhaustion. Added to this he suffered a brutal attack while preaching in the town of Bala, which seemed to have affected his brain.

During Whitefield's periods of absence in the colonies Wesley preached strongly and widely against what he termed the "hellish infection of predestination".[44] Whitefield's continuing response was that he preached Christ "promiscuously to all" since "we know not who are the elect, and who reprobate... For the word may be useful, even to the non-elect, in restraining them from much wickedness and sin."[45] After nearly a decade of theological conflict the two factions began to recognize that their enmity was hindering the progress of the gospel. This led to Harris, Whitefield, and John and Charles Wesley meeting together in conference at Bristol in August 1749 in the hope of working in closer union. No formal arrangements were made but it brought the leaders into a somewhat improved working relationship. Over time, generally speaking, the English Calvinistic Methodists tended to suffer from a variety of clashes and minor factions while their Welsh counterparts enjoyed a much greater basic unity. By 1750 there were more than 420 Calvinistic Methodist societies in South Wales alone. This was probably due to their more collegiate style of leadership which included Whitefield, and provided greater accountability.[46] In England Whitefield appears not to have given the same degree of effective leadership to his societies due to his many preaching commitments and his concern for his London churches and the Savannah orphan house.

The Countess of Huntingdon

Alongside Whitefield's close friendship with Howell Harris he entered into a long and symbiotic relationship with the Countess of Huntingdon. With the passing of the years Whitefield was able to support some of her enterprises and encourage her in the reformed faith. She, for her part, gave him public recognition and affirmation by inviting him to preach to members of the nobility in her chapels and private residences.

Lady Selina Shirley was born at Stanton Harold, the seat of the Shirley family, on 24 August 1707. She was educated as befitted the aristocracy of the time. On 3 June 1728 she married Theophilus, the ninth Earl of Huntingdon, a man who could claim royal descent from the Plantagenet Duke of Clarence. By these means Lady Selina came to move in high society and court circles. By this time Methodism was beginning to make an impact on the aristocracy and Selina's sister-in-law, Lady Margaret Hastings, came to a personal faith in Christ through the preaching of Benjamin Ingham. At some point in the summer of 1739, as the result of a serious illness and Margaret's spiritual concern, the countess herself experienced the new birth and was restored to perfect health.[47] Much like John Wesley she came to regard herself as "a brand plucked from the burning". Members of the nobility were bemused at the sudden change which had taken place in her.

After her conversion the Countess of Huntingdon's visits to the court were less frequent and she and Lord Huntingdon began to attend the Methodist Society which had been formed in London's Fetter Lane. Here, in the autumn of 1740, she encountered a number of celebrated preachers, including John and Charles Wesley, and later George Whitefield, on his return from America in March 1741.

The countess first met Howell Harris on 26 August 1743 when she visited Enfield Chase, a small village to the north of London.[48] Through their friendship the countess began to attend worship at Moorfields Tabernacle where she also heard Whitefield preach on a number of occasions. She was greatly impressed and began to persuade her friends to go with her to hear his sermons. Among those who accepted her invitations were Sarah Churchill, Duchess of Marlborough, the Duchess of Ancaster, Lady Townsend, and Lady Cobham. The latter two she wrote "were exceedingly pleased with many observations in Mr Whitefield's sermon in St Sepulchre's Church".[49]

The countess also struck up a close friendship with John Wesley who noted in his diary that he paid at least six visits to her between April and August 1741.[50] She soon began to support Methodist societies in the area close to the family's Donnington Hall estate. In addition she and the Earl had a London house in Downing Street and a mansion in the peaceful village of Chelsea. She was wholly committed to using every opportunity to influence and persuade her friends and acquaintances to hear the Wesleys and later Whitefield at gatherings which she held in their London residence. A. H. New wrote, "The good effect of the Countess of Huntingdon was very great, and through her persuasions, numbers of the aristocracy were brought within the sound of the faithful preaching of the Gospel."[51] Her drawing rooms were often filled with lords, ladies, politicians, and the great and good.

The countess's life was a sad one. Two of her sons died of

smallpox at the ages of eleven and thirteen and her husband, Lord Huntingdon, died of apoplexy a short time later on 13 October 1736. The countess found great solace in her Christian faith. She was particularly caring of the servants and labourers who worked for her. In this she was a kindred spirit with the Wesleys and Whitefield, who constantly carried the needs of the poor on their hearts. She became a mother to the poor wherever she encountered them, praying for them in their times of sickness and ensuring their basic needs were attended to. She also saw the importance of using her home as a base for spreading the Christian message although this was not without its problems. On one occasion when Whitefield was preaching there riots broke out and some of the congregation were threatened on their way home.[52]

Invitations to the great and the good

The Countess of Huntingdon was undeterred by the comments of those who did not share her Christian faith and was gradually devising ways to bring them to Christ. On Whitefield's arrival back in London from America on 5 July 1748 the countess summoned him to her home. During the following weeks she invited various members of the aristocracy to hear him preach.[53]

As a peeress of the realm Countess Selina had the legal right to appoint two chaplains who would be responsible to attend to the spiritual needs of her household wherever she might be living. She therefore invited Whitefield to be her personal chaplain.[54] This position was the only title that Whitefield ever had and he took great pride and encouragement from it. Her trust in him increased his self-confidence and was the start of a lifelong spiritual friendship in which they became co-workers. Whitefield's appointment happened just at the point when he was about to set off for Scotland but he immediately wrote a letter to her on 1 September, expressing his gratitude for the recognition she had given him.

> I dare not leave town without dropping a few lines gratefully to acknowledge the many favours I have received from your Ladyship, especially the honour you have done me in making me one of your Ladyship's chaplains. A sense of it humbles me in making me pray more intensely for grace to walk worthy of that God who has called me to his kingdom and glory. As your ladyship has been pleased to confer this honour upon me, I shall think it my duty to send you weekly accounts of what the Lord Jesus is pleased to do for and by me.[55]

Whitefield's status as chaplain was a sign that the countess valued his preaching and doctrine. She invited many distinguished people to come and hear him preach in her home. Among those who came were the Duchess of Queensbury and those who had previously heard Whitefield preach before at the countess's invitation: Lady Townsend and the Duchess of Marlborough. There were times when Whitefield found himself in high demand. He wrote in a letter, "Good Lady Huntingdon is to come to town, and I am to preach at her Ladyship's house twice a week to the great and noble. O that some of them may be effectually called, and taste of the riches of redeeming love!"[56] One of those who was singularly impressed by Whitefield's endeavours was Lord Bolingbroke, a man who had little sympathy with the Christian message. He nevertheless acclaimed Whitefield as "the most extraordinary man of our times".[57] Another who heard him was Lord Chesterfield, a self-confessed atheist, who enjoyed good oratory. On one occasion he was so impressed by Whitefield's description of a beggar tottering on the brink of a precipice, that he inadvertently leapt to his feet and called out "Good God, he's gone!"[58] Neither of the two men, it should be said, appears to have come to any kind of faith. Among those who did, however, were Lord St John, the Earl of Bath, and William Pulteney, who attended worship at Whitefield's Tottenham Court Road chapel. Lady Chesterfield and Countess Delitz, both illegitimate daughters of George I by his mistress the Duchess of Kendal, also experienced the new birth.[59]

In fact Tyerman listed more than fifty aristocrats and notable men and women of distinction who heard Whitefield speak in one or other of the countess's residences.[60] Whitefield rejoiced in these meetings and wrote in a letter dated 30 December 1748, "O how is the power of the Redeemer's resurrection displayed in Lady Huntingdon. She is a mother in Israel indeed. It would please you to see the assemblies in her Ladyship's house."[61] The countess was also well acquainted with some of the Scottish nobility who had been converted through Whitefield's preaching north of the border, and when they came to London they visited her and took part in her meetings.

While very few embraced Evangelical religion, the majority were impressed by Whitefield and the message he brought. On a positive note it made the ruling classes aware that Methodism was not a vehicle for "enthusiasm" as popularly understood, extreme radicalism, or rebellion. Writing of these occasions, he noted, "I go with fear and trembling, knowing how difficult it is to speak to the great so as to win them to Jesus Christ."[62] Whitefield was always respectful and deferential toward the countess. In fact he has been criticized for his self-deprecation which is seen in the way he signed off his letters with expressions such as "I am your Lady's most dutiful – most unworthy servant".[63] Writing to her in May 1755 he wrote, "How shall I express my gratitude? – Tears trickle down my eyes, whilst I am thinking of your Ladyship's condescending to patronize such a dead dog as I am… Ever honoured Madam excuse me. Tears flow too fast for me to write on!"[64]

Protector of Methodism

By the later 1740s Methodism was expanding rapidly through the influence of Whitefield and the Wesleys, but also other Church of England clergy and lay helpers. Methodist people were frequently maligned and their societies denounced by the Church of England authorities. It often happened that local magistrates refused to take action on behalf of those who were being unjustly treated. The Countess of Huntingdon therefore took it upon herself to intervene whenever she had the opportunity. In 1745 she appealed to Lord Carteret, the secretary of state, who in turn brought the matter to King George. The king required him to forward a reply to the countess in a letter dated 19 November 1745, in which he asserted that he would tolerate no persecution on grounds of religion and requiring that all magistrates afford protection to all who were engaged in religious observances.[65]

A. H. New wrote of the countess: "She heeded not the sarcasms or witticisms of the gay, nor the stern opposition of the world. The anathema of the worldly-minded priests fell powerless upon her… She cast a shield of protection around her own ministers… her very name was sufficient to strike terror into the enemies of the cross, and to attract thousands to see the illustrious lady."[66] Her protection was indeed needed for a season in the autumn of 1760 when London's Drury Lane theatre was staging a play called "The Minor" in which George Whitefield was being ridiculed. The countess protested on his behalf to the Lord Chamberlain, the Duke of Gloucester, and later met with the celebrated actor David Garrick (1717–79), who acknowledged the offensive nature of the performances and agreed to use his influence to have them halted.

The Countess's Calvinistic chapels

The Countess of Huntingdon was a member of the established Church of England and it was never her intention to leave its bounds. However, many of the Methodists whom she befriended and whose ministries she supported were increasingly persecuted or expelled from its Anglican links. As a result she felt impelled to devote a considerable portion of her personal wealth to the building of chapels which would be preaching places for such men – and in some cases women – as well as centres for worship and for encouraging and building up new converts. In 1753 the countess gave generously to the building of a commodious chapel in Bristol which was designed for the people who clamoured to hear Whitefield preach. A similar venture followed at Norwich in 1755; it was intended for people to hear the preaching of James Wheatley who had earlier worked with the Wesleys.[67] In 1761 a chapel was built next to the Countess's Brighton home. Initially this, along with her other places of worship, were served solely by ordained clergy from the Church of England.

Among those who preached and taught there were William Romaine, John Berridge, John Venn, and John Fletcher. The building was enlarged in 1767 and Whitefield preached at its reopening from the text of 2 Peter 3:18, "Grow in the grace and knowledge of our Lord and Saviour Jesus Christ" (NIV). Other chapels followed at Oat Hall in Sussex and at Tunbridge Wells in July 1769, with Whitefield once again preaching from Genesis 28:17, "How dreadful is this place! This is none other than the house of God, and this is the gate of heaven" (ASV). The countess was also responsible for building chapels at Lewes and Bath. Others followed in the years after Whitefield's death including Birmingham, Bootle, Hereford, Hull, Reading, St Ives, Westminster, and Worcester. Her chapel in Bath proved to be a particularly valuable means of reaching out to the wealthy and the aristocracy. The Countess of

Huntingdon informed John Wesley, who had offered to preach there, of the importance of the season "when the great of this world are in reach of the sound of the gospel".[68] In 1781 these chapels were finally forced to sever their links with the Church of England and became a separate denomination which later became known as "The Countess of Huntingdon's connection".[69] The major reason for this was that they had contravened the parochial system and the right of Anglican incumbents to have sole charge over worship in their parishes. Early in 1782 the countess finally seceded from the Church of England.[70]

Whitefield's separation from Harris

With the passing of time Harris emerged as an increasingly controlling leader and often crossed swords with Daniel Rowland,[71] the other generally accepted leader of the revival in Wales. Harris often reminded people that he was the first in the field and considered himself to be the originator of the Welsh outpourings. His orthodoxy was also questioned on account of his preaching and holding a form of patripassianism[72] with Harris maintaining that both the human and the divine nature of Jesus suffered and died on the cross. On the other hand, those who followed Rowland, including Whitefield, maintained that only the human nature of the Lord was crucified.[73] The issue brought about a split in Welsh Methodism which lasted for nearly twenty years. The two groups became known as "Harris's People" and "Rowland's People."[74]

It was at this point that Harris then allowed himself to fall into an inappropriate relationship with Mrs Sidney Griffiths, the wife of a dissolute Welsh squire. Harris had first met her briefly while preaching in North Wales in 1748. She fled from her husband to Trevecca, and Harris, with his wife's consent, took her into their home. His relationship with "Madam Griffiths" was not sexually immoral, but it was nevertheless ill-advised. Harris took her with him on some of his evangelistic preaching engagements and came to believe that she had apostolic preaching gifts and the discernment of spirits. This caused his expulsion from the Welsh Association in 1750 and resulted in a major split in the work with the majority siding with Rowland. Whitefield, needless to say, expressed his rank disapproval of Harris's behaviour as contrary to God's Word and refused to allow him to preach at the Tabernacle.[75]

Harris's lapse was a devastating blow to Whitefield since, for the previous eleven years, he had been his closest friend and fellow worker. They were of one mind in matters of doctrine and strategy and they had laboured together in prayer and preaching. As we have noted, in 1743 they had brought together the English and Welsh societies with Whitefield as moderator and Harris acting in his absence.[76] Whitefield therefore had to sever their relationship and this in turn meant that he had to reassume responsibility for the London Tabernacle and his societies which he had also entrusted to Harris's pastoral oversight. In the event he was unable to find one preacher to assume total responsibility for the preaching at Moorfields and he left the societies to take care of themselves. With the passing of time Whitefield's relationships with the Wesleys improved and some of his societies placed themselves in their pastoral care. In this matter Whitefield was clearly deficient in management and organizational skills.

Harris's condition and mental instability lasted for about two years, after which time he began to return to better health and well-being. Harris subsequently retreated to Talgarth where many recent converts were settling. He formed them into a religious community similar in ethos to those of the Moravians with agricultural activities and workshops with a variety of manual trades. He recognized and apologized for his former lapses in behaviour and resumed preaching in 1763. His relationship with Whitefield was restored and in 1767 he spent some time with him at the Tabernacle and the two of them went together to Wesley's annual Conference. Harris built up his community and continued to travel in Wales preaching and building up the societies. When he died ten years later it is said that 20,000 attended his funeral. In summary, there can be no doubt, as Dallimore wrote, that "Whitefield was profoundly influenced by Harris's example."[77] He was the pioneer of field preaching and the first to form a number of societies into a connexion.

Trevecca College

Since her conversion the countess constantly looked for ways to extend the gospel and this led to her interest in training men for the ministry. In 1753 a deputation arrived in England in an endeavour to raise funds for a college in New Jersey, founded to train men for the ministry of the Presbyterian Church. Whitefield was a keen supporter of this project, which later became Princeton University, and the countess gave considerable financial support to it. She also supported Dartmouth College, which was granted a charter by George III.

In 1768 six students were expelled from St Edmund Hall, Oxford. They were dubbed "enthusiasts" on account of their practice of extempore prayer and other Methodist practices. Whitefield staunchly defended the students in a strongly worded pamphlet entitled *A Letter to the Reverend Dr Durell, Vice-Chancellor of the University of Oxford*. It was a lengthy piece of some thirty pages with a gamut of arguments in defence of both the expelled students and Methodism in general. He demonstrated that the prayers we read in Scripture "which availed much with God, were all of an extempore nature". He pointed out that receiving the witness of the Spirit was no reason for these students to be dubbed enthusiasts. "Did not the Church of England ordination service," he wrote, require students "to be inwardly moved by the Holy Spirit?"[78] In defence of Methodists in general Whitefield pointed out that they "dearly love and honour their king, their rightful sovereign King George" and stressed that "every additional proselyte to true Methodism is an additional loyal subject to King George the Third."[79] Whitefield ended his pamphlet with the words of the first-century rabbi Gamaliel, "And now I say unto you, refrain from these men, and let them alone; for if this council or work be of men, it will come to nought; but if it be of God, ye cannot overthrow it; lest haply ye be found to fight against God."

The Countess of Huntingdon was deeply perturbed that such good men should be treated in this way and made her views widely known. After giving the matter serious consideration she purchased Trevecca House in 1767 and converted it into a theological college. It was situated close to the village of Talgarth in Wales, where Harris's community was established. This enabled him to take an interest in the college's life and activities.

Whitefield preached at the official opening of the college on 24 August 1768 and chose as his text Exodus 20:24, "In all places where I record my name, I will come unto to thee, and I will bless thee." On the Sunday following Whitefield preached to a congregation of several thousand who had come together in the courtyard in front of the college. He based his message on 1 Corinthians 3:11, "other foundation can no man lay than that is laid, which is Jesus Christ."

The curriculum at Trevecca was noteworthy for its academic content which included Greek, Latin, ecclesiastical history, natural philosophy and geography, but with a strong influence on the spiritual life and active evangelistic activities. All students were vetted by the countess herself. John Fletcher, the incumbent of Madeley, was given the responsibility of overseeing the college and given the title "President", although he did not reside on the premises but instead visited the college for extended periods of time. Fletcher resigned his position in 1771 on account of the struggles between the Calvinists and Arminians. Following this the countess personally supervised the college and invested much time in maintaining its work. She took strenuous efforts to ensure that the students became effective preachers. In the disputes which took place between Wesley and Whitefield over predestination the countess did her best to act as a mediator. In reality her sympathies were with Whitefield and, following a stormy encounter at Bristol in August 1770, Wesley's preachers were excluded from her pulpits. The eventual outcome of this debacle was a clearly defined separation between the Wesleyans and the Calvinistic Methodists.

At the time of her death the countess had opened 200 chapels and mission stations. She set up a scheme by which she divided them into twenty-three districts, each with its own representatives who were to be sent to an annual Conference. Her Connexion flourished and in 1828 there were 35,000 regular worshippers and 72 officiating ministers.[80]

In all of this there seems little doubt that Whitefield was the most influential of the countess's chaplains. He received frequent invitations to her homes to address the great and the good and there was constant correspondence between them. Even when Whitefield was far from home preaching in Scotland or in America it was clear she was never far from his thoughts. It became increasingly clear that she favoured his Calvinistic theology; indeed she and her advisers drew up "Fifteen Articles of Faith" to which all her societies were committed. Article 6 "Of Predestination and Election", clearly stated, "Although the whole world is thus become guilty before God, it hath pleased him to predestinate some unto everlasting life." The strong ties between Whitefield and the countess were made abundantly obvious when, in 1771, Cornelius Winter, who had accompanied Whitefield to America, returned carrying his will. By this Whitefield left her his orphan house in Georgia. The countess took an immediate interest in the project and purchased additional land in the colony.

In 1766, at the countess's suggestion, John and Charles Wesley met in conference with herself and Whitefield. Although no decisive action resulted their relationships became more cordial and they reached a general agreement to avoid rivalry. Charles Wesley declared that a threefold cord had been established which "we trust will nevermore be broken".[81] When Whitefield died four years later, his relationship with the Wesleys was somewhat restored. Indeed he had specifically requested that John Wesley should preach at his funeral service.

In summary, it is clear that Whitefield played a hugely significant role in the early days of Methodism and set up a connexional organization before John Wesley. He emerged as the eighteenth century's most forthright champion and leader of the Calvinistic Methodists. He was the acknowledged leader of English Calvinistic Methodists and indeed the Welsh at least in the early years of the revival. His very close relationship with the Countess of Huntingdon enabled him to influence a significant section of the English aristocracy and others in high places. Whitefield's preaching, teaching, and writing enabled him to strengthen the impact of reformed theology on the countess's Connexion, her chapels, and her college. In fact Whitefield became the eighteenth century's most high-profile Evangelical exponent of the Reformed faith.

Chapter 6 notes

1   M. H. Jones, *The Trevecca Letters* (C.M. Book Agency, Caernarvon, 1932) p. 209, cited A. Dallimore, op. cit., p. 237.
2   H. J. Hughes, *The Life of Howell Harris the Reformer* (London, James Nisbet, 1892), p. 294.
3   *Journal*, Wednesday 7 March 1739.

4   *Letter to Mr H*, 27 January 1739, *Works*, Vol. 1, p. 47.

5   *Journal*, Wednesday 7 March 1739. See also H. J. Hughes, *Life of Howell Harris* (London, James Nisbet & Co, 1892), p. 81.

6   D. C. Jones et al., *The Elect Methodists: Calvinistic Methodism in England and Wales 1735–1811* (Cardiff, University of Wales, 2016), p. 24.

7   Ibid.

8   See Bennet, "The Early Life of Howell Harris", in D. C. Jones et al., op. cit., p. 135.

9   *Journal*, Wednesday 7 March 1739.

10 Ibid, Friday 9 March 1739.

11 *A Short Account*, Section 3, p.18.

12 See D. C. Jones, op. cit., for a list of Whitfield's societies in 1747 in Appendix A pp. 263–64.

13 D. C. Jones, op. cit., p. 45.

14 See C. D. Field, "The social composition of English Methodism to 1830: a membership analysis", *Bulletin of John Rylands University Manchester Library*, 76 (Spring 1994) and D. Hempton, Methodism: Empire of the Spirit (New Haven, CT, Yale University Press, 2005), p. 5 in D. C. Jones et al., op. cit., p. 48.

15 Whitefield had married Elizabeth James on 14 November 1741.

16 D. Rowlands, *Letter to George Whitefield*, 2 February 1743 in L Tyerman, op. cit., Vol. 1, p 50.

17 H. Harris, *Letter to the Rev George Whitefield*, 12 February 1743, *Life and Times of Howell Harris*, p. 130 in L. Tyerman, op. cit., Vol. 1, p. 51.

18 H. Harris, *Letter to the Rev George Whitefield*, 1 March 1743 in *Life and Times of Howell Harris*, p. 130 in L. Tyerman, op. cit., Vol. 1, p. 52.

19 *Records of Associations*, II, p. 9, Calvinistic Archives, National Library of Wales in D. C. Jones et al., *The Elect Methodists*, p. 73.

20 *Christian History* was discontinued in July 1748. The last page of the 23 June 1748 issue states, "This is the last number of *Christian History* that will be printed."

21 *Christian History*, 15 November 1744.

22 Ibid.

23 Ibid, 7 January 1745.

24 D. C. Jones, op. cit., p. 21.

25 A. Dallimore, op. cit., p. 157.

26 A. Dallimore, op. cit., pp. 157–58. In a *Letter to Captain W——*, on 29 November 1748, Whitefield stated that he had given over the immediate care of all his societies to Harris.

27 Perhaps it was the case that Whitefield could initiate but not sustain societies. Wesley was able to do both.

28 L. Tyerman, op. cit., Vol. 1, p. 530.

29 *Letter to Gilbert Tennent*, 19 November 1741, *Works*, Vol. 1, pp. 338–39. See also *Gentleman's Magazine*, 1742, p. 608.

30 *Letter to the Reverend Mr O——*, 30 December 1741.

31   H. S. Stout, *The Divine Dramatist: George Whitefield and the Rise of Modern Evangelicalism* (Grand Rapids, William B. Eerdmans Publishing Company, 1991), p. 171.
32   *Letter to the Right Honourable Lady Dartmouth,* 22 November 1741.
33   *Letter to the Rev. Mr. S,* 12 November 1748.
34   *Letter to Mr C—,* 30 March 1754.
35   *Letter to the Reverend Mr H—,* 9 September 1747 and *Mr and Mrs F—,* 9 September 1747.
36   *Letter to Mr T—E—,* 27 November 1741.
37   D. C. Jones et al., op. cit., p. 31, makes the point that after 1740 Methodism effectively split into three distinct factions: Moravians, Wesleyan, and Calvinist.
38   *Letter to Mr S—M—,* 27 April 1741, *Works,* Vol. 1, p. 259.
39   *Letter to Howell Harris,* 28 April 1741, *Works,* Vol. 1, p. 259.
40   H. H. Hughes, *Life of Howell Harris,* p. 307.
41   Trevecca Letter 1306 James Erskine to Howell Harris, 20 March 1745, National Library of Wales in C. R. Jones, *The Elect Methodists,* p. 145.
42   Trevecca MSS, cited H. H. Hughes, op. cit., p. 309.
43   H. H. Hughes, op. cit., p. 310.
44   L. Tyerman, op. cit., Vol. 1, p. 465.
45   Whitefield, *A Letter to the Rev. Mr John Wesley,* 9 August 1740 in *Whitefield's Journals* (Banner of Truth Trust, 1965), p. 575.
46   C. R. Jones, *The Elect Methodists,* p. 78.
47   F. Cook, *Selina, Countess of Huntingdon* (Edinburgh, The Banner of Truth Trust, 2001) p. 51.
48   Ibid, p. 85.
49   A. C. H. Seymour, *The Life and Times of Selina* (London, 1839), Vol. 1, p. 25 cited in F. Cook, *Selina,* p. 92.
50   F. Cook, op. cit., p. 58.
51   A. H. New, *The Coronet and the Cross,* cited in G. W. Kirby, *The Elect Lady* (Trustees of the Countess of Huntingdon's Connexion, 1972), p. 19.
52   G. W. Kirby, *The Elect Lady,* p. 22.
53   F. Cook, *Selina,* pp. 110–11.
54   Ibid, p. 156.
55   *Letter to Lady Huntingdon,* 1 September 1748.
56   G. W. Kirby, op. cit., p. 26.
57   *Letter to Lady B—,* 30 December 1748.
58   G. W. Kirby, op. cit., p. 26.
59   F. Cook, op. cit., p. 122.
60   L. Tyerman, op. cit., Vol. 2.
61   *Letter to Lady B—,* 30 December 1748.
62   A. C. H. Seymour, op. cit., Vol. 2, pp. 209–10.
63   *Letter to the Countess of Huntingdon,* 24 February 1749.
64   Ibid, 27 May 1755.
65   G. W. Kirby, op. cit., p. 28.

66   A. H. New, *The Cornet and the Cross*, cited in G. W. Kirby, op. cit., p. 28.
67   F. Cook, op. cit., p. 155.
68   Wesley, *Journal* (London, Kelly, 1909–1916 – 8 Vols) Vol. 5, pp. 182–83.
69   The first ordinations took place in 1783 with the result that most of the
     countess's chaplains withdrew from her service. See G. W. Kirby, op. cit.,
     p. 34.
70   F. Cook, op. cit., p. 380.
71   Also sometimes spelled Rowlands.
72   Patripassianism derived from the Latin literally meaning "the Father
     suffers".
73   Rowlands published a pamphlet on this issue in 1749 entitled *Orthodox
     Methodist*.
74   H. H. Hughes, op. cit., p .360.
75   A. Dallimore, op. cit., Vol. 2, p. 300.
76   L. Tyerman, op. cit., Vol. 2, pp. 49–50; A. Dallimore, *George Whitefield*,
     Vol. 2, p. 157.
77   A. Dallimore, op. cit., Vol. 1, p. 249.
78   *A Letter to the Reverend Dr Durell, Vice-Chancellor of the University of
     Oxford occasioned by the Expulsion of Six Students from Edmund Hall*
     (1768) X 3, Works, Vol. 3, p. 326.
79   Ibid.
80   G. W. Kirby, op. cit., p. 54.
81   C. Wesley, *Journal*, Vol. 2, p. 247.

Chapter 7

Trapped in the Homeland

Although Whitefield had America, Georgia, and his beloved Bethesda orphan house constantly on his heart and mind, suddenly he found himself confined to British soil. Between 1756 and 1763 the great powers of Europe were engaged in a conflict that affected Europe, the Americas, West Africa, India, and the Philippines. The hostilities, which became known as the Seven Years' War, divided Europe into two main coalitions. On the one side were the French, who resented the growing colonial power of Georgian Britain. Britain, on the other, was supported by Prussia and some of the smaller German states, including Hanover, which was under the British crown. France formed a grand alliance with Austria and succeeded in bringing other European powers to their side. In the resultant conflict, however, they were defeated by the Anglo-Prussian coalition. Britain then used her dominant position at sea and attacked disputed French positions in North America. On 28 May 1754 British forces defeated the French at the Battle of Jumonville Glen in Pennsylvania. In the subsequent fighting Britain gained the greater part of French-held territories as well as Spanish Florida and some of the Caribbean islands too.

The extent of the war meant that travel was not an option for Whitefield and he therefore remained in Britain until the fighting was finally brought to a halt by the Peace of Paris on 10 February 1763. He nevertheless followed the conflict with a keen interest organizing fast days, gatherings for prayer and collections of money for the needy, and refugees. We catch a glimpse of Whitefield's wartime fundraising efforts when on 6 February he wrote to a friend that he had organized a collection at his Tabernacle which raised eighty pounds for the persecuted Protestants of France. It was entrusted to Mr A in Fleet Street to take the donation to them.[1]

Whitefield saw the Anglo-Prussian alliance as a divinely inspired Protestant instrument in the fight against the corruptions of the papacy and the Roman Catholic Church. Set against the fears of Britain being invaded Whitefield published on 23 February 1756 *A Short Address to Persons of all Denominations, Occasioned by the Alarm of an Intended Invasion.* The pamphlet, of which he sent a copy to the Dean of Westminster, Bishop Zachary Pearce (1690–1774), had large sales in both England and America, being reprinted six times in 1756 alone. In it Whitefield wrote of the "artful insinuations" of the French and of their having "unjustly invaded his Majesty's dominions in America". Then he referred to the recent earthquakes in Lisbon describing them as judgments from God. He asserted they would be "but small in comparison to our hearing a French army, accompanied with a popish contender, and thousands of Romish priests, was suffered to invade England". "Read," he continued, "the shocking accounts of the horrid butcheries and cruel murders committed on the bodies of many of our fellow-subjects in America, by the hands of savage Indians, instigated thereto by more than savage popish priests."[2] Whitefield reminded his readers of the sixteenth-century Protestant martyrs and the thousands of Protestants slaughtered on the streets of Paris. His language was strong and doubtless infuriated Catholics who were provoked into writing hostile letters. At the close of October

1757 Whitefield organized a solemn fast during which he preached three times. Thousands attended and he expressed the hope that their prayers "reached the ears of Lord of Sabaoth". He went on, however, to report "More bad news from America for our fleet: God humble and reform us, for his infinite mercy's sake."[3]

Though these attacks must have caused Whitefield considerable hurt he took encouragement from the progress of the Prussian armies in Europe. An issue of the *Gentleman's Magazine* for 1758 noted that on Monday 2 January a day of thanksgiving had taken place at the chapel in Tottenham Court Road "for the signal victories gained by the King of Prussia over his enemies".[4] In March of the same year Whitefield observed in a letter to a Professor F— that "thousands and thousands are now praying daily for success to the Prussian and Hanoverian armies... He that wrought such wonders for the Prussian monarch last year, can repeat them this. Lord, we believe, help our unbelief!"[5] During his visit to Scotland in August 1759 he devoted his energies to stirring the people's support for King George II and preached a thanksgiving sermon for the victory of Prince Ferdinand of Brunswick over the French at Minden on 31 July.[6]

The following month (18 and 19 August), Admiral Edward Boscawen and the British fleet first successfully blockaded the French in Toulon and then defeated them in the open sea off the coasts of Spain and Portugal, in what became known as the Battle of Lagos. Then, on 13 September, the British, under General James Wolfe, won a dramatic victory over the French, scaling the heights of Abraham in the Battle of Quebec. Whitefield being too impulsive to wait for the royal proclamation preached three thanksgiving sermons attended by numerous persons of distinction on Friday 19 October. Two addresses were given in the morning at Moorfields and one in the afternoon at Tottenham Court Road Chapel. Whitefield was doubtless untroubled when he was roundly rebuked by Dr John Free, the vicar of East Coker in Somerset, "for not having the decency to wait till his Majesty appointed a day of thanksgiving".[7]

In March 1760 Whitefield published a twenty-four-page pamphlet entitled *Russian Cruelty* which highlighted instances of extreme savagery handed out by Russian troops in Germany. In the preface Whitefield asked for practical help for distressed German Protestants. In a sermon preached before a very large congregation on 14 March he denounced the brutality of the Russian cossacks on the inhabitants of the Duchy of Mecklenburg. He commended a collection for their relief to be held on the coming day of the public fast. A total of £400 was then donated at Tottenham Court Road Chapel and the Moorfields Tabernacle.[8] The following year Whitefield wrote that on the fast day held on Friday 13 February 1761 near £600 was collected for the plundered Protestants of Brandenburg and the relief of distressed inhabitants of New England. Many aristocrats attended one or other of the three services. They included the Countess of Huntingdon, Lord Bute, the Duke of Grafton, Prime Minister William Pitt, and Lord Villiers.[9] After this time Whitefield's correspondence becomes more focused on his extensive travels in Britain and matters relating to Georgia and the orphan house. Finally, on 15 January 1763, he wrote that the situation was set to enable him to visit America.

Work in London and travels in the British Isles

During his enforced stay in Britain Whitefield made London his base. On 6 June[10] he wrote to Governor Belcher in Boston, "Just this day a month ago did I arrive in this metropolis [London], where, glory, glory be to the head of the church! The word hath still free course. The poor despised Methodists are as lively as ever, and in several churches the gospel is now preached with power."[11] In a letter to a Mr C, written in the same month, he wrote that "it will rejoice you to hear that his glorious gospel of Jesus Christ gets ground apace".[12]

In 1756 Whitefield took steps to build a place of worship in Tottenham Court Road. When the new chapel was first constructed it was 70 feet (21 metres) square on the inside. The foundation stone was laid at the beginning of June. Whitefield preached from the text of Ezra 3:11, "They sang together by course in praising and giving thanks unto the Lord; because he is good, for his mercy endureth for ever toward Israel. And all the people shouted with a great shout, when they praised the Lord, because the foundation of the house of the Lord was laid." Whitefield wrote to the Countess of Huntingdon, "Blessed be God, a new building is now erecting at Tottenham Court Road."[13] The chapel was opened for public worship on 7 November 1756 with Whitefield preaching a sermon based on 1 Corinthians 3:11, "Other foundation can no man lay than that is laid, which is Jesus Christ." Two years later twelve almshouses and a residence for the minister were added.

About a year later the building was found to be too small and was lengthened to 127 feet (38 metres) with the width remaining at 70 feet (21 metres). Whitefield had hoped that it would be possible for the chapel to be connected with the Church of England and even consulted the House of Commons with that intention. In the end the difficulties proved insurmountable and it was licensed as a Dissenting Meeting House.[14] Beneath the building was a vault for the burial of the dead where Whitefield intended that he himself would be buried. The initial opening of the Tottenham Court Road chapel coincided with a season of renewed spiritual life and Whitefield, writing on 15 December, observed that there was a wonderful stirring of the dry bones with some great people asking if they might have a regular seat.[15] At the end of the year Whitefield was still much encouraged and wrote:

God is doing wonders in the new chapel. Hundreds went away last Sunday morning, who could not come in. On Christmas Day and last Tuesday night (the first time of burning candles), the power of the Lord was present, both to wound and to heal. A neighbouring doctor has baptised the place calling it "Whitefield's Soul-Trap". I pray that it may be a soul trap indeed, to many wandering sinners. Abundance of people round about, I hear, are much struck.[16]

A year later the situation was still one of great encouragement, with Whitefield noting on 3 November 1757 that "thousands went away last Sunday evening from Tottenham Court, for want of room" and "that every day produces fresh accounts of good being done".[17] He wrote again later in the same month that in "Tottenham Court chapel, as well as the Tabernacle, the word runs and is glorified".[18] In mid-December he expressed his hope that the chapel debts would be discharged by New Year's Day, writing that "every day proves more and more that it was built for the glory of Christ, and the welfare of precious immortal souls".[19]

London, as the administrative centre from which Whitefield's societies were managed, also remained the central focus of Whitefield's labours during this time – and it was there that his preaching attracted large and growing congregations over the seven years in which he was confined to Britain. It was there that he was able to impact the aristocracy and men and women of distinction with the Evangelical Christian faith. While only a few experienced the new birth there is no doubt that numbers were moved by Whitefield's patriotic sermons on behalf of British and Prussian troops. Many gave generous financial support to his collections.

Long Acre Chapel and persecution

During this time Whitefield's public profile reached its zenith. So too did the amount of verbal and written hostility and the degree of physical attacks he encountered. One of the worst episodes, which combined all three of these aspects of persecution, came to the fore when he began preaching at Long Acre Chapel in London. For some while Whitefield had hoped to establish a chapel in the West End where the theatres and places of entertainment were based. It was there that the celebrated David Garrick managed the theatre in Drury Lane and well-known actors and actresses of the day such as John Rich "the Harlequin", Catherine Clive, and Samuel Foote wowed their audiences. Since his youth Whitefield had been drawn to the stage, first as a participant but now in his later years as a growing critic. He was still possessed with acting talents but employed them solely for promoting the cause of Christ. He knew himself to be an entertainer with gifts of voice and the ability to dramatize his message. Indeed David Garrick had once exclaimed, "I would give a hundred guineas if I could say 'Oh!' like Mr Whitefield." He felt that here was the place in the heart of the nation's capital that he could herald the gospel message.

By what seemed to Whitefield to be a divine incident the Revd John Barnard vacated his pastorate at Long Acre Chapel and Whitefield was invited to read prayers and preach there twice a week. The Dean of Westminster, Dr Zachary Pearce,[20] who was also Bishop of Bangor, as well as having held the lucrative living of St Martin-in-the-Fields for the previous twenty-three years, claimed to exercise jurisdiction over the building.[21] He clearly had an inbuilt dislike for both Whitefield and Methodism in general although he seems not to have entered into any conflict with Wesley who had a chapel close by. Pearce's hostility to Whitefield may in part have been due to his more puritanical views. Indeed, earlier in 1753, the owner of a Glasgow theatre came to have serious moral doubts about the stage after hearing Whitefield's preaching. This led him to dismantle his playhouse in the city. Rumours spread that Whitefield was responsible for this.[22]

From the outset of his ministry at Long Acre Chapel Whitefield encountered forthright opposition. On 29 January 1756 he reported to the Countess of Huntingdon that a number of people had caused a disturbance outside the chapel during the time of public worship and had been called before a justice of the peace. Strangely the same individuals had also been summoned by the bishop who had inquired as to the address of Whitefield's residence.[23] The following day Whitefield wrote again to the countess and thanked her for "the care and zeal you have expressed in suppressing the late disorders at Long Acre Chapel".[24]

However, a day or so later, Whitefield received a letter from the bishop ordering him to desist from preaching in Long Acre Chapel. But by this time Whitefield was a seasoned campaigner when it came to defending himself and his rights. He replied in firm but gracious terms pointing out that the building was unconsecrated and properly licensed and that the previous occupant of the pulpit was a Dissenting minister who had preached unhindered for a number of years. He trusted that "your Lordship will be so good as to inform yourself and me more particularly about this matter" and anticipated that "the irregularity I am charged with, will appear justifiable to every true lover of English liberty". In light of this Whitefield stated that he had given notice that he would preach in the chapel every Tuesday and Thursday while he was in town.[25]

The bishop responded with a further missive that Whitefield was unable to publish since the prelate claimed his right as a peer of the realm to forbid it. Whitefield who was ever at the ready when it came to letter writing replied in an expansive answer of six folios in length. Among many other things he reminded the bishop that he was an ordained minister of the Church of England and that for nearly twenty years he had conscientiously defended the Articles of Religion and the Book of Homilies. He also pointed out that he continued to use the church's liturgy wherever a church or chapel allowed him to do so and assured his Lordship that he would continue to adhere to the doctrine of the church until his dying day. He also reminded the bishop that he had recently published a small tract (a copy of which he begged him to receive) in which he recommended the Communion office of the Church of England.[26] Whitefield's letter was forthright, earnest, and respectful.

However, when Whitefield returned to London from a visit to Bristol a month later he found it necessary to write again to the bishop. He discovered that the disturbances had increased, and more than that, it appeared that "persons from your Lordship's vestry" were responsible for "such irregular proceedings".[27] So strong was the bishop's hostility both to Methodism and to Whitefield that he was unwilling to let the matter pass. He wrote again and although the content of his letter is not known it seems from Whitefield's reply that he was encouraging the troublemakers. Whitefield pointed out that what was happening during the time of divine worship was more than mere noise, it was, in fact, "premeditated rioting".

> Drummers, soldiers, and many of the baser sort, have been hired by subscription. A copper furnace, bells, drums, clappers, marrow-bones and cleavers, and such-like instruments have been provided for them, and repeatedly have been used by them, from the moment I have begun preaching, to the end of the sermon. By these horrid noises, many women have been almost frightened to death, and mobbers

encouraged thereby to come and riot at the chapel door during divine service, and insult and abuse me and the congregation after it hath been over. Not content with this, the chapel windows, while I have been preaching, have repeatedly been broken with large stones of almost a pound in weight (some of them lying before me) which levelled at, providentially missed me, but at the same time sadly wounded some of my hearers.[28]

Whitefield ended this letter by requesting the bishop to instruct the individuals who were from his parish of St Martin-in-the-Fields to "henceforward desist from such unchristian, such riotous and dangerous proceedings".[29] The whole affair was clearly distressing to Whitefield who informed the Countess of Huntingdon in the following April that the noise of the rabble had been infernal and that he felt they were laying plans to kill him.[30] While the theatres were in part responsible for the noises around Long Acre there seems little doubt that Bishop Pearce was also behind the actions of the troublemakers. The debacle prompted one very significant result in that it led Whitefield to take steps to build his aforementioned Tottenham Court Road Chapel.

Hostility from London's clergy and theatres

During his visit to Philadelphia in 1744 Whitefield had landed himself in hot water by making strong pronouncements against theatres and dance halls.[31] It was inevitable that Whitefield would experience similar hostility from the London stage for toward the end of 1760 he preached a sermon against those who attended the theatres. This soon stirred up a veritable hornet's nest and provoked a response entitled *A discourse concerning plays and players*. The writer of this piece described himself as a Methodist who had long held an ignorant zeal against theatres but had recently been cured of his ignorance as a result of conversations with a comedian, and since seeing Garrick perform on stage.

A succession of hostile pronouncements followed in the wake of these two documents. The year 1760 was marked by the burlesquing of Whitefield. Prominent among them was a series of performances by a certain Samuel Foote. Oxford-educated Foote had originally intended to become a lawyer but having squandered much of his wealth he was driven to take up acting. In 1747 he opened a small theatre in the Haymarket. There, in 1760, he published and performed a profane burlesque of Whitefield and his followers. Entitled *The Minor* it was noted for Foote's extraordinary mimicry and the profane obscenity of its language. Even *The Monthly Review*, which was no friend of the Methodists, denounced it as "unjust to Mr Whitefield".[32] In August it was also opposed by the Reverend Martin Madan (1726–90), in a pamphlet entitled *Christian and Critical Remarks on a Droll or Interlude called the Minor.*[33] The writer, it stated, has gone "beyond any of his competitors in debauching and debasing the stage".[34]

Shortly after this the public were treated to a hostile composition entitled, *A Satyrical Dialogue between the celebrated Mr F___te and Dr Squintum* which was performed at Garrick's theatre in Drury Lane. The use of the word "Squintum" was a reference to Whitefield's weak eye. At one point in the lewd production Whitefield was represented as duping the public of their money with love feasts and other baits. Even *The Monthly Review* condemned "The impudence of our low dirty hedge-publishers" which is "risen to a most shameful height."[35]

The Minor was again on stage in November 1760 in Drury Lane. In this performance Mrs Cole, the bawd, is made to say, "Dr Squintum washed me with the soap-suds and scouring sand of the Tabernacle, and I became as clean and bright as a pewter platter." From this time Foote began to take in a substantial income from mocking and ridiculing Whitefield in public. At this point, however, Madan stepped forward once more and denounced Foote for "a Dramatic Libel against the Christian Religion". He blushed, he wrote, for his countrymen who attended "this vile stuff" for "above thirty nights".[36]

Foote's relentless hostility toward Whitefield continued into 1761, when three new additions were made to the script of *The Minor*.[37] In one of them, *The Register Office: A Farce in Two Acts*, Whitefield is presented as "Mr Watchlight" instead of "Dr Squintum" and other dramatis personae included "Lady Wrinkle" and "Mrs Snareswell". Another hostile piece, *The Methodist: a Comedy: Being a Continuation and Completion of the Plan of the Minor*, was suppressed on account of its offensive content and so failed to achieve a stage performance.[38] Matters didn't end at this point and the hostile Foote continued to hound Whitefield even after his death. Gillies recorded that at the first night of a performance of *The Minor* in the winter of 1770 there was a "pretty throng, as people fond of any novelty were led to it without knowing any thing of the nature of the performance". However, when the public became aware of the level of impurity and indecency, only ten women appeared for the second night's performance. In the aftermath a dispute arose among those who had seen the play as to "whether it was proper to bring Mr Whitefield upon the stage, as he was now dead?" On the Sunday following several of the city's leading ministers used their pulpits to condemn the play out of hand. One of their number Mr Baine of the Scottish Relief Church concluded his sermon on the matter stating, "How base and ungrateful is such treatment of the dead" and "How illiberal such usage of one, whose indefatigable labours of his beloved King and Country are well known."[39]

Samuel Foote's vehement hostility toward Whitefield was not a lone voice; there was much more opposition that he had to endure. On Whitsunday 1758 Dr John Free, preached a hostile sermon before the University of Oxford which consisted chiefly of extracts from Whitefield's journals. Among a number of warnings he declared "Methodists experiment upon women in hysteric fits, and upon young persons in convulsions, under the pretence of exorcising devils." He also asserted that Whitefield had "attempted to set up a new form of church government". Dr Free's sermon was later published under the title, *Rules for the discovery of false prophets; or the dangerous impositions of the People called Methodists.*[40] The Revd John Downes, Rector of St Michael's Wood Street, and lecturer at St Mary-le-Bow, London, published *Methodism Examined and Exposed*[41] in which both Whitefield and Wesley were openly abused.[42]

There were many other sermons, hostile tracts, and newspaper articles too numerous to record in the present context. Mention should be made of two of them. First, *A Journal of the Travels of Nathaniel Snip, a Methodist Teacher of the Word.* This was a burlesque in which the puppet, Punch, appeared in the guise of Dr Squintum who picked the pockets of his hearers while they were looking heavenward. Second was Bishop John Green of Lincoln's *The Principles and Practices of the Methodists farther considered; in a Letter to the Reverend Mr George Whitefield.*[43] Green, who had been Regius Professor of Divinity, was a more erudite critic although part of his argument was based on Whitefield's views as expressed in his *Short Account of God's Dealings with him* some of which he had retracted. He denounced Whitefield as "a spiritual pickpocket" and pointed to instances where orators had been known to dissolve their hearers into tears without their having understood a word they had spoken.[44]

Although outwardly Whitefield most often appeared resilient and forthright in his public responses to persecution and criticism he must surely have been brought low in his spirit by this level of public mockery. His first mention of the matter is found in a letter he penned on 15 August 1760, where he noted, "Satan is angry. I am now mimicked and burlesqued upon the public stage. All hail such contempt! God forbid that I should boast, save in the cross of Jesus Christ."[45] In the spring of 1761 he referred to himself as "a worthless worm".[46]

Travels outside London

Having to withstand such levels of opposition from the stage, bishops, and other hostile pamphleteers Whitefield was no doubt encouraged by the growing numbers who heard him preach at Moorfields Tabernacle and his Tottenham Court Road Chapel and elsewhere. "It was," he wrote, "the prayers of God's people that have brought me back from the borders of the eternal world."[47] He would of course have garnered strength from the Countess of Huntingdon, other members of the aristocracy and distinguished people who supported his ministry. It was also apparent that his many successful preaching journeys to other parts of the British Isles regenerated his own spiritual and emotional energy. He wrote in June 1761 that "through the divine mercy I am somewhat improved in my health since leaving London".[48] A further encouragement was the increasing number of clergy who began to align themselves with Whitefield's Evangelicalism. Some of them such as William Grimshaw of Howarth, John Berridge of Everton, and William Talbot of Kineton rode out with him and shared in the preaching.

During Whitefield's confinement in Britain, London was his base particularly in the winter months when the weather made travel considerably more difficult. It wasn't until the 1820s that

John MacAdam brought significant improvements to the nation's highways using crushed stone. Before then travel at any time could be hazardous and Whitefield himself suffered falls from horses and accidents with his one-horse chaise. In a letter to "Captain H__" Whitefield wrote that "the Welsh roads have almost demolished my open one-horse chaise, as well as me."[49]

Most often Whitefield organized his preaching into short periods of between three weeks to sometimes as much as three or four months if Scotland, Ireland, or North Wales happened to be his chosen destination. Even on these occasions he tended to base himself primarily in one central location such as Edinburgh, Bristol, Gloucester, or Dublin. From there he would then take off for short periods into the surrounding towns and countryside. This development of circuits became a popular mission strategy among the early Methodist followers of both Whitefield and the Wesleys. With the passing of time the circuit emerged as the centrepiece of Methodist organization. It enabled the preacher to return to the scene of his or her former labours and encourage and exhort recent converts to meet in class and strengthen their faith and commitment. It cannot have escaped Whitefield that here was a strategy of revisiting and pastoral care that resonated with the ministry of Paul's missionary journeys, and the travels of other apostolic leaders of the New Testament church.

We see instances of Whitefield's circuit-style preaching strategy in his visits to the West Country, Yorkshire, and Scotland in particular. In August 1756 he wrote as follows in a letter addressed to a Mr Z:

> It is now a fortnight since I came to Leeds. On the Sunday evening, a few hours after my arrival, many thousands were gathered in the fields, to whom Jesus enabled me to speak with some

degree of power. The following week, I preached in and about Leeds, thrice almost every day, to thronged and affected congregations... at seven in the evening at Birstal... The next morning... at Tadcaster... On Tuesday, I preached twice at York... On Wednesday, at Warstall, about fifty miles off; on Thursday, twice at Yarm; and last night and this morning here (back in Leeds).[50]

One of the places "about Leeds" which he visited and mentions in the above letter without further comment was the small town of Howarth, later to be made famous as the home of the Brontë sisters. Here the incumbent was the rugged and forthright William Grimshaw. St Michael's Parish Church had a capacity of about 525 seats, but often a thousand or more crowded into the building on a Sunday.[51] On the occasion of Whitefield's visit a scaffold was erected in the churchyard from which he preached on the text of Zechariah 9:12, "Turn you to the stronghold, ye prisoners of hope."[52] Samuel Whitaker, a young Yorkshire man, got among the crowd nearly under the scaffold and described it "as the most affecting time I ever experienced".[53] A commemorative tablet in Howarth Methodist Church records that Whitefield made five visits to the parish although it has been suggested there were probably as many as seventeen in all.[54]

It happened once or twice that Whitefield's coming coincided with one of the three Sundays in the year when the sacrament of Communion was appointed. This doubtless helped to swell the already large numbers who attended. About 6,000 hearers assembled in the churchyard to listen to Whitefield in September 1749, and over a thousand took Communion. In 1753 Whitefield once again proved to be a crowd-puller with Grimshaw writing, "we have lately had Mr Whitefield in these parts... In my church he assisted me in administering the Lord's Supper to as many communicants as sipped away 35 bottles of wine within a gill. It was a high day indeed, a Sabbath of Sabbaths." On this occasion communicants filled the church four times one after another. [55]

In May 1758 Whitefield based himself in Bristol, "where I propose staying till Sunday: then for Wales".[56] A month later he was back in Bristol and reported to the Countess of Huntingdon that he had just returned from Wales in what "proved a most delightful trying circuit".[57] He also penned another letter to Captain H, thanking him for the gift of a close chaise which he liked "exceedingly well" and which doubtless made his future travels considerably easier and more comfortable.[58]

Of all the destinations Whitefield took from his London base Scotland seemed to stir his spirit the most, bringing him the greatest encouragement. Part of the reason for this may have been the Scottish Presbyterian commitment to the doctrines of election and final perseverance which were close to his own heart. Whitefield set out for Scotland on Monday 25 April 1757 and arrived in Edinburgh sixteen days later where he immediately began preaching twice a day in the Orphan Hospital Park. From 19 to 30 May he attended all the debates of the General Assembly of the Church of Scotland. Many of the topics considered were at the centre of his personal faith and provided a daily recreation between his morning and evening sermons.[59]

During this time in Edinburgh Whitefield demonstrated the huge energy he devoted to his preaching. In a letter dated 9 June 1757 he wrote that he had come to the city "on the 12 May, and left 6 June and preached fifty times". He added that the Lord High Commissioner had invited him to dine and that "Thousands and thousands among whom were a great many of the best rank daily attended on the word preached."[60] Having preached his way to Glasgow Whitefield made a visit of two or three weeks to Ireland and ministered in Athlone, Limerick, Cork, and Dublin where he preached "near fifty times and had Cambuslang seasons".[61] His very large Dublin congregations caused him only minor molestation. "Now and then," he reported, "a few stones and clods of dirt were thrown at me." However, one evening he was trapped by a group of Catholics as he was going alone to his residence after the meeting was ended and was lucky to escape with his life.

> Vollies of hard stones came from all quarters, and
> every step I took, a fresh stone struck, and made
> me reel backwards and forwards, till I was almost
> breathless, and all over a gore of blood. My strong
> beaver hat served me as it were for a scull cap for
> a while; but at last that was knocked off, and my
> head left quite defenceless. I received many blows
> and wounds; one was particularly large near my
> temples.[62]

Eventually he managed to escape when a Methodist preacher with two friends brought a coach alongside and he was able to leap into it.

Whitefield was once more in Edinburgh in August 1758, where he preached twice every day "to enormous congregations" for nearly a month "despite physical weakness".[63] In September he wrote that "Jesus owned my feeble labours in Glasgow. Indeed we had some good seasons: some quite remarkable."[64] In July 1759 Whitefield travelled to Scotland again and reported, "I preach, and the people flock as usual; but Scotland is not London."[65] That said, he seemed in reasonably positive mood when he wrote on the course of his homeward journey that Jesus' "power hath been made known in Scotland for these six weeks".[66] Yet once again we find record of Whitefield north of the border in September 1762 and preaching every day to large congregations in Glasgow, twice speaking at Cambuslang.[67]

There were other occasional high spots in England including a remarkable glorious "mission week" in Cheltenham in 1757. Whitefield had been invited by Lord Dartmouth to come and preach in the town. When the revivalist arrived accompanied by Lord and Lady Dartmouth an immense crowd had gathered anticipating that he would preach in the church. However the door was locked. Never at a loss when it came to finding a pulpit Whitefield took his stand on a nearby tombstone and preached to a company which filled the entire churchyard. At one point "his words cut like a sword, and several of the congregation burst out into the most piercing bitter cries" and the preacher himself then "burst into a flood of tears". It was reported that when the sermon was ended the people seemed "chained to the ground". Whitefield preached again on the following day to another very large congregation on Isaiah 55:6.[68] It is strange that Whitefield left no mention of this remarkable happening or made any reference to it in his correspondence.

Failing health and a yearning for America

These seven years in Britain were a period in which Whitefield grossly overworked. In consequence he suffered almost total physical and emotional burnout. He had the capacity to drive himself well beyond the limits of what anyone could normally be expected to be able to cope with. Far from Jesus' burden being light and his yoke easy Whitefield's life in this period was often one of continuous exhaustion. He was constantly weighed down with concern for his Georgia orphanage house and solicited funds for it from time to time both in London and on his travels elsewhere in the country. Alongside this he was anxious about Britain's role in the war, raising money for building Tottenham Court Road Chapel and almshouses for pious widows, serving as the Countess of Huntingdon's chaplain, and writing letters by the boxful – often late into the night. He does on occasion mention concern for his wife but it seems they must have been separated from one another for long periods. Doubtless this would have caused him further worry. On top of all of this he was mocked by pamphleteers, mimicked by stage players, frequently physically assaulted by "papists" and mobsters, besides being hounded by bishops and other clergy. Such being Whitefield's lot it comes as no surprise to find his letters and the public press punctuated with details of his ill health and periods of incapacity.

Whitefield made mention of his sickness and physical ailments in more than thirty of his letters during this period. Gillies, commenting on his return to London in October 1757, stated that his health was "greatly impaired" and that "he was troubled by continuous vomitings, got little sleep, and had no appetite".[69] In June 1758 Whitefield wrote to the Countess of Huntingdon, "I suppose your Ladyship hath heard how low I have been in body, scarce ever lower; not able to sit up in company all the time, yet strengthened to travel without food."[70] By August the same year he was more downbeat about his health and wrote that "for above these three months last past, I have been so weak in my animal frame, that I can scarcely drag the crazy load along." That said, he was still positive in his spirit and a sentence later exclaimed, "Blessed be God, the work prospers in London more than ever."[71] The following July, however, Whitefield began to recognize that he was putting on a good deal of weight and wrote, "I am growing fat; but I take it to be a disease, I hope I shall go home sooner."[72]

After this time Whitefield made increasing references to his concern about his size, along with comments that suggest he was suffering from some kind of nervous disorder. In February 1760 he noted, "I am growing very corpulent, but, I trust, not too corpulent for another voyage, when called to it."[73] A month later he caught a cold which so seriously affected his health that one of the London papers even inadvertently announced his death.[74] In the July following he bemoaned, "I grow fatter and fatter every day. Lord help me to work it down! but it seems working will not do."[75] In October 1761 Whitefield anxiously wrote, "A sea voyage seems more necessary now than ever. I know now what nervous disorders are."[76] In the following year he evidently felt much greater concern about his condition, writing from Bristol in April, "You would scarce know me I am so swollen with wind, and so corpulent." He nevertheless added "With some difficulty I preach four or five times a week."[77]

The war having come to an end Whitefield set matters in order in London and journeyed to Edinburgh expecting to sail from there to America in April. A change in circumstances led to his voyage being delayed until 4 June. During this unexpected delay his long-standing friend John Wesley came to Scotland and they spent some time together. Wesley noted in his journal, "At Edinburgh I had the satisfaction of spending a little time with Mr Whitefield. Humanly speaking, he is worn out; but we have to do with Him who hath all power in heaven and earth."[78]

The *Lloyds Evening Post* for 6 June announced that the Revd Mr Whitefield had been too ill to embark on his voyage to America but undeterred he had sufficiently recovered and boarded the *Fanny* under Captain Galbraith bound for Rapanach in Virginia.[79] This, his eleventh voyage across the Atlantic, marked the end of a sustained period of intensely demanding labour in his homeland.

This period during which Whitefield was confined to the

homeland was one of extensive travelling and preaching tours. His forthright open-air preaching provoked considerable hostility from bishops and members of the establishment. In response Whitefield stood firm and justified his actions declaring himself to be a loyal member of the Anglican Church. His preaching in London, which included attacks on the theatre generated hostility in the form of stage plays and mimicry. The war years marked Whitefield's entry into the political arena. His strongly expressed Protestant sympathies provoked considerable opposition from Catholics in Ireland. Understandably during these years of constant travel, preaching and writing into the night, Whitefield's health began to fail.

Chapter 7 notes

1   *Letter to Mr B—*, 9 February 1756.
2   Anon, *A Brief View of the Conduct of Pennsylvania for the Year 1755* (London, R. Griffiths, 1756), pp. 13–14. Text available at: https://archive.org/details/cihm_20196/page/n7.
3   *Letter to the Reverend Mr M—*, 3 November 1757, *Works*, Vol. 3, p. 218.
4   Cited in L. Tyerman, op. cit., Vol. 2, p. 404.
5   *Letter to Professor F—*, 5 March 1758, *Works*, Vol. 3, p. 230.
6   J. Gillies, op. cit., p. 239.
7   L. Tyerman, op. cit., Vol. 2, p. 343.
8   *Lloyd's Evening Post*, 17 March 1760, cited in L. Tyerman, op. cit., Vol. 2, p. 424.
9   *Letter to Mr K—*, 21 February 1761, *Works*, Vol. 3, p. 263.
10 Not 14 May as Tyerman stated in op. cit., Vol. 2, p. 341.
11 *Letter to Governor Belcher*, 6 June 1755, *Works*, Vol. 3, p. 121.
12 *Letter to Mr C—*, 7 June 1755.
13 *Letter to Lady Huntingdon*, 4 June 1756, *Works*, Vol. 3 p 182.
14 Ibid.
15 *Letter to Mrs G—*, 15 December 1756 *Works*, Vol. 3, pp 195–96.
16 *Letter to Mrs B—*, 30 December 1756, *Works*, Vol. 3, p 196.
17 *Letter to Rev. Mr. M—*, 3 November 1757, *Works*, Vol. 3, p. 217.
18 *Letter to Mr D—*, 12 November 1757, *Works*, Vol. 3, p. 219.
19 *Letter to Mrs B—*, 14 December 1757. *Works*, Vol. 3, p. 222.
20 Bishop of Bangor (1748–56); Dean of Westminster 1756–68; Bishop of Rochester 1756–74.
21 This may have been on account of a family connection, the chapel having been constructed by Matthew Pearce.

22 A. Dallimore, op. cit., Vol. 2, p. 383.
23 *Letter to Lady Huntingdon*, 29 January 1756, *Works,* Vol. 3, p. 156.
24 Ibid, 30 January 1756, p. 156.
25 *Letter to the Bishop of Bangor,* 2 February 1756, *Works,* Vol. 3, pp. 156–57.
26 Ibid, 16 February 1756, *Works,* Vol. 3, p. 159.
27 Ibid, 20 March 1756, *Works,* Vol. 3, p. 369.
28 Ibid, 25 March 1756, *Works,* Vol. 3 pp. 168–69.
29 Ibid, pp. 168–69.
30 *Letter to the Countess of Huntingdon,* 10 April 1756, *Works,* Vol. 3, p. 172. See also *London Gazette,* 1 May 1756: "the said letters contained threats of injury and destruction to the Reverend Mr George Whitefield".
31 See, for example, D. A. Copeland, *Debating Issues in Colonial Newspapers* (Westport, CT., Greenwood Press, 2000), p. 104.
32 *The Monthly Review,* July 1760, cited in Tyerman, op. cit., Vol. 2, p. 431.
33 Anon, *Christian and Critical Remarks on a Droll or Interlude called the Minor* (London, 1760), p. 41.
34 Ibid.
35 *The Monthly Review,* July 1760 cited in Tyerman, *Life,* Vol. 2, p. 431.
36 M. Madan, *A Letter to David Garrick, Esq occasioned by the intended Representation of the Minor at the Theatre Royal in Drury Lane,* cited in L Tyerman, *Life,* Vol. 2, p. 434.
37 These were *An Additional Scene to the Comedy of the Minor* (London, 1761), pp. 19; *The Register Office: A Farce in Two Acts* (London, 1761) and *The Methodist: A Comedy: Being a Continuation and Completion of the Plan of the Minor written by Mr Foote* (London, 1761).
38 Cited in L. Tyerman, *Life,* Vol. 2, p. 438.
39 J. Gillies, op. cit., p. 233.
40 J. Nichols, *Literary Anecdotes of the Eighteenth Century* (London, Nichols, Son and Bentley, 1812), Vol. 5, p. 695.
41 J. Downes, *Methodism Examined and Exposed* (London, 1759), p. 106.
42 L. Tyerman, *Life,* Vol. 2, pp. 446–47.
43 J. Green, *The Principles and Practices of the Methodists farther considered; in a Letter to the Rev. Mr. George Whitefield* (Cambridge, 1761), p. 74.
44 L. Tyerman, *Life,* Vol. 2, pp. 450–51.
45 *Letter to Mr D——,* 15 August 1760, *Works,* Vol. 3, p. 262.
46 *Letter to the Rev. Mr. G——,* 2 May 1761, *Works,* Vol. 3, p. 267.
47 *Letter to the Rev. Mr. T——,* 27 April 1761, *Works,* Vol. 3, p. 266.
48 *Letter to Mr S——S——,* 5 June 1761, *Works,* Vol. 3, p. 267.
49 *Letter to Captain H——,* 16 June 1758, *Works,* Vol. 3, p. 236.
50 *Letter to Mr Z——,* 14 August 1756, *Works,* Vol. 3, p. 381.
51 F. Baker, *William Grimshaw* (London, Epworth Press, 1963), p. 186.
52 *Methodist Magazine,* 1819, p. 56.
53 *Letter to Lady Huntingdon,* 17 June 1758, *Works,* Vol. 3, p. 236.
54 F. Baker, *William Grimshaw,* p. 239.

55 G. R. Balleine, *A History of the Evangelical Party in the Church of England* (London, Longmans, Green and Co, 1933), p. 71. See also *Letter*, 19 September, *Proceedings of the Wesley Historical Society*, Vol. XVIII, p. 125.

56 *Letter to Mr—* (no name or initial) 22 May 1758, *Works*, Vol. 3, p. 232.

57 *Letter to Lady Huntingdon*, 17 June 1758, *Works*, Vol. 3, p. 237.

58 *Letter to Captain H—*, 16 June 1758, *Works*, Vol. 3, p. 236.

59 *Letter to the Rev. Mr. T—*, 31 May 1757, *Works,* Vol. 3, p 203.

60 *Letter to Mr—* , 9 June 1757, *Works*, Vol. 3, p 203.

61 *Letter to the Rev. Mr. G*, 7 August 1757, *Works*, Vol. 3, p. 210.

62 *Letter to Mr—*, 9 July 1757, *Works,* Vol. 3, p. 207.

63 *Scot's Magazine*, 1758, p. 388, cited in L. Tyerman, *Life*, *Works*, Vol. 2, p. 410.

64 *Letter to Mr T—*, 9 September 1758, *Works*, Vol. 3, p. 242.

65 *Letter to The Rev. Mr. G—*, 7 July 1759, *Works*, Vol. 3, p. 252.

66 *Letter to Mr D—* ,16 August 1759, *Works*, Vol. 3, p. 255.

67 *Letter to The Rev. Mr. T—*, 2 September 1762, *Works*, Vol. 3, p. 280.

68 A. C. H. Seymour, *The Life and Times of Selina* (London, 1991), Vol. 1, p. 431.

69 J. Gillies, op. cit., p. 226.

70 *Letter to Lady Huntingdon*, 17 June 1758, *Works*, Vol. 3, p. 237.

71 *Letter to the Rev. Mr. G—*, 10 August 1758, *Works,* Vol. 3, p. 239.

72 *Letter to Mr S—*, 3 July 1759, *Works*, Vol. 3, p. 251.

73 *Letter to Mr D—*, 5 February 1760, *Works*, Vol. 3, p. 259.

74 *Lloyds Evening Post* cited in L. Tyerman, *Life*, Vol. 2, p. 441. See also Whitefield's reference to the matter in a later *Letter to Mrs C—*, 24 October 1761, *Works*, Vol. 3, p. 271.

75 *Letter to Mr D—*, 8 July 1760, *Works*, Vol. 3, 262.

76 Ibid, 24 October 1761, *Works*, Vol. 3, p 270.

77 *Letter to Mrs C—*, 4 May 1762, *Works,* Vol. 3, p. 277.

78 J. Wesley, *Journal*, 22 May 1763.

79 *Letter to the Rev. Mr. T—*, 4 June 1763, *Works*, Vol. 3, p. 293.

Chapter 8

The Grand Itinerant

Immediately following his ordination in June 1736 Whitefield had embarked on an itinerant ministry with preaching tours to Bristol and Kingswood. Then shortly afterwards he made his first visit to Savannah and Georgia. Following his return from the colony he became an incessant traveller in both the British Isles and the American colonies. In so doing he became one of the best known people on both sides of the Atlantic. By the time of his later visits to America in the 1750s and 1760s he came to be widely viewed as a celebrity figure accorded the status of "Grand Itinerant".

Whitefield's last four journeys to the colonies

Whitefield's last four journeys to America were short; his fourth from 1751 to 1752 being a mere six months and his fifth from 1754 to 1755 lasted just ten months.[1] His sixth visit, which began in Virginia was a mere two years from 1763 to 1765. His final journey began when he arrived at Charleston in the first week of December 1769 and ended when he died on 30 September 1770 at Newburyport. It is easy to overlook the fact that the length of Whitefield's ministry in the British Isles was therefore more than twice the time he spent in America.[2] That said, he proved to be one of the most significant figures in American history. His influence profoundly impacted the religious and social life of the colonies, which, in turn, if we are to follow Winthrop Hudson and others, helped to fuel the spirit and desire for liberty. Hudson cited the *Origin and Progress of the American Rebellion,* a book published by the arch-Tory Peter Oliver (1713–91) in 1781 in which he suggested that "if one wished to understand the inflamed public opinion which swept the colonies into war one must look to… 'the dissenting clergy'. They certainly were key figures, for their influence penetrated remote communities that were seldom reached by newspapers and books."

Hudson went on to cite the opinion of James Otis (1725–83), a Boston lawyer, "who was one of the most conspicuous leaders in arousing anti-British sentiment". For both Oliver and Otis the role of the clergy was "not restricted to fostering and perpetuating notions of fundamental and 'inalienable' rights… they provided active support by 'preaching up' the Revolution with innumerable 'fast days' and recruiting sermons."[3] Care must be taken, however, not to attribute too much directly to Whitefield although he certainly expressed his thankfulness when the Stamp Act of 1765 by which the colonists were to be taxed was repealed.[4] Kidd wisely cautioned that during the crisis between Britain and the colonies Whitefield "remained occupied primarily with evangelistic and educational affairs".[5]

By the time of these later travels Whitefield, as we have seen, was all too aware of his failing health. He worried about his growing corpulence, frequent vomiting, and breathlessness. In a number of his letters he wrote that he felt the remaining time of his ministry might be short. On days when he was in a particularly low and weak state he even expressed the hope that the Lord might call him home. For this reason his aim and plan on these later travels was twofold: to visit and encourage his family at his Bethesda orphan house in Georgia, and to revisit the major towns and cities in the north where his preaching had already given him a celebrity status.

He was now fast becoming the "Grand Itinerant" whose preaching was eagerly sought after. Local clergy of all denominations, with the exception of most of the Church of England, welcomed him to their pulpits. Ministers, clergy, and others often travelled with him in support of him but also to learn from him, and to seek his advice.

It appeared that Whitefield had planned his fourth, but unexpectedly short journey, to follow the same pattern as his previous three. On his arrival in Savannah he found "the Orphan-house in as good a situation as could be expected. The children have much improved in learning; and I hope the new foundation is now laid for a useful seminary."[6] Two months later, on 1 February 1752, now that matters at Bethesda were settled, he wrote, "I purpose setting out upon my Spring campaign."[7] This must necessarily have been short for he boarded ship for England at the beginning of April. It seems, as Gillies stated, that he took note of the warnings he had received that the hot summer climate might further damage his weak state of health and decided to return home.[8] His correspondence provides no information as to his activities. Even Gillies merely commented that "from November 1751 to the beginning of the following April, he was partly at Bethesda, and partly in South Carolina, still at full stretch in his Master's work".[9]

In each of his last three journeys to America Whitefield's correspondence gives ample detail to show that he followed this same pattern of checking out the situation at his orphan house in Savannah and then making major preaching tours to the growing towns and cities in the north. If time permitted he used these locations as a base and journeyed out into the surrounding areas. Significantly, on all three of his last short visits to the colonies he made New York, Philadelphia, and Boston the central focus of his ministry.

New York seems to have accorded Whitefield warm receptions.

On his fifth journey he arrived in the city by water in July 1754 and preached backwards and forwards from New York to Philadelphia till the middle of September. "Everywhere," he wrote, "a divine power accompanies the word, prejudices have been removed, and a more effectual door opened than ever for preaching the everlasting gospel."[10] When he returned eight years later he was welcomed once again and wrote, "I am able to preach thrice a week" and "such flocking of all ranks, I never before saw at New York."[11] In June 1770, on his final journey, Whitefield's health appeared to have improved considerably and he wrote of being "enabled to ride and travel cheerfully".[12] On his arrival in New York he found "congregations are rather larger than ever" and that "invitations [were] coming from every quarter". He also expressed the hope of being able to visit the Oneida Indians in the northerly part of the colony.[13] The following July Whitefield reported, "this month I have been above a five hundred miles circuit, and have been enabled to preach and travel through the heat every day". The congregations in twelve places in particular were "very large and attentive, and affected".[14]

The people of Philadelphia also appear to have received him favourably. He arrived in Philadelphia at the beginning of his fifth journey in August 1754. Despite being taken "with a violent cholera morbus"[15] he reported ten days later that "thousands flock daily to hear the word preached".[16] On his return to the city in November 1763 he recorded that his weak state of health limited his preaching but "many of various ranks seem to be brought under conviction".[17] The following October, in 1764, Whitefield was welcomed to the Philadelphia College by the provost who read prayers for him before he addressed the staff and pupils. Both the present and the previous governors as well as the head and the leading people of the city attended the occasion.[18] His last preaching in the city began on 7 May when he was enabled to speak to "a large auditory" and reported that "Pulpits, hearts and affections, seem to be as open and enlarged to me, as ever."[19] A short time later he wrote, "I have now been here three weeks... A wide and effectual door, I trust, hath been opened in this city. People of all ranks flock as much as ever."[20] He was also encouraged to report that churches and other denominational meeting houses were opened to him.[21]

Boston was always among Whitefield's favoured places. He spent nearly two weeks in the city in October 1754. When he arrived thousands eagerly flocked to hear his message. Among other places he preached at both the Old and New North Churches. At seven in the morning there were "generally three thousand or more at the Old North and many cannot come in".[22] On one of these occasions such was the crush of people that Whitefield had to be helped into the building through a window![23] During his sixth visit to the colonies in 1764 Whitefield returned to Boston in March and "was received with the usual warmth of affection".[24] He based himself in the city till the beginning of June and made a number of short preaching excursions from there into the surrounding countryside to Concord, Providence, Newport, Portsmouth, and elsewhere. He reported that "Invitations come so thick and fast from every quarter, that I know not what to do."[25] Despite having to be cautious on account of the spread of smallpox through the town Whitefield was amazed that the people earnestly begged him for a six o'clock morning lecture.[26] He noted in a letter, "Every day I hear of some brought under concern; and trust, whenever I remove, a blessing will be left behind."[27]

Just ten days before his death the great preacher made his last and brief visit to Boston. There is only a passing reference to it in his correspondence but Gillies noted that from 17 to 20 September, he preached daily in the town, and then on the 21st "set out upon a tour to the eastward, pretty much indisposed."[28]

Impacting America

Whitefield clearly sensed he had a divine calling to America. No sooner was he back on British soil than he began to feel the pull of the colonies once more. His preaching drew people from across the entire social hierarchy. As was true of his divine master, the majority of the common people heard Whitefield gladly while on the other hand some of the religious leaders eschewed his preaching. Such seems to have been more marked during his earlier visits to New England. Gillies observed "the uncommon desire that all sorts of people expressed to attend his preaching; and that not upon the first or second visit only, but every succeeding opportunity". He continued, "Wherever he went, prodigious numbers flocked to hear him. His congregations upon some occasions have been computed to be from twenty to thirty thousand."[29]

Charles Chauncy (1705–87), a Boston Congregational clergyman and an opponent of the revival, wrote to a British colleague expressing his regret at Whitefield's popularity. "When he came to town," Chauncy lamented, "he was received by the churches as though he had been an angel of God… he was strangely flocked after by all sorts of persons, and much admired by the vulgar, both great and small."[30] Chauncy was not alone among New England clergy in his dislike of Whitefield's preaching. The Revd Nathaniel Henchman, pastor of the First Church in Lyn, wrote a letter on 3 January 1745 to the Revd Stephen Chase of Lyn End, in which he gave his reasons for declining to invite Whitefield to his pulpit. He resented Whitefield's "slanderous treatment of our colleges" and "the insufferable pride of the man". "Who," he wrote, "ever equalled him in vain-glorious boasting?" He then added with disdain, "In one country, he is a true son of the Church of England; in a second, a staunch Presbyterian; and in a third, a strong Congregationalist." He suspected Whitefield of coming to America on a begging mission for the poor little ones of his orphan house.[31] Nathaniel Henchman also addressed a letter to Whitefield through the columns of the *Boston Evening Post* accusing him of having "sown pernicious seeds of separation, contention and disorder among us; and by cherishing the separatists, and your injurious insinuations respecting ministers as unacquainted with Christ".[32]

The Revd Nathaniel Eells of Scituate wrote in April 1745 that Mr Whitefield "did not stand right in the gospel of Christ; for by his episcopal ordination he received no authority to itinerate". He "was no real friend to the ministers and churches of this land". "Furthermore," Eells added, "he favoured disorders in public worship such as screaming etc."[33] Eells' reference to Whitefield being "no friend to the ministers and churches" was doubtless a reference to Whitefield's denunciations of unregenerate clergy. Yet with the passing of the years and Whitefield's later visits his preaching became increasingly accepted by growing numbers of clergy.

Whitefield's preaching contributed to a growing democratic spirit among the inhabitants of the colonies as they were taught to recognize their equality before God, all loved and all standing in need of his forgiveness. Whitefield's lifelong friend, Benjamin Franklin recorded his growing celebrity status in the following lines.

> The multitudes of all sects and denominations that attended his sermons were enormous, and it was a matter of speculation to me, who was one of their number, to observe the extraordinary influence of his oratory on his hearers. From being thoughtless or indifferent about religion, it seemed as if all the world were growing religious so that one could not walk through the town in an evening without hearing psalms sung in different families of every street.[34]

Harry Stout, in his study of Whitefield, suggested that his preaching came to have "an almost hypnotic effect" over the crowds who came to hear him. He cited the case of a German woman who could speak no English "but such was the power of his gestures, expressions, look and voice" that she had "a quickening, edifying experience" such as she had "never in all her life before".[35]

Whitefield travelled continuously up and down the east coast of America from New England in the north to Georgia in the south so that with the passing of time he became the best-known person in America. His frequent appearances and repeated preaching of the "new birth" and personal faith to hundreds of thousands across the individual colonies bound them together in a shared faith and experience. Indeed his constant travels gradually generated a cohesive national consciousness. Denominational walls were broken down and the distinction between lay people and ordained clergy was considerably diminished. Whitefield readily spoke from any available pulpit whether Anglican, Presbyterian, Congregational, Baptist, or Dutch Reformed. Preaching from the court house balcony in Philadelphia he declared:

> Father Abraham, whom have you in heaven? Any Episcopalians? No! Any Presbyterians? No! Any Independents or Methodists? No! No, no, no! Whom have you there? We don't know those names here. All who are here are Christians... Oh is this the case? Then God help us forget party names and to become Christians in deed and truth.[36]

Whitefield's preaching together with his published sermons generated a shared religious experience which connected large swathes of people across the American colonies. For the first time disparate groups of Christians attached to distinct cultural settlement groups and different Christian churches began to feel united and a part of a wider whole. In this were the seeds of a nascent national consciousness. That said, E. L. Hyatt's view that "the Declaration of Independence of 1776 was a result of the evangelical preaching of the revivalists of the Great Awakening" needs tempering.[37]

Undermining the Anglican Church

When Whitefield had first visited the colonies he found that many Anglican churches were closed to him. This was largely on account of his having been dubbed an "enthusiast" by the English bishops and others and because of his attacks on liberal-minded Church of England clergy. Undeterred Whitefield adopted his practice of taking to the towns and city squares and the open fields. He shared the views of the American revival preachers who had spoken out against the nominal Christianity of many of the American Anglican incumbents. Indeed he had stood behind his friend Gilbert Tennent's sermon on *The Dangers of an Unconverted Ministry* which he had preached at Nottingham, Pennsylvania on 8 March 1740. The sermon ended with an exhortation to quit the ministry of "natural men" and join a church where they would receive genuine Christian instruction. Whitefield, it should be said, paid tribute to the general level of religious life in New England but he was nevertheless of the view that the majority of those who preached lacked an "experimental knowledge" of Christ.[38]

Whitefield's views in support of Tennent were further confirmed by disparaging comments he had written in the published journal of his New England tour. And that was not all since, at the beginning of the same year, he had published a small pamphlet entitled *Three Letters from the Rev. Mr George Whitefield*. In the third of these he justified his conviction that Archbishop Tillotson "knew no more about Christianity than Mahomet".[39] At the time of his comments Tillotson's writings were still much valued by many of the American clergy of the established church and at Harvard. But it was Tillotson's contradiction of Whitefield's understanding of the "new birth" that led to his opposition to the former Archbishop of Canterbury. In this heated controversy the vast majority of the population of the colonies, however, sided with Whitefield's preaching and teaching. In this way the undermining of the established English church contributed to the gradual undermining of the social order and established British government.[40]

Truly the "Grand Itinerant"

Whitefield truly deserved to be accorded status as the Grand Itinerant. He was an inveterate traveller who covered thousands of miles often on horseback and sometimes in treacherous conditions. Wherever he found himself he was always thinking ahead and planning his next move. He was of course profoundly aware of his great speaking and teaching gifts and was clearly impelled to devote them to bringing the gospel message to the major towns and cities of the east coast of America.

Whitefield's itinerant ministry and travels were made even more widely known by his constant use of printed media as Frank Lambert's study, *Pedlar in Divinity*, has so well demonstrated. He made a careful examination of Whitefield's use of press adverts detailing his forthcoming preaching venues. He also noted the constant flow of newspaper and journal articles recounting Whitefield's recent successes. All of these helped to enhance Whitefield's status as a travelling celebrity. Lambert also demonstrated that Whitefield made sermons "a vendable commodity".[41] He showed that *The Pennsylvania Gazette* devoted 75 per cent of its coverage to Whitefield between 1739 and 1740,[42] and that *The New York Gazette* often had Whitefield on its front page.[43] Whitefield himself constantly sold his books and extracts from his journals and there was a big demand for them on his preaching tours,[44] causing Charles Chauncy to denounce him for pedalling the gospel.[45] Whitefield's close friend Benjamin Franklin did good business, publishing details of Whitefield's movements.[46]

As we have seen, ill health tended to dog Whitefield; sometimes in the form of colic, and at other times vomiting or loss of breath. He occasionally suffered intense soreness of the throat and experienced bouts of a severe nervous disorder. This latter condition probably stemmed from sheer exhaustion. He was eventually to die of asthma at the comparatively young age of fifty-six. On a number of occasions having been almost totally incapacitated by breathlessness or colic Whitefield had the extraordinary ability to suddenly drag himself back up and journey on or take to the field once again and preach to thousands.

Thus it happened that while journeying to New York in the summer of 1754 Whitefield wrote, "My health is wonderfully preserved – My wonted vomitings, have left me, and though I ride whole nights, and have been frequently exposed to great thunders, violent lightnings [sic], and heavy rains, yet I am better than usual, and as far as I can judge not yet to die."[47] The week following he wrote near the end of a letter, "Keep me travelling, keep me working, or at least beginning to begin the work for thee till I die!"[48] In November 1754 Whitefield recorded that he had been able to preach a hundred times in places in New England in the previous month.[49] At the end of the same year he wrote a letter from Maryland noting, "I may have rode near two thousand miles, and preached about two hundred and thirty times; but to how many thousand souls cannot well be said."[50]

During his final journey Whitefield was once again at full-stretch. He wrote from Philadelphia that he had "just returned from a hundred and fifty miles circuit, in which, blessed be God! I have been enabled to preach every day."[51] On 30 June 1770 we find Whitefield writing from New York, "I have been here just a week… Congregations are larger than ever… numerous invitations from every quarter I am daily receiving."[52] A month later on 29 July he wrote, "I have been above a five hundred miles circuit, and have been able to preach and travel through the heat every day."[53]

By any stretch of the imagination Whitefield was a remarkable inveterate traveller. He travelled enormous distances on land in both America and the British Isles. He made fifteen visits to Scotland, two journeys to Ireland and one each to Bermuda, Gibraltar and the Netherlands. No Christian preacher in the days before mechanized transport ever travelled comparable distances on land and sea. After Whitefield's death a monument was erected in his honour at Newbury Port, part of which read, "He crossed the Atlantic Thirteen times, preached more than Eighteen Thousand sermons… Gave unexampled energy. No other man ever preached to so large assemblies with an influence so powerful."[54]

Chapter 8 notes

1   These times represent the time he was actually on American soil. Each Atlantic crossing typically amounted to between eight and twelve weeks.
2   From the time of his ordination in 1736 until his death in 1770 Whitefield spent roughly twenty-three years in the British Isles and approximately ten years in America.
3   W. Hudson, *Religion in America* (New York, Charles Scribner's Sons, 1965), pp. 96–97. See especially his section "The Winning of Independence", pp. 94–105.
4   T. Kidd, *George Whitefield*, p. 242.
5   Ibid.
6   *Letter to Mr T——*, 20 November 1751.
7   *Letter to the Rev. Mr. H——*, 1 February 1752.
8   J. Gillies, op. cit., p. 196.
9   Ibid.
10   *Letter to Lady Huntingdon*, 30 September 1754.
11   *Letter to Mr H——*, 8 December 1763.
12   *Letter to Mr R——K——*, 14 June 1770.
13   Ibid, 30 June 1770.

14 *Letter to Mr R—K—*, 29 July 1770.
15 *Letter to Mr R—*, 7 August 1770.
16 *Letter to Mr E—*, 17 August 1770.
17 *Letter to Mr R—K—*, 14 November 1763.
18 Ibid, 19 October 1764.
19 Ibid, 9 May 1770.
20 Ibid, 24 May 1770.
21 Ibid.
22 *Letter to Mr V—*, 14 October 1754.
23 *Letter to Mr S—*, 14 October 1754.
24 *Letter to Mr R—K—*, 3 March 1764.
25 Ibid.
26 Ibid, 19 May 1764.
27 *Letter to C—H—*, 1 June 1764.
28 J. Gillies, op. cit., p. 269.
29 J. Gillies, op. cit., pp. 282–83.
30 J. Ripper, *American Stories: Living American History* (London, Routledge, 2008), Vol. 1, p. 46.
31 L. Tyerman, *Life*, Vol. 2, p. 137.
32 *Boston Evening Post*, 15 July 1745.
33 L. Tyerman, *Life*, Vol. 2, p. 140.
34 *Memoirs of the Life and Writings of Benjamin Franklin* (London, 1818), Vol. 1, p. 410, cited in L. Tyerman, *Life*, Vol.1, pp. 338–39.
35 H. Stout, *The Divine Dramatist*, p. 251.
36 Cited in W. S. Hudson, *Religion in America*, pp. 80–81.
37 Cited in E. L. Hyatt, *Pilgrims and Patriots: The Radical Roots of American Democracy and Freedom* (Hyatt Press, 2006), p. 100.
38 W. D. Hudson, *Religion in America*, pp. 70–71.
39 L. Tyerman, *Life*, Vol. 2, p. 360.
40 See G. B. Nash, *The Unknown American Revolution: The Unruly Birth of Democracy and the Struggle to Create America* (New York, Penguin Books, 2006), pp. 9–10, and T. S. Kidd, *God of Liberty: A Religious History of the American Revolution* (New York, Basic Books, 2010), pp. 16–19.
41 F. Lambert, *Pedlar in Divinity: George Whitefield and the Transatlantic Revivals, 1737–1770* (New Jersey, Princeton University Press, 1993), p. 106.
42 Ibid.
43 Ibid.
44 Ibid, p. 86.
45 Ibid, p. 93.
46 Ibid, p. 110.
47 *Letter to Mr C—W—*, 20 July 1754.
48 *Letter to Mr S—*, 27 July 1754.
49 *Letter to Mr G—*, 25 November 1754.
50 *Letter to Mrs C—*, 27 December 1754.
51 *Letter to Mr R—K—*, 14 June 1770.

52   Ibid, 30 June 1770.
53   Ibid, 29 July 1770.
54   R. Philip, op. cit., p. 551.

Chapter 9

Preacher Extraordinaire

From the day he gave his very first sermon as an ordained clergyman Whitefield became a preaching phenomenon. His first endeavour took place in the church where he had been baptized as an infant with his family and childhood friends surrounding him. It was by all accounts an impressive debut which set the pattern for a supremely powerful preaching ministry which was to impact hundreds of thousands in both the British Isles and the American colonies. Whitefield gave details of it in a letter he wrote to a friend on 30 June 1736 stating that "some mocked, but most for the present seemed struck".[1]

From this point on Whitefield began to preach whenever and wherever the opportunity arose. In a letter to John Wesley he wrote, "I intend to go about preaching the Gospel to every creature."[2] Although he was not against preparing and writing out sermons he was strongly of the view that expounding and praying extempore were both preferable and more effective. On an October day in 1740 he jotted in his journal, "God grant I may pursue the method of expounding and praying extempore."[3] In an entry in his journal for 21 October 1740 he wrote, "Though not all are to be condemned who use notes, yet it is a symptom of the decay of religion when reading becomes fashionable where extempore preaching did once prevail."[4]

On his arrival in Georgia in 1735 Colonel William Stevens, the colonial secretary, noted in his journal, "May 21. Mr Whitefield officiated this day at the church, and made a sermon very engaging to the most thronged congregation I had ever seen there." On 4 June he added, "Mr Whitefield's auditors increase daily, and the place of worship is far too small to contain the people who seek his doctrine", and then "June 18. Mr Whitefield went on moving the people with his captivating discourses."[5]

The following year, on 15 November, Whitefield arrived in New York, where being refused the use of the established church, he preached in the evening in the Presbyterian church. One of those present, quite possibly the minister, Dr Pemberton, recorded his impressions in a letter to the *New England Journal*.

> I never in my life saw so attentive an audience. Mr Whitefield spoke as one having authority: all he said was demonstration, life and power. The people's eyes and ears hung on his lips. They greedily devoured every word. I came home astonished. Every scruple vanished; I never saw or heard the like; and I said within myself, Surely God is with this man of a truth!... Mr Whitefield is a man of middle stature, of a slender body, a fair complexion and a comely appearance. He is of a sprightly cheerful temper and acts and moves with great agility... His wit is quick and piercing... He has a most ready memory and, I think, speaks entirely without notes. He has a clear and musical voice, and a wonderful command of it. He uses much gesture, but with great propriety. Every accent of his voice, and every motion of his body, speaks, and both are natural and unaffected. He has a great mastery of words, but studies

much plainness of speech... He speaks much
the language of the New Testament; and has an
admirable faculty in explaining the Scriptures...
He declares that his whole view in preaching is
to bring men to Christ... and to revive primitive
Christianity among them.[6]

Just over two weeks later Benjamin Franklin heard Whitefield
preach a sermon to upwards of 10,000 at White Clay Creek and
noted that "3,000 came on horse back". The noise created by
watering and feeding such a large number of animals must indeed
have been immense.[7]

On a later occasion in 1740 Franklin attended one of Whitefield's
sermons in Philadelphia during which it became clear there would
be a collection at the end on behalf of the orphan house. Franklin
resolved that he would give nothing. At the time he had in his
pocket a handful of copper money, three or four silver dollars, and
five pistoles [European coins] in gold. As the sermon progressed
Franklin found himself warming to the preacher and concluded
that he would donate the copper. After a little more of Whitefield's
inspiring oratory he decided to give the silver. The end of the
discourse was so compelling that he emptied the entire contents of
his pocket into the collecting dish, gold and all![8]

Something of the huge drawing power of Whitefield's preaching
was captured by Nathan Cole, a local farmer, who took his wife to
hear the great revivalist preach on the day he visited Middletown,
Connecticut, on 23 October 1740. Writing some time after the
event Cole recounted.

Then on a sudden, in the morning all on a
sudden, about 8 or 9 o'clock there came a

messenger and said Mr. Whitefield preached at Hartford and Wethersfield yesterday and is to preach at Middletown this morning [23 October 1740] at ten of the Clock. I was in my field at work. I dropped my tool that I had in my hand and ran home to my wife telling her to get ready quickly to go and hear Mr. Whitefield preach at Middletown, then ran to my pasture for my horse with all my might fearing that I should be too late. Having my horse I with my wife soon mounted the horse and went forward as fast as I thought the horse could bear... As I came nearer the Road [to Middletown], I heard the noise of horses' feet coming down the road and this cloud was a cloud of dust made by the horses' feet... As I drew nearer it seemed like a steady stream of horses and their riders, scarcely a horse more than his length behind another, all of a lather and foam with sweat, their breath rolling out of their nostrils every jump; every horse seemed to go with all his might to carry his rider to hear news from heaven for the saving of Souls. It made me tremble to see the sight, how the world was in a struggle... When we got to Middletown old meeting house there was a great multitude; it was said to be 3 or 4,000 of people assembled together. We dismounted and shook off the dust, and the ministers were then coming to the meeting house. I turned and looked towards the Great River and saw the ferry boats running swift backward and forward bringing over loads of people; the oars rowed nimble and quick. Everything, men horses and boats seemed to be struggling for life. The land and banks over the river looked black with people and horses; all along the 12 miles I saw no man at work in his field, but all seemed to be gone. When I saw Mr. Whitefield come upon the Scaffold he looked almost angelical, a young, slim slender youth, before some thousands of people with a bold undaunted countenance. And my hearing how God was with him everywhere as he came along, it solemnized my mind, and put me into a trembling fear before he began to preach; for he looked as if he was clothed with authority from the Great God, and a sweet solemn solemnity sat upon his brow, and my hearing him preach gave me a heart wound. By God's blessing my old foundation was broken up, and I saw that my righteousness would not save me.[9]

In July 1740 the Revd Joseph Smith, the minister of the Independent Church at Charleston preached a sermon entitled "The Character, Preaching, etc., of the Rev Mr Whitefield, Impartially Represented and Supported". In it he declared that Whitefield "is certainly a finished preacher and a great master of pulpit oratory" and that "his discourses were very extraordinary". He also reported "how earnestly did he press Christ upon us! …So charmed were the people with his manner of address, that they shut up their shops and forgot their secular business, and the oftener he preached, the keener edge did he put on their desires of hearing them again." Smith summed up Whitefield as "the wonder of the age".[10]

Whitefield's voice

Benjamin Franklin noted that Whitefield

> had a loud clear voice, and articulated his words and sentences so perfectly, that he might be heard and understood at a great distance... By hearing him often, I came to distinguish easily between sermons newly composed and those which he had often preached in the course of his travels. His delivery of the latter was so improved by frequent repetition, that every accent, every emphasis, every modulation of the voice, was so perfectly well turned and well placed, that, without being interested in the subject, one could not help being pleased with the discourse.[11]

Gillies wrote of his "strong and musical voice" and of "his wonderful command of it". His charm was "nothing less than the power of his irresistible eloquence".[12]

Sarah, the wife of Jonathan Edwards of Northampton, was struck by Whitefield's captivating voice and wrote that "he is a born orator" with a "deep toned yet clear melodious voice. It is perfect music". She continued, "It is wonderful to see what a spell he casts over an audience by proclaiming the simplest truths of the Bible. I have seen upwards of a thousand people hang on his words with breathless silence, broken only by an occasional half-suppressed sob."[13]

On one occasion David Garrick said that Whitefield could move men to tears just by pronouncing the word "Mesopotamia". He thought it truly wonderful that Whitefield could cast such a spell over people by proclaiming the simplest truths of the Bible.[14]

Lord Bolingbroke wrote in a letter to his wife that "Mr Whitefield is the most extraordinary man of our times. He has the most commanding eloquence I ever heard in any person; his abilities are very considerable – his zeal unquenchable and his piety and excellence genuine and unquestionable."[15] The Earl of Chesterfield was of like opinion and stated, "Mr Whitefield's eloquence is unrivalled – his zeal inexhaustible; and not to admire both would argue a total absence of taste and an insensibility not to be coveted by anybody."[16] The philosopher, David Hume heard Whitefield on several occasions and thought him the most ingenious preacher he had ever heard and that it was worth going twenty miles to hear him.[17]

The content of Whitefield's sermons

Whitefield published a small number of his hand-written sermons in the early years of his ministry. Joseph Gurney, the Holborn bookseller, published eighteen of his sermons in 1771 but without Whitefield's permission. He asserted that they had been taken down verbatim in shorthand and faithfully transcribed. Whitefield raised strong objections to one of them claiming, "It is not verbatim" and "in some places Mr Gurney makes me speak false concord, and even nonsense". It is clear that these later sermons were inferior in content to those Whitefield had himself published in earlier times. Tyerman nevertheless asserted that "though they might not have been reported with perfect accuracy they may be taken as a specimen – though an imperfect one – of Whitefield's style of preaching during the last few years of an eventful life".[18]

In 1768 Whitefield took into his paid employment Cornelius Winter, a young man who had been converted under his preaching some years earlier. Winter had his residence close to the Tabernacle and gradually accepted more responsibilities, including preaching on two mornings during the week. Winter has left us a number of reflections on his new employer's preaching. He never knew Whitefield to have composed and written out a sermon unless he was on board ship. In fact he went further and declared that he had never even seen the skeleton of a sermon among his papers with which he was permitted to be familiar. He also related that it was Whitefield's custom to spend an hour or two on his own before going into the pulpit on the Lord's Day. These were devotional times when he was accustomed to have Clarke's Bible, Matthew Henry's Commentary and Cruden's Concordance to hand. From Winter we also learn that much of what Whitefield preached came to him in the late evening or during the night hours when he was awakened from his sleep.[19]

An analysis of Whitefield's fifty-nine sermons, which were gathered and published in volumes 5 and 6 of his works, yielded some clear characteristics of his preaching. Sixteen of the sermons were based on Old Testament themes and the rest taken from passages or verses in the New Testament, twenty-five being from the Gospels. This latter fact is significant because Whitefield's preaching was avowedly Christocentric with a strong emphasis on faith and the new birth. There are not many references in his preaching to God and Jesus together or the Trinity. This should not surprise us since his aim was always to bring the heart of the Christian faith – commitment to Christ – to ordinary people who had only a limited knowledge of Christianity. Whitefield knew the necessity of keeping his message straightforward and easy to understand. Of the fifty-nine published sermons forty were on the practical outcomes of being a Christian and only eight on explicitly doctrinal topics. Of the fifty-nine sermons only five were verse-by-verse expositions of a biblical passage of eight or more verses. The rest were based on one or two verses which were central to the theme or title. Only five out of the entire total were explicitly on specific doctrines: imputed righteousness, the incarnation, eternal punishment, justification, and regeneration.

As one would expect Whitefield's aim was, in his own words, "to offer Christ to all" – but as a Calvinist, on the majority of occasions, he did this in an oblique way. Twenty-seven of the sermons have nothing that could be considered an exhortation to his hearers to be converted or make a commitment to Christ. It is clear that Whitefield expected Jesus to take hold of those elect who had been chosen to be his followers rather than that he should endeavour to persuade them to take hold of Jesus of their own will and volition. Thirteen of the sermons conclude with what might be considered a gentle exhortation for his hearers to recognize the divine hand on their lives while the remaining nineteen endings appear to be a little more forthright.

Typical of the gentle exhortations are the following. At the conclusion of his sermon entitled *The Care of the Soul as the One Thing Needful* he concluded with the words, "If you are disposed to sit down at Christ's feet, he will teach you by his word and spirit."[20] Coming to the end of his address entitled *Christ the only Preservative against a Reprobate Spirit* Whitefield said, "But I hope better things of most of you, even that you will turn unto the Lord of love, the Jesus who died for you that… you may hear his voice, 'Come ye blessed of my Father, enter into the kingdom prepared for you before the foundation of the world.'"[21]

In contrast on some occasions, Whitefield closed on a more forceful note, as, for example, at the end of his sermon *Christ the best Husband*: "methinks I could speak to you till midnight, if it would bring you unto the Lord Jesus Christ, and make you espoused to him."[22] In his sermon on Jesus bringing rest to the "weary and heavy-laden" Whitefield spoke in words that might have come from any

Arminian revivalist: "Come, all ye drunkards, swearers, Sabbath-breakers, adulterers, fornicators; come, all ye scoffers, harlots, thieves, and murderers, and Jesus Christ will save you; he will give you rest, if you are weary of your sins."[23] Concluding his address on the wise and foolish virgins Whitefield cried out, "If you believe on Jesus Christ, and cry out to him with the same faith as the expiring thief, 'Lord remember me, now thou art in thy kingdom', I will pawn my eternal salvation upon it, if he does not shortly translate you to his heavenly paradise."[24] He ended his homily on *The Power of Christ's Resurrection* with the words, "Let us cry instantly to Him that is mighty and able to save."[25] In the sermon preached in the last year of his life before the governor, the Council and the House of Assembly of Georgia, Whitefield ended with a challenge to them to "Come unto him, all ye that are weary and heavy laden, he will give you rest; rest from the guilt, rest from the power, rest from the punishment of sin; rest from the fear of divine judgements here, rest with himself eternally hereafter."[26]

Whitefield's preaching was often focused around a particular biblical theme. His very first sermon was entitled *He that is in Christ is a new creature*. Among others which are known were *Walking with God*, *The Great Duty of Family Religion*, *What think ye of Christ?*, *Saul's Conversion*, *The Marriage of Cana* and *The Conversion of Zacchaeus*. They were very simply told in unsophisticated language and filled with anecdotes and simple homely stories. They were messages in which Jesus was fully proclaimed and offered to all who would come to him. Christ as the only way to find forgiveness, justification, and the new birth were recurring themes in all his sermons, and Jesus was always presented as both fully human and fully divine. It is therefore no surprise that Whitefield frequently referred to Jesus in both his letters and sermons as "our glorious Emmanuel".

Whitefield had a great ability to provide simple but memorable illustrations. Speaking at Moorfields Tabernacle on 30 August 1769 he said, "Sheep love to be together. They don't love to be alone. You rarely see a sheep by itself; and Christ's people may well be compared to them in this."[27] In his sermon on *The Necessity and Benefits of Religious Society*, Whitefield pointed out that

> kindled coals, if placed asunder, soon go out, but if heaped together, quicken and liven each other and afford a lasting heat. The same will hold good in the case now before us. If Christians kindled by the grace of God unite, they will quicken and enliven each other, but if they separate asunder, no marvel if they soon grow cold and tepid.[28]

In his sermon entitled *Thy Maker is Thy Husband*, Whitefield used the example of household fire insurance. He pointed out how the owner in any populous town or city "takes out an insurance policy for his house from the fire-office to insure it, in case of fire". What foolishness is this "to be anxious to secure their ships against a storm, and their houses against a fire, and at the same time fail to take a policy out of the assurance-office of heaven."[29]

The impact of Whitefield's preaching on the clergy

During his second visit to America in the middle of October 1740 Whitefield journeyed to Northampton, where his preaching rekindled the revival under Jonathan Edwards, which was then beginning to dwindle. Edwards recorded that Whitefield's sermons "were suitable for the circumstances of the town" and that they immediately impacted the minds of the people in general.[30] Indeed

Whitefield's visit changed Edwards' conception of what made preaching effective.[31] Prior to Whitefield's arrival preachers in the old school Calvinist tradition tended to be doctrinal and rational in emphasis. As Stout aptly put it, "He restored narrative to the centre of preaching. No longer was Scripture primarily a set of doctrines, now it became a dramatic script with a cast of characters whose lives served as role models."[32] Indeed Whitefield preached in what came to be regarded as "plain style". His aim, much like that of John Wesley, was to preach "the plain truth to the plain man". Whitefield sought always to speak to ordinary men and women in the language they could readily understand. He made use of stories and homely everyday illustrations. His influence on American clergy was felt far and wide as they took to his straightforward approach.[33] Charles Chauncy, an "Old Light"[34] and minister at First Church, Boston, for sixty years, was disturbed by the number of ministers in the town who "venerated" Whitefield and invited him to preach before their congregations. He complained that "evening lectures were up in one place and another; no less than six in this town, four weekly, and two monthly ones, though the town does not consist of above 5,000 families."[35]

The dramatist

In his youth Whitefield both loved to read and act in plays but following his conversion he turned away from the stage believing it to have a degenerating effect on people's moral behaviour. That said, it is clear that Whitefield never altogether laid aside his natural dramatic gifts. Instead he channelled them into his public preaching. In so doing his sermons became a form of entertainment, albeit godly entertainment. As Stout observed, "Whitefield managed to fuse a public amalgam of preaching and acting that held audiences spellbound."[36] He became "at heart", Stout went on to assert, "an actor-preacher, as opposed to a scholar preacher".[37] However, Stout's assertion that Whitefield was driven by a craving for power, respect, and personal egotism[38] needs to be set alongside other motivating factors. Whitefield had a vivid, almost physical sense, of the presence of Christ. At times he felt an overwhelming presence of the Holy Spirit which gave him the passion and the drive to share his experience of the new birth with all who would listen, regardless of their station in society whenever the opportunity arose. Along with many eighteenth-century Christians Whitefield also had a strong sense of duty which compelled him to fulfil his calling. If Whitefield was driven by a craving for respect it certainly didn't show in his attitude to Roman Catholicism, unregenerate clergy, the Church of England hierarchy, and those who spent their time at the theatre or on the dance floor.

Like many great orators he made very frequent use of gestures with his hands, a trait that is seen in many of the paintings, engravings, and other depictions of him. With the passing of the years Whitefield preached some of his sermons several hundred times such that he not only knew them off by heart, but also found himself able to dramatize them. A hearer described attending one of his sermons on a stormy day in Boston and the powerful effect that it had upon him. Whitefield began with a lengthy opening prayer after which "he knelt for a long time in profound silence" which so powerfully affected "even the most heartless of his audience, that a stillness like that of a tomb pervaded the entire assembly". As the sermon progressed Whitefield became powerfully direct and called out "O sinner! by all your hopes of happiness, I beseech you to repent. Let not the wrath of God be awakened! Let not the fires of eternity be kindled against you! See there! He cried out with passion and pointing to a flash of lightning, proclaimed, 'It is a glance from the angry eye of Jehovah! Hark!' He then raised his little finger in a listening attitude, as the thunder broke in a tremendous crash, and declared, 'it was the voice of the Almighty as He passed by in His anger!'"[39]

On another occasion, addressing a large gathering, Whitefield made a solemn pause and then described an angel about to leave earth and ascend into heaven. "Will he bring good news of one sinner among all this multitude reclaimed from the errors of his way?" To give powerful effect to this answer he stamped his foot, lifted his eyes to heaven and streaming with tears, cried out, "Stop Gabriel! Stop Gabriel! Stop, ere you enter the sacred portals, and yet carry with you the news of one sinner converted to God!"[40]

Emotional phenomena

Such was the compelling power of Whitefield's preaching that his hearers often cried out and went down on their knees in repentance. William McCulloch, who heard many of Whitefield's sermons at Cambuslang, reported that several were "crying out" and "a very great but decent weeping and mourning was observable throughout the auditory".[41] Thomas Rankin, who heard Whitefield in Edinburgh, wrote, "The sermon exceeded all the sermons I ever heard. About the middle of it, I ventured to look up, and saw crowds around Mr Whitefield bathed in tears."[42]

For the greater part Whitefield was little troubled by these expressions of emotion on the part of his hearers. Cornelius Winter recorded that he hardly ever knew Whitefield to go through a sermon without weeping and that he truly believed his tears were tears of sincerity. He stated that "his freedom in the use of his passions, often put my pride to the trial. I could hardly bear such unreserved use of tears, and the scope he gave to his feelings, for sometimes he wept, stamped loudly and passionately, and was frequently so overcome, that, for a few seconds, you would suspect he never would recover; and when he did, nature required some little time to compose herself."[43]

Because Whitefield spoke to such large crowds and often for quite long periods of time he expended huge amounts of energy. He himself wrote, and doubtless said on a number of other occasions, "I preach till I sweat through and through."[44] As the years passed by and, as we have seen, his health deteriorated he was often laid extremely low, suffering from a nervous disposition, vomiting, flatulence, and excessive soreness in his throat. His journals and letters abound with details of his failing health. For example in a letter from London in October 1761 he wrote: "I have not preached a single sermon for some weeks. Last Sunday, I spoke a little; but I feel its effects ever since."[45]

Cornelius Winter observed the last years of Whitefield's ministry and wrote of the ways he found preaching to be increasingly physically and emotionally draining. As soon as his preaching was done and the worship concluded he noted that Whitefield often suffered a vast discharge from his stomach, usually with a considerable quantity of blood. Only then was he able to speak. Unsurprisingly he also recalled that Whitefield was averse to much singing after the preaching because it detracted people from the content of his sermon. After having given his all to proclaim the gospel message he would hardly have wanted to diminish its impact. Gillies poignantly commented, "he wore himself away in the service of souls; and when he died, he died quite exhausted by much speaking".[46]

It has been suggested that the pace at which Whitefield lived during his thirty years of ministry meant that he was speaking more than he was sleeping. Henry Venn, the vicar of Huddersfield, knew him well and wrote, "Who would think it possible that a person... should speak in the compass of a single week (and that for years) in general forty hours, and in very many sixty, and that to thousands; and after this labour, instead of taking any rest, should be offering up prayers and intercessions, with hymns and spiritual songs, as his manner was, in every house to which he was invited."[47]

Much has been written by Lambert and Stout in particular about the ways in which Whitefield's effectiveness was greatly strengthened by his use of print media in what was an age of growing consumerism.[48] Nevertheless the fact remains that it was his preaching that drew and magnetized thousands. Had he not been a unique and captivating orator no amount of press releases and advertising would continue to bring the crowds for more than thirty years. Significantly none of the obituarists who Gillies included at the end of his biography of Whitefield[49] made any mention of the impact of Whitefield's writings. But they all, including John Wesley, Benjamin Coleman and Ebenezer Pemberton of Boston, Josiah Smith of Charleston, and John Newton and Henry Venn in England, stressed his gifts as an orator.

The impacts of Whitefield's itinerant preaching

Whitefield's preaching had a major impact on society, education, and culture in both the American colonies and in the British Isles. These issues are treated in detail in the following chapter. The remainder of this chapter is concerned with Whitefield's influence on clergy and the life and worship of the churches.

Whitefield's proclamation of the Christian message utilized new means of communication. He made extensive use of publicity by printing and circulating his journals, tracts, and pamphlets and by constantly writing letters to the local and national press. When he arrived at Newport, Rhode Island in September 1740 his arrival had already been well-publicized. Boston newspapers contained advertisements of numerous books by and about Whitefield.[50] He was ever ready to respond to hostile pamphlets or episcopal and ecclesiastical sanctions. Add to this the enormous number of sermons he preached and his oratorical gifts of voice and dramatization coupled with his practice of singing hymns in public roads and we are seeing the beginnings of modern mass communication. As Mark Noll aptly put it, "Whitefield seemed intuitively to grasp that in the new era of commerce, trade, growing cities, and the breakdown of European traditions, dynamic new techniques were needed to promote the Christian message."[51] The Christianity of Whitefield and the revival preachers with its minimalist ecclesiology and doctrine together with its emphasis on a "new birth" experience and fresh forms of singing was ideally suited to the raw conditions of the frontier and the new colonial settlements.

By these means many thousands testified to having been converted and of experiencing the new birth. In Boston alone thirty new societies attached to local churches were founded in the wake of Whitefield's several visits to the town. There were also societies for children, young people, and women. In addition there were some mixed societies for black and white people. A similar picture emerged in both Philadelphia and New York.[52] Significantly, Anthony Benezet, a prominent Philadelphia Quaker who became the champion of the black African cause and a powerful advocate of abolition, testified that it was Whitefield's ministry that had motivated him.[53] In addition the Great Awakening also planted the seed that the Methodists began to harvest in the later part of the eighteenth century. The number of Methodists in America grew from about 2,000 in 1773 to 9,000 in 1777. By 1791 the number had hugely increased to more than 75,000.[54]

Major themes in Whitefield's preaching such as the new birth, opposition to nominal established religion, and freedom in Christ must in some measure have imbued the colonists with the hope of freedom from British oppression and taxation. It was this that prompted Mahaffey to suggest that Whitefield facilitated "the first uniquely American collective experience".[55] Indeed he contended that without George Whitefield American independence "would have come much later, if at all".[56]

There can be no doubting but that Whitefield and the revival preachers made a significant impact on the manners and cultural and social life of the colonies. This is considered in more detail in Chapter 11. Suffice it to say at this point that during his time in America Whitefield spoke out strongly against the misuse of alcoholic beverages, the lack of education, the evils of the dance floor, the neglect of the poor, and the brutalities of the slave owners.[57] Whitefield urged humane treatment of slaves and made numerous collections for the poor and the victims of the Seven Years' War.

Whitefield was undoubtedly one of the most remarkable, able, and energetic preachers the world has seen. He preached an estimated 18,000 formal sermons and gave many hundreds of shorter talks and addresses in prisons, places of learning, private homes, and on board ships. During his ministry he did produce a number of full-manuscript sermons, seventy-eight of which were published. Most of these he memorized, dramatized, and preached many hundreds of times, delivering them extempore doubtless with new material, alterations, and fresh illustrations as appropriate to the circumstances. In addition there were many sermons which were simply born of his own meditations or his readings from Matthew Henry's Commentaries. Perhaps the one thing, though, that stands out is Whitefield's unique gifts of language and speaking (some would term it an "anointing"), which enabled his hearers to encounter Christ's presence. The manuscripts of Whitefield's published sermons don't strike the reader as exceptional but it was his delivery of them, which made for compelling listening. He had an intense experience of Jesus' presence which enabled him to communicate the gospel message with passion and sincerity. It is said that the philosopher David Hume was once observed hurrying to hear George Whitefield preach. When he was asked if he really believed what the great evangelist preacher taught, Hume replied "certainly not! But he does, and I want to hear a man who truly believes what he says."[58] Speaking of Whitefield's preaching on another occasion Hume wrote: "In the most simple but energetic language [he] described what he called the Saviour's dying love to sinful men, so that almost the whole assembly was melted to tears. This address was accompanied with such animated yet natural action that it surpassed anything I ever saw or heard in any preacher."[59]

Chapter 9 notes

1   *Letter to Mr H—*, 30 June 1736. See also J. Pollock, *George Whitefield* (Christian Focus, 2009), p. 38; R. Davies, *Methodism* (Harmondsworth, Penguin Books, 1964), p. 66.

2   *Letter to Rev. Mr. John Wesley*, 1 September 1748.

3   *Journal*, 7 January 1739.

4   Ibid, 21 October 1740.

5   *Collections of the Georgia Historical Society, The Journal of Secretary Stephens*, Supplement to Vol. 4, entries of dates indicated, 1738 in A. Dallimore, op. cit., Vol. 1, pp. 202–03.

6   *New England Journal*, taken in shortened form from A. Dallimore, op. cit., Vol. 1, pp. 434–36.

7   A. Dallimore, op. cit., Vol. 1, p. 441.

8   Taken from Seward's *Journal*, p. 7, in L. Tyerman, *Life*, Vol. 1, p. 374.

9   Eyewitness account of Whitefield's visit to Middletown, Connecticut, 23 October 1740, taken from "The Spiritual Travels of Nathan Cole" reprinted in *The William and Mary Quarterly*, 3rd Series, VII (1950), pp. 590–91. The book was published in 1761. Nathan Cole was a farmer from Middletown, Connecticut, who heard George Whitefield preach in 1740. The experience convinced Cole to find salvation and become born-again.

10 J. Smith, *The Character, Preaching etc., of the Reverend Mr George Whitefield*, 26 March 1740 in A. Dallimore, op. cit., Vol. 1, p. 514.

11 B. Franklin, *Memoirs of the Life and Writings of Benjamin Franklin* (London, 1818), Vol. 1, p. 284.

12 J. Gillies, op. cit., p. 284.

13 S. Edwards, *Letter to Brother James*, 24 October 1740, cited in L. Tyerman, *Life*, Vol. 1, pp. 428–29.

14 M. A. G. Haykin, *The Revived Puritan: The Spirituality of George*

Whitefield (Evangelical Press, 2004), pp. 35–37.

15 A. C. H. Seymour, *The Life and Times of Selina, Countess of Huntingdon* (London, 1840), Vol. 1, p. 179. See also F. Cook, op. cit., p. 121.

16 A. C. H., Seymour, op. cit., Vol. 2, p. 379.

17 F. Cook, op. cit., p. 121.

18 L. Tyerman (London, Hodder and Stoughton, 1877), Vol. 2, p. 461.

19 W. Jay, *Memoirs of the Late Reverend Cornelius Winter* (Bath, 1808) 99 19–20 and 66–69. Cited in L. Tyerman, *Life*, Vol. 2, pp. 510–13; A. Dallimore, op. cit., Vol. 2, pp. 477–82; T. S. Kidd, *George Whitefield*, pp. 240–41 and 245–47.

20 Whitefield, *The Care of the Soul as the One Thing Needful*, Sermon 31, *Works*, Vol. 5, p. 474.

21 Whitefield, *Christ the Only Preservative Against a Reprobate Spirit*, Sermon 51, *Works*, Vol. 6, p. 300.

22 Whitefield, *Christ the Best Husband: Or an Invitation to Young Women to Come to See Christ*, Sermon 5, *Works*, Vol. 5, p. 77.

23 Whitefield, *Christ the Only Rest for the Weary and Heavy-Laden*, Sermon 21, *Works*, Vol. 5, pp. 317–18.

24 Whitefield, *The Wise and Foolish Virgins*, Sermon 25, *Works*, Vol. 5, p. 387.

25 Whitefield, *The Power of Christ's Resurrection*, Sermon 53, *Works*, Vol. 6, p. 328.

26 Whitefield, *A Sermon Preached before the Governor, and Council, and the House of Assembly, in Georgia, on January 28, 1770*, Sermon 57, *Works*, Vol. 6, p. 387.

27 L. Tyerman, *Life of Whitefield*, Vol. 2, p. 564.

28 Whitefield, *The Necessity and Benefits of Religious Society*, Sermon VIII, *Works*, Vol. 5, p. 112.

29 Whitefield, *Thy Maker is Thy Husband*, Sermon 12, *Works*, Vol. 5, p. 179.

30 J. Edwards, *An Account of the Revival of Religion in Northampton in 1740–42, as Communicated in a Letter to a Minister in Boston* (Edinburgh, The Banner of Truth Trust, 1991), p. 149.

31 G. Marsden, *Jonathan Edwards: A Life* (New Haven, Yale University Press, 2003), pp. 219–20.

32 H. Stout, *The Divine Dramatist*, p. xx.

33 J. H. Smith, *The First Great Awakening: Redefining Religion in British America 1725–1775* (Madison, Farleigh Dickinson University Press, 2015), pp. 1–3.

34 "Old Lights" were those who stood against the revival.

35 J. Ripper, *American Stories*, Vol. 1, p. 46.

36 H. Stout, *The Divine Dramatist*, p. xviii.

37 Ibid.

38 Ibid, pp. 36 and 55.

39 J. B. Wakeley, *Anecdotes of the Rev George Whitefield* (London, Hodder, 1900), pp. 344–47, in A. Dallimore, op. cit., Vol. 1, p. 543.

40 A. C. H. Seymour, op. cit., Vol. 1, pp. 98–99.

41 D. Macfarlan, *Revivals of the Eighteenth Century* (London and Edinburgh, undated), pp. 73–74 in A. Dallimore, *George Whitefield*, Vol. 2, p. 128.
42 T. Rankin, MS *Journal* in Tyerman, *The Life of Whitefield*, Vol. 2, p. 393.
43 W. Jay, *Memoirs of the Late Cornelius Winter*, cited in L. Tyerman, *The Life*, Vol. 2, p. 511.
44 *Letter to Mr H——*, 27 April 1739.
45 *Letter to Mr K——*, 13 October 1761.
46 J. Gillies, op. cit., p. 335.
47 Cited in J. I. Packer, "The Spirit with the Word; The Reformational Revivalism of George Whitefield" in *The Collected Shorter Writings of J. I. Packer* (Carlisle, Paternoster Press, 1999), p. 40.
48 H. Stout, *The Divine Dramatist*, pp. xx–xxiii and F. Lambert, op. cit., pp. 54–57 and 63–76.
49 J. Gillies, op. cit., pp. 282–83.
50 W. S. Hudson, *Religion in America*, p. 68.
51 M. A. Noll, *The Old Religion in a New World* (Grand Rapids, William B. Eerdmans Publishing Company, 2002), p. 53.
52 A. Dallimore, op. cit., Vol. 1, pp. 588–89.
53 Ibid, p. 588, note 1.
54 See "Table of American Methodists 1773–1791" in M. A. Noll, *The Old Religion in a New World*, p. 205.
55 J. D. Mahaffey, *The Accidental Revolutionary* (Baylon, 2011) p. 58.
56 Ibid, p. xi.
57 Whitefield, it should be noted, was in favour of slavery with the proviso that slaves were treated with respect and kindness.
58 Source unknown.
59 F. Cook, *Selina*, p. 121 citing J. B. Wakely, *Anecdotes of George Whitefield* (London, Hodder and Stoughton, 1879) p. 210.

Chapter 10

Social Gospeller

Charity preaching in London and elsewhere

Almost as soon as he had been made a deacon in June 1736 Whitefield had several short periods of ministry in different places, including London, the South East, and Bristol. Some of these assignments were taking services and preaching for clerical friends who were away from their parishes and others were by invitation from clergy who wanted to check out his rapidly growing reputation as a preacher. Whenever it seemed appropriate it became the young Whitefield's practice to take collections for those in need. Understandably there were soon numerous occasions when critics accused him of mishandling such monies but Whitefield kept careful accounts and despite his continuing the practice to the end of his days he was never convicted of dishonesty.

In February 1737, while he was in Bristol, he wrote to a close friend, "Methinks it would be almost sinful to leave Bristol at this critical juncture, there being now a prospect of making a very considerable collection for the poor Americans."[1] On 23 May 1737 he returned for a second visit and reported that "multitudes came to meet him including many in coaches a mile outside the city". He preached five times a week there and collected "for the poor prisoners in Newgate... twice or thrice a week".[2] In a letter sent from London at the end of the same year Whitefield wrote: "Great things have been done for us here. Perhaps upwards of a thousand pounds have been collected for the poor, and the charity schools, and I have preached above a hundred times, since I have been here."[3] The following year he calculated that his charity sermons had raised "near a thousand pounds Sterling for the children belonging to the charity schools of London and Westminster".[4] Back in London in January 1739 Whitefield made a brief note in his journal, "preached a charity sermon".[5] In his desire to establish schools for the poor he was doubtless helped by William Seward (1711–40), a young, very wealthy, widower, who had devoted much time and money to promoting charity schools. He placed both himself and his fortune at Whitefield's disposal. Tragically he was killed following an assault by an anti-Methodist mob in Wales in May 1740.

On his arrival in Bristol on 17 March,1739 Whitefield wrote that God rewarded him "by giving me such extraordinary power at the Poor-house this afternoon, that great numbers were quite melted, and dissolved into tears".[6] Shortly after this time on 28 March Whitefield dined with some of the colliers who had been powerfully impacted under his preaching and who had collected over twenty pounds in money, as well as having raised more than forty pounds in subscriptions toward the building of a local charity school. He encouraged them in their plan and expressed the view that the project would prosper. Less than a week later, a man had given the group the necessary ground required for the building and Whitefield laid a stone, knelt down, and prayed to God that the gates of hell might not prevail against the school.[7]

When he first arrived in Savannah Whitefield immediately saw the crucial importance of schooling. He wrote on 10 June 1738 "I am settling up little schools in and about Savannah; that the rising generation may be bred up in the nurture and admonition of the Lord."[8] Throughout his ministry his journal and his many published letters are punctuated with references to his raising money for a variety of needs including schools, the poor, prisoners, refugees, the hungry, destitute, and victims of war. Twenty years later a letter he penned in 1760 provides a glimpse of his ongoing concern for the marginalized. A meeting of the freeholders and other inhabitants unanimously expressed the town's thanks to the Revd George Whitefield, "for his charitable care and pains in collecting a considerable sum of money in Great Britain, for the distressed sufferers by the great fire in Boston. A committee was formed to wait on Mr Whitefield and to inform him of the vote and present him with a copy of it."[9]

Bethesda orphan house

J. H. Overton, writing in the later nineteenth century, somewhat unkindly described the orphan house which Whitefield founded as "his hobby", stating that "it was only one out of a thousand instances of his benevolence".[10] In reality, however, it turned out to be a lifelong project which absorbed huge amounts of his emotional and physical energy. It also had the effect of keeping Whitefield's constant focus on the needs of the poor and marginalized.

Throughout all the years of his ministry, travelling and preaching in both the British Isles and America, the orphanage was never far from his mind. Whitefield was continuously collecting money for the home from wealthy benefactors and those who came to listen to his preaching. Funds were constantly needed to extend the buildings and to purchase more land on which to produce milk, meat, grain, fruit and vegetables to feed the staff and the children. For the duration of Whitefield's entire life hardly a month passed by in which he didn't write a letter mentioning the needs of his house. There were requests for prayer for God's blessing on the spiritual needs of the children and staff. Added to this were the constant need for material resources that included anything from wood, tools, reading books, pens, and paper to shoes and rolls of cloth to be made into clothes.

In addition to the huge amount of energy that Whitefield expended on the orphan house he took care to publish accounts of the amounts he had taken and of the ways in which it was spent as there was a constant need for strict and careful handling of the money he received from public collections. He was rarely one who would take adverse criticism and in response to the hostility of his critics he wrote two lengthy pamphlets detailing the affairs and management of the home. These included plans of the estate, land usage, financial statements, and the daily activities of the community. The first document consisting of thirty-one folios was published in January 1741 and entitled *An Account of the Orphan House in Georgia*.[11] A second followed in March 1746 under the caption, *Continuation of the Account and Progress, &c. of the Orphan House*.[12]

When Whitefield returned to America in 1738 he began the project by renting a large house and taking in all the orphans he could find in the colony. Most were poor and their total number during that year varied between sixty and seventy. He also set up an infirmary where sick people could be treated and taken care of without charge. Whitefield had applied for a grant of 500 acres of land on which to construct the new buildings and begin to provide food for residents of the Bethesda orphan house. In March 1746 he was able to report that they had recently begun to put some of the land under the plough and hoped to have many acres of good oats and barley. At the same time he stated that they now had "near twenty sheep and lambs, fifty head of cattle, and seven horses". The gardens were flourishing and producing all sorts of greens. In addition he stated, "We have plenty of milk, eggs, poultry, and make a good deal of butter weekly."[13] By the spring of 1741 the superintendent, James Habersham, mentioned in a letter that the garden and plantation were now able "to afford us many things, and in great plenty. Our stores are yet well-stocked with flour and beef, &c."[14] All the children were given a rudimentary education and taught practical life skills. The overriding vision on which Whitefield founded the institution was that each individual would "be able to give a reason for the hope that is in them". Whitefield also constantly instructed them in the Church of England's Articles.[15] The children had daily worship, which included singing and prayers, and they attended church on Sundays.

The institution operated under a fairly strict regime, which included the following. Morning Prayer was to begin, consistently every day, at half-past five o'clock and Evening Prayer every night. On Sundays full prayers with a sermon were held at ten in the morning and three in the afternoon. Rule 2 was that "Great care be taken that all can read, write, speak and behave properly." Rule 4 read, "No cards, dice or gaming of any kind be allowed, on pain of expulsion; and no music but divine psalmody." Rule 8: "No one suffered to go to Savannah without leave." Rule 10: "All orphans and students to learn and repeat the *Thirty Nine Articles*." Rule 11: "The *Homilies* to be read publicly, every year, by students, in rotation." Rule 13 stated, "The young negro boys to be baptised and taught to read; the young negro girls to be taught to work with the needle." Taken as a whole these regulations give a reflection of the Holy Club and early Methodist disciplines.[16] For all his warm relationships with Dissenters Whitefield ran and organized Bethesda on strictly Anglican lines.

In his two written accounts of Bethesda not only did Whitefield highlight the criticisms about the handling of the finances but he also opined that, "Great calumnies have been spread abroad concerning our management of the children." Whitefield did his best to meet these criticisms and was glad to cite the case of one gentleman critic who he had invited to see for himself and was so impressed he desired to come and live in the community.[17]

The amounts of money which Whitefield raised through the many collections he made from the crowds who came to hear him preach can be judged from the following:

> Sunday 20th May, 1739 Preached at Moorfields and Kennington Common, and, at both places collected very near £50 for the Orphan House.[18] Sunday 28 September 1740: Preached at Dr Sewall's meeting-house [Roxbury, New England] to a very crowded auditory, and £555 were collected for the Orphan House.[19] 6 October 1740: I preached on the common [Boston], to about fifteen thousand people, and collected upwards of £200 for the Orphans. 13 October 1742: I collected last week £128 [at Edinburgh] for my poor orphans.[20]

It is noticeable that after 1750 Whitefield continued to mention the orphan house and its needs but rarely mentioned the sums of money he collected. This may have been to avoid details being inadvertently being passed on to his critics. It may well indicate that the institution was becoming more self-sufficient in terms of food and also that income was being generated through project work being done by the children and other members of the community.

It is clear from Whitefield's voluminous correspondence that Bethesda was a lifelong burden which at times weighed on him considerably. This was particularly the case in the first years of the project when there were large debts to be paid off. Yet as late as 27

November 1767 we find him writing, "None but God knows what a concern lies upon me now, in respect to Bethesda. Friends can guess, and a little sympathise, and I thank them for it; but the friend of sinners alone can shew what is to be done. At present, as to this particular, I walk in darkness, and have no light."[21] Set against the enormous energies he expended on travelling, preaching, writing, and involvement in church and local and national affairs, it is difficult to understand why he didn't release the entire orphanage project into the hands of another. He did, after all, resign the living of the parsonage of Savannah in November 1739.[22] That said, one of the great impacts of Bethesda, as Dallimore so clearly pointed out, was that it "had awakened the Christian conscience to a concern for orphans and for the needy in general".[23] Philanthropic Christian endeavour of the kind seen in Bethesda helped to bring about more humane and caring frontier communities. It also helped to make practical caring social action a key aspect of the Evangelical gospel.

Whitefield and the slavery question

Whitefield's management of the orphan house raised a matter which became the source of considerable debate, both nationally and internationally. This was the issue of slavery. At the time of Whitefield's arrival in 1739 there were estimated to be about 150,000 black African slaves in America.[24] Somewhat surprisingly the Governor of Georgia, General Oglethorpe, had, in 1733, outlawed the use of slaves in the colony. The settlers, however, were of a different view, protesting that English men and women would not be able to cope in the fields during the hot summer months. They backed their claim citing the colonies of Carolina and Virginia which were prospering on account of slave labour. Slavery was taking place in parts of England and the West Indies at this time. Very few Christian leaders spoke out in condemnation of the practice and English ships were bringing in thousands of black slaves from West Africa every year. In a fairly short time Whitefield, who himself suffered greatly in the hot climate, became increasingly sympathetic to the views of the Georgian settlers. However, it must immediately be said that he was both forthright and vigorous in his denunciation of the cruelties perpetrated against slaves.

His views on the matter were immediately apparent when in June 1740 he published *A Letter to the Inhabitants of Maryland, Virginia, North and South Carolina.* This was a truly hard-hitting piece. In the first paragraph Whitefield wrote, "I think God has a quarrel with you for your abuse and cruelty to the poor negroes." He went on to be more specific.

> Your slaves, I believe, work as hard, if not harder, than the horses whereon you ride. These after they have done their work, are fed and taken proper care of; but many negroes, when wearied with labour in your plantations, have been obliged to grind their own corn after they return home. Your dogs are caressed and fondled at your tables; but your slaves, who are frequently styled dogs or beasts, have not an equal privilege.[25]

Whitefield continued with the same degree of vehemence declaring "my blood has frequently run cold within me, to consider how many of your slaves had neither convenient food to eat, nor proper raiment to put on, notwithstanding most of the comforts you enjoy were solely owing to their indefatigable labours."[26] He denounced the owners for keeping their slaves "ignorant of Christianity and so profaning the Lord's day". He warned them that judgment would in the future befall their land just as the Lord had later visited the land of Israel in the time of King David, on account of their earlier brutal treatment of the poor in the time of King Saul (2 Samuel 21:1). Judgment, he asserted, had already begun in the case of the people of South Carolina: "their houses having been depopulated with small pox fever, and their own slaves have risen in arms against them".[27] The *Letter* was printed in the newspapers and published by Benjamin Franklin as a pamphlet with the consequence that it became widely known in the colonies.

Whitefield didn't content himself with a written protest alone. He had a deep compassion for the slaves, many of whom wept as he left Philadelphia. On 21 April 1740 he recorded in his *Journal*:

> This day I bought five thousand acres of land on the forks of Delaware, and ordered a large house to be built thereon, for the instruction of these poor creatures. The land, I hear is exceedingly rich. It is a manor... I took up so much because I intend settling some English friends there, when I come next from England. I have called it Nazareth; and I trust, in a few years, the Lord will let us see much good come out of it. Amen, Lord Jesus, Amen.[28]

The friends who Whitefield had in mind were people who had sought his assistance to emigrate to America. Some of their number might well have included Methodists seeking to escape from persecution and looking to improve their lot in the world. His plan also included establishing schools for black African slaves on this plantation.[29] In addition to initiating this demanding scheme to improve the slaves' quality of life Whitefield adopted the practice of addressing his preaching as much to them as to white men and women in Charleston and elsewhere, and "preached in such language that the meanest servant may understand".[30] This was an important step since many of the slave traders believed black African people to be somewhere above animal but less than human. Whitefield concluded his sermon *The Lord Our Righteousness* with the following words:

> Here then I could conclude; but I must not forget the *poor negroes*; no, I must not. Jesus Christ has died for them, as well as for others. Nor do I mention you last, because I despise your souls, but because I would have what I shall say, make a deeper impression upon your hearts. O that you would seek the Lord to be your righteousness... Did you never read of the eunuch belonging to the queen of Candace? A negro like yourselves. He believed and was baptised. Do you also believe, and you shall be saved.[31]

Despite being deeply concerned for the welfare of slaves, Whitefield realized that he had large debts to pay off at Bethesda, as well as more than a hundred hungry mouths to feed. He increasingly came to the view that to have slave labour carefully managed and respectfully treated could solve the problem. Since slavery continued to be outlawed in Georgia, James Habersham, together with Hugh and Jonathan Bryan, planned and purchased a plantation in South Carolina where slave-ownership was legal. The food and resources generated from this estate would supply the needs of the orphan house. Whitefield wrote from Charleston:

> God has put it into the hearts of my South-Carolina friends, to contribute liberally towards purchasing

> a plantation and slaves in this province; which I
> purpose to devote to the support of Bethesda –
> Blessed be God, the purchase is made – I last week
> bought, at a very cheap rate, a plantation of six
> hundred and forty acres of excellent land, with a
> good house, barn, and out-houses, and sixty acres
> of ground ready cleared, fenced and fit for rice,
> corn, and every thing that will be necessary for
> provisions. One negro has been given to me. Some
> more I propose to purchase next week. An overseer
> is put upon the plantation, and I trust a sufficient
> quantity of provision will be raised this year.[32]

In June the same year, following a collection made in Charleston, Whitefield purchased "a plantation and some slaves" which, he stated, "I intend to devote to the use of Bethesda." He was hopeful that the income and resources raised would remove the burden which lay "as a dead weight" upon him.[33] Gillies, while recording the purchase, passed no judgment on the matter,[34] though it should be added that Whitefield opened a school in Charleston to teach black children to read.[35]

Thus it happened that for all his expressed concern for the black African communities Whitefield became an owner of slaves. Despite his intention to treat them with kindness and bring them under the influence of the gospel he had in fact made himself a partner in the practice of slavery. It was a trade which his friend and fellow Methodist, John Wesley described as "the execrable sum of all villainies".[36]

Whitefield persisted in his assertions that some form of slavery would greatly improve the quality of the colony and be of great personal benefit to his orphan house. In December 1748 he penned a lengthy letter from Gloucester to the trustees on a number of issues, including that of the slave question. Referring to his struggles to maintain Bethesda in "the wilderness" he stressed that "had a negro been allowed, I should have had a sufficience [sic] to support a great many orphans, without expending above half the sum which hath been laid out". He went on to remind them of the success of his use of black labour on his plantation in South Carolina. This, he maintained, confirmed his view that Georgia would never be a flourishing province without slavery being allowed. He asked them to consider the possibility of "a limited use of negroes", informing them that in time this would enable the orphan house to become "not only a receptacle for fatherless children, but also a place of literature and academical [sic] studies".[37]

There can be no doubting that Whitefield's compassionate and caring attitude to the black African slaves resulted in their much better treatment in many places. However, the fact remains that Whitefield failed to see the need for the total abolition of slavery. So many people looked to him as their moral guide and spiritual leader that he could easily have persuaded them that Christian justice demanded equal rights for black and white peoples of the colonies.

Concern for the Native American Indian communities

The town and parish of Savannah to which Whitefield initially came to serve as parish priest and in which he established the orphanage was surrounded by Native American Indian settlements. Whitefield immediately did his best to show friendship and reach out to them. As mentioned earlier, it was just a few days after his arrival in Georgia that he went to visit the Native American chief Tomochichi, who was dangerously ill. From that time on the Native American communities were never far from Whitefield's heart.

He was particularly encouraged by a Native American trader who came to visit him on 8 May 1740 when he was in Philadelphia. This man had been praying with, and exhorting all, who were willing to listen. Whitefield took their meeting to be an encouragement of what might be in the future.[38] On 19 May, while he was still in the city, Whitefield was again visited by the same Native American tradesman whom he subsequently addressed as "Mr M—". Whitefield expressed the hope that "the Lord would open a door" among Indians and wrote to the trader offering some straightforward advice on how best to convey the Christian faith to his communities.[39] Two days later Whitefield addressed the entire Allegany Indian community giving them a simple but profound and forthright summary of the heart of the Christian faith.[40] Among a number of key doctrines Whitefield explained to them that Jesus was "God and man in one person, that God and men might be happy together again." He continued addressing them as "My dear brethren" and stated that "these are strange things" but that if you are willing "the Holy Spirit will teach you".[41]

The Native Americans, it seems, were never far from Whitefield's thoughts. In October 1763, while he was based in New York, Whitefield preached a sermon for the benefit of Eleazar Wheelock's Indian School at Lebanon in New England. Notwithstanding the prejudices against the Native Americans he was gratified to collect the sum of £120.[42] In the spring of 1766 Samson Occum (c. 1723–92), a Native American preacher, made the voyage to England accompanied by the Revd Nathaniel Whitaker to collect money for Wheelock's Indian college. Occum had been converted through the preaching of Whitefield and Gilbert Tennent.[43] Whitefield was "much pleased" with Occum's spirit and preaching and did all he could to assist him. Between 16 February and 22 July 1766 Occum preached more than 300 sermons – many of them to packed congregations. His Majesty, King George III, subscribed £200 and the total amount raised came to £12,500.[44] Whitefield's assistance to Wheelock's school proved to be of lasting value with the money raised eventually leading to the establishment of Dartmouth College.[45] After his return to America, Occum spent most of his days in missionary labours among the Native Americans of Stockbridge. Upwards of 300 Native Americans attended his funeral when he died in 1792.

On 30 June 1770, just three months before his death, we find Whitefield planned to journey to Albany, New York, in the hope of visiting Oneida, where a large Indian Congress was planned to take place.[46] His next letter, written a month later, listed twelve places where he had preached to large numbers including Albany, but he made no mention of the Native Americans.[47] There can be no doubting that Whitefield and the revival preachers had generated a serious concern for the well-being and compassionate treatment of their communities.

Constant concern for the prisoner and the condemned

From his earliest days as an undergraduate student at Oxford Whitefield had also been deeply concerned about the plight of the prisoner. Shortly after his ordination he made early contact with Bristol's Newgate prison since its keeper, Abel Dagge, had been converted under his preaching. Newgate had a reputation for brutality and filthy conditions but since his conversion Dagge instigated an immediate change. Such was the transformation that even Dr Samuel Johnson wrote of the wholesome change in both the jailer and the jail.[48] In August and September 1736 Whitefield preached in London's Ludgate prison "every Tuesday".[49] Two and a half years later, on 15 February 1739, he recorded in his journal,

"I preached a sermon on the Penitent Thief to the poor prisoners of Bristol and collected fifteen shillings for them. Many seemed much affected, and I hope the power of the Lord was present to awaken them."[50] The following day he noted, "Began this morning to settle a daily exposition, and reading prayers to the prisoners in Newgate."[51] On 23 February 1739, he again noted, "Preached a written sermon at Newgate and collected £2 5s for the prisoners. Many I believe were affected. To God be all the glory!"[52] In March the same year the prisoners had petitioned the mayor to appoint Whitefield to teach and visit them. He, however, employed a fellow clergyman in preference to Whitefield.[53]

Education

As has been noted at the beginning of this chapter, Whitefield, along with other leading Methodists and revivalists, was concerned to promote education at all levels. He made frequent collections for charity schools for young children and established schools himself. At home in England, for example, "on Sunday 29 July 1739 the morning congregation at his Moorfields Tabernacle gave a total of £24.9s for the school at Kingswood".[54] Whitefield also set up schools for children in Georgia and Savannah. Later he wanted to transform his orphan house into a college but was unable to agree the terms of the charter because some of the trustees of Georgia insisted that the principal should be a member of the Church of England and Whitefield could not agree that this should be enshrined in the foundation deed, particularly because much funding had been received from Dissenters.

Impact on the colleges

Whitefield and the revivalists not only multiplied the number of churches and the size of their congregations, they also generated a need and a desire for education and institutions of higher learning. The great majority of clergy, in America, received Whitefield with enthusiasm. During his second journey to the colonies both Harvard and Yale opened their doors to him. Despite the fact that Whitefield challenged the level of Harvard spirituality and the latitudinarian literature in the college library, his visit proved to be highly positive.[55] He returned to the college a second time and preached on Noah as an example of a preacher of righteousness.[56] He also visited Yale College in New Haven where he dined with the principal, Thomas Clapp, and spoke to the students on "the dreadful and ill consequences of an unconverted ministry".[57]

Whitefield's aspersions against an unconverted ministry unsurprisingly stirred up hostility on the part of both colleges and on the clergy of the surrounding areas. Both Harvard and Yale made strong pronouncements against him. Edward Wigglesworth, professor of divinity at Harvard, denounced him as an "enthusiast" whose "pernicious reflections on the ministers and churches of New England" had prejudiced people against their ministers.[58] On 25 February the faculty of Yale endorsed their brethren of Harvard College and denounced Whitefield for his assertion that "the generality of ministers were unconverted" and for his assertion that in a very short time they could expect "a supply of minsters from his Orphan House".[59] To his credit, Whitefield, who was only thirty at the time and still full of youthful zeal, later admitted that he had spoken in haste and taken too much note of hearsay. In 1756 he added a footnote to his journal that he had been "rash and uncharitable" and asked for "public pardon".[60] Subsequently Whitefield did his best to seek ways of improving relations and when the Harvard library was burned down in 1764 he was able to provide the college with a number of useful books. Happily, some four years later the president and fellows of the college expressed their gratitude to him for his "former kindness" and "generosity".[61]

Whitefield had an altogether more positive relationship with the College of New Jersey (Princeton) which had been established in 1746 by the Synod of New York, and which became a leading Presbyterian place of education. Whitefield devoted time and effort to raising capital in support of the New Jersey College where his close friend, Gilbert Tennent, was one of the trustees. He encouraged Tennent and Samuel Davies to embark on a fundraising mission to the British Isles. While they gained very little help from their fellow Presbyterians they were warmly supported by Methodists and Church of England clergy who had embraced the Evangelical revival. Davies later wrote "of the remarkable interposition of providence in favour of the college". A sum of about £4,000 was raised during the ten-month visit, which resulted in the building of Nassau Hall at Princeton.[62]

Whitefield's close association with the College of New Jersey was further deepened when he was invited to preach at their commencement in September 1754. The president and the trustees used the occasion to thank him for his ministry and the encouragement he had given to the college. They honoured him with the degree Master of Arts.[63] Whitefield later wrote, "I was exceedingly delighted at New Jersey commencement. Surely that college is of God."[64] In May 1755, and back on English soil, Whitefield wrote to the Marquis of Lothian thanking him for his "great zeal in promoting the welfare of the college" and asking him to see if he could procure a Doctor of Divinity degree for Abraham Burr, "the college's worthy president" as this would enhance the status and reputation of the college.[65] Lord Lothian replied stating that the University of Edinburgh had asked him to provide some details of Burr's achievements and literary output. Although Whitefield replied, it appears that Burr had nothing in print but "a little pamphlet lately published".[66] Nevertheless Whitefield kept in close contact with Burr who died three years later.

Whitefield called the college "a glorious plan set on foot" and asserted that "the spreading of the gospel in Maryland and Virginia in a great measure depends upon it".[67] Murray pointed out that Whitefield's convictions were soon fulfilled in that 500 of the first 2,500 graduates became preachers of the gospel.[68] When Whitefield returned to America in 1763 he reported on 14 November, "I am now about to make my fifth excursion to New Jersey College."[69] The following month he recalled that they had had "some sweet seasons" there,[70] and described the college as "a blessed nursery; one of the purist perhaps in the universe. The worthy President and three tutors, are all bent on making the students both saints and scholars."[71]

In June 1764, when Whitefield was on his way south toward Georgia, he received an invitation to preach at New Haven College. Just as he was about to leave the president informed him that the students had been "so deeply impressed by the sermon", that they were gone into the chapel and were begging for more. Needless to say Whitefield was only too happy to oblige.[72]

There were a number of other colleges which emerged from the revival. Baptists founded Rhode Island College (later Brown University) in 1764 and the Dutch Reformed Churches established Queen's College in 1769. In his later years Whitefield planned that his own Bethesda orphan house should become a college modelled on the plan of the New Jersey College. Proposals were made to James Wright, the Governor of Georgia, the Lord President, and the Archbishop of Canterbury. Whitefield's endeavours extended even further when he presented a document entitled "To the King's most Excellent Majesty. The Memorial of George Whitefield, Clerk."[73] In it he begged leave to inform the monarch that "there is no seminary for academical [sic] studies as yet founded, southward of Virginia". There was an extended correspondence between the interested parties, which was concluded with a letter sent by Whitefield to the archbishop on 16 October 1767. The negotiations finally broke down because the British authorities were adamant that the head of the college should be a member of the Church of England and that "public prayers should not be extempore ones, but the liturgy of the Church or some other settled form". Whitefield could not agree to either of these restrictions because he wanted the college to be founded upon "a broad bottom, and no other".[74] Whitefield's attempt to change Bethesda into a seminary is significant in that it is clear he saw the need to contain the revival within the boundaries of biblical orthodoxy. Unlike other revivalists he saw clearly that a properly trained ministry was the way to achieve this end.

Whitefield played a significant role in the foundation of the University of Pennsylvania. In 1740 those who had been inspired and converted under his ministry erected what became known as "The New Building" for him to use for preaching whenever he came to the city. It was underused, and eventually, in 1749, Benjamin Franklin proposed that an academy should be established and be operated from it. Planning was fairly quickly in place and Whitefield became one of the trustees. Franklin consulted him for suggestions concerning both the management and the administration. Whitefield wrote to Franklin on 26 February the following year and urged that the most important thing was "to have proper masters that are acquainted with this world, with themselves and with God, and who will naturally care for the welfare of the youth that shall be committed to their care."[75] He added a plea "for the free education of the poorer sort, who should appear to have promising abilities".[76] Whitefield was invited to preach at the college in October 1764. The provost led the prayers and both the current and previous governors and head gentlemen of the city attended the occasion.[77] The academy proved highly successful and eventually became the University of Pennsylvania.

Whitefield continued to pursue this broad-based social activism for the whole of his ministry. He personally supervised or involved himself in many different projects. In addition, as we have seen, he raised huge sums of money in collections and donations, the like of which had not been seen before, for a variety of needs. These included charity schools and the victims of war, famine, fire, and sickness. There was also funding for prisons, almshouses, libraries and book and tract distribution on a very wide scale. As Stout appositely stated, "Whitefield pioneered a new type of philanthropy or charity unrivalled in its variety and extent."[78]

Impact on manners and culture

Very early in his ministry Whitefield spoke out strongly against dysfunctional behaviour. On Friday 17 March 1738, when crossing the Atlantic, Whitefield preached a sermon against drunkenness to the soldiers and others on board. He also offered books in exchange for playing cards, which he threw overboard.[79] In March 1739 Whitefield preached to about 2,000 colliers on Coal-Pit Heath about seven miles from Bristol, and warned them of "misspending their time in revelling and dancing".[80] Preaching to upwards of 10,000 at Hackney Marsh in July 1739 Whitefield condemned horse-racing.[81] As we saw in Chapter 7, Whitefield also emerged as a vehement opponent of the theatres. During his visit to Gloucester early in 1739 he spoke out strongly against the local magistrates for allowing stage-players to act in the city asserting that in law they were "stiled [sic] sturdy beggars". "Their meetings," he contended, were "nurseries of debauchery." Such individuals are "the pest of our nation and the bane of true Christianity".[82] He felt so strongly against these activities that later in the autumn of the same year he issued a strong warning against them in "A Letter Addressed to the Religious Societies of England". "Balls, plays and horse-races," he wrote are "unchristian and fatal entertainments" which few have the courage to suppress.[83] In 1840 the *Pennsylvania Gazette* reported that "Since Mr Whitefield's preaching here, the Dancing School, Assembly and Concert Room have been shut up."[84] More than a decade later in Glasgow, in August 1753, he preached against playhouses and "their pernicious influence on religion and morality, especially in a populous, commercial city, and the seat of a University".[85]

In his *Remarks on a Pamphlet entitled The Enthusiasm of Methodists and Papists Compared.*[86] Whitefield expressed the view that the clergy should be examples to the rest of society by not "drinking... playing at dice, cards, or tables, or any other unlawful game... and doing the things that appertain to honesty and endeavouring to profit the church of God."[87] In a letter written in March 1744 to the Bishop of London and several of his close associates on the episcopal bench Whitefield urged that it would be "more becoming to your Lordships [sic] characters to put your clergy on preaching against revelling, cock-fighting, and such like, than to move the government against those who preach the love of God to precious souls".[88] Writing to the Native Americans communities, Whitefield explained that "true Christians are sober, chaste and holy. They will not get drunk, they will not play the whore, they will not cheat, lie, curse or swear; but they will bless and praise God, keep the Sabbath, and do all the good they can; for thus Jesus Christ, their Lord and master, lived when he was here on earth."[89] In a powerful sermon entitled *The Great Duty of Charity Recommended* Whitefield had strong words for those "rolling in your coaches and taking your pleasure". They "indulge themselves in the follies of life...while the poor all around them are not thought to be worthy to be set with the dogs of their flock". He said, "I speak particularly to you, my rich brethren, to intreat you to consider those that are poor in this world, and help them from time to time, as their necessity calls for it."[90] In view of this it is not surprising to read comments such as those of Benjamin Franklin that "it was wonderful to see the change in the manners of the inhabitants. From being thoughtless or indifferent about religion, it seemed as if all the world were growing religious, so that one could not walk through the town in an evening without hearing psalms sung in different families of every street."[91]

Together with Wesley, the other members of the Holy Club and the early Methodists, Whitefield constantly asserted by his teaching and example that the words and works of Jesus must be seen in concert. He was clear that while good works could not contribute anything towards a person's acceptance by God they were nevertheless the evidence of holiness and a lively faith. He contended that while we value "faith in Christ, the love of God, and being born again are of more infinite worth; you cannot be true Christians without having charity to your fellow creatures, be they friends or enemies, in distress".[92]

Chapter 10 notes

1   *Letter to Mr H—*, 10 February 1737.
2   Whitefield, *A Further Account of God's Dealings (June 1736–December 1737)*.
3   *Letter to Mrs H—*, 23 December 1737.
4   Whitefield, *Continuation of the Account and Progress, &c, of the Orphan House, Works*, Vol. 3, p. 463.
5   *Journal*, 24 January 1739.
6   Ibid, 17 March 1739.
7   Ibid, 28 March 1739.
8   *Letter to Mr H—*, 10 June 1738.
9   *Boston Gazette*, February 1764 in R. Philip, *Life and Times*, p. 469.
10 C. J. Abbey and J. H. Overton, *The English Church in the Nineteenth Century (London, Longmans, Green and Company,* 1878) Vol. 2, p. 98.
11 Whitefield, *An Account of the Orphan House in Georgia*, January 1741.
12 Whitefield, *Continuation of the Account and Progress, &c of the Orphan House, Works*, Vol. 3.
13 The information in this paragraph is taken from Whitefield, *Continuation of the Account, Works*, Vol. 3, pp. 463–68.

14 J. Habersham, *Letter to George Whitefield*, 11 June 1741, in Whitefield, *Works*, Vol. 3, pp. 441–42.

15 Whitefield, *An Account of the Orphan House*, *Works*, Vol. 3, p. 433.

16 L. Tyerman, op. cit., Vol. 2, pp. 582–83.

17 Whitefield, *An Account of the Orphan House*, *Works*, Vol. 3, p. 435.

18 *Journal*, 20 May 1739.

19 Ibid, 28 September 1740.

20 *Letter to Mrs Ann D—*, 13 October 1742.

21 *Letter to Mr R—K—*, 27 November 1767.

22 *Letter to Mr Wm D—*, 10 November 1739.

23 A. Dallimore, op. cit., Vol. 1, p. 588.

24 Ibid, p. 431.

25 *A Letter to the Inhabitants of Maryland, Virginia, North and South Carolina*, *Works*, Vol. 4, p. 37.

26 Ibid, p. 38.

27 Ibid, p. 41.

28 *Journal*, 22 April 1740. See also F. Lambert, op. cit., p. 82. He held services in Moorfields to raise money for this particular project.

29 *Journal*, 9 May 1740.

30 F. Lambert, op. cit., pp. 153–54.

31 Whitefield, *The Lord our Righteousness*, *Works*, Vol. 5, p. 234.

32 *Letter to a generous Benefactor unknown*, 15 March 1747.

33 *Letter to Mr H—*, 1 June 1747. See also J. Gillies, op. cit., p. 151.

34 J. Gillies, op. cit., p. 151.

35 F. Lambert, op. cit., p. 139.

36 J. Wesley, *Thoughts on Slavery*, 1744.

37 Information taken from Whitefield, *Letter to the Trustees of Georgia*, 6 December 1748.

38 *Journal*, 8 May 1740.

39 *Letter to Mr M—, an Indian Trader*, 19 May 1740.

40 *Letter to Mr G—L—*, 22 May 1740.

41 *Letter to the Allegany Indians*, 21 May 1740.

42 J. Belcher, *Life of Whitefield*, p. 378. See also *Boston Gazette*, 23 January 1764.

43 L. Tyerman, *Life*, Vol. 2, p. 494.

44 "Occum Circle Personography", *Dartmouth College Collections*, where Occom appears to be the preferred spelling: https://collections.dartmouth.edu/occom/html/ctx/personography/personography.html?ographyID=pers0036.ocp? See also R. Philip, op. cit., p. 484.

45 A. Dallimore, op. cit., Vol. 2, p. 430.

46 *Letter to Mr R—K—*, 30 June 1770.

47 Ibid, 29 July 1770.

48 A. Dallimore, op. cit., Vol. 1, p. 254.

49 *Journal*, 8 August 1736.

50 Ibid, 15 February 1739.
51 Ibid, 16 February 1739
52 Ibid, 23 February 1739.
53 Ibid, 17 March 1739.
54 Ibid, 29 July 1739.
55 See Chapter 4, "Awakening in America".
56 *Journal*, 11 October 1740.
57 Ibid, 24 October 1740.
58 L. Tyerman, op. cit., Vol. 2, p. 134.
69 Ibid, p. 138.
60 See footnote Whitefield, *Journal*, 24 September 1740.
61 *Letter to Mr S—S—*, 10 March 1764, J. Gillies, op. cit., p. 241.
62 I. Murray, *Revival and Revivalism* (Edinburgh, The Banner of Truth Trust, 1994), pp. 15–16.
63 See J. Gillies, op. cit., p. 213; A. Dallimore, op. cit., Vol. 2, p. 370; T. Kidd, *George Whitefield*, p. 210.
64 *Letter to The Rev. Mr. G—*, 25 November 1754.
65 *Letter to the Marquis of Lothian*, 14 May 1755.
66 L. Tyerman, op. cit., Vol. 2, p. 342.
67 I. Murray, *Revival and Revivalism*, p. 38.
68 Ibid.
69 *Letter to Mr R—K—*, 14 November 1763.
70 *Letter to Anon.*, 1 December 1763.
71 *Letter to the Rev. Mr. G*, 18 December 1763.
72 *Letter to Mr R—K—*, 25 June 1764.
73 Whitefield, "To the King's Most Excellent Majesty. The Memorial of George Whitefield, Clerk", *Works*, Vol. 3, pp. 473–75.
74 *Letter to the Archbishop of Canterbury*, 16 October 1767, *Works*, Vol. 3, pp. 480–82.
75 *Letter to Benjamin Franklin*, 26 February 1750.
76 Ibid.
77 *Letter to Mr R—K—*, 10 October 1764.
78 H. Stout, Review of "George Whitefield and Benjamin Franklin: Thoughts on a Peculiar Friendship", *Proceedings of the Massachusetts Historical Society*, Third Series, Vol. 103 (1991), p. 11.
79 *Journal*, 18 March 1738.
80 Ibid, 30 March 1739.
81 Ibid, 26 July 1739.
82 *Letter to Mr N—*, 10 November 1739.
83 *A Letter to the Religious Societies of England* (November 1739), *Works*, Vol. 4, p. 23.
84 *Pennsylvania Gazette*, 1 May 1740 in F. Lambert, op. cit., p. 11. See also p. 79. The dancing masters and the jewellers in the city complained of loss of business.
85 *Newcastle Journal*, 11 August 1753 in J. Gillies, op. cit., p. 204.

86 Whitefield, *Remarks on a Pamphlet entitled The Enthusiasm of Methodists and Papists Compared*, *Works*, Vol. 4, p. 237.

87 Ibid.

88 *A Letter to the Right Reverend the Bishop of London*, March 1744, *Works*, Vol. 4, p. 138.

89 *Letter to the Allegany Indians*, 21 May 1740.

90 Whitefield, *The Great Duty of Charity Recommended*, *Works*, Vol. 6, p. 230.

91 *Memoirs of the Life and Writings of Benjamin Franklin* (London, 1818), Vol. 1, p. 410.

92 Whitefield, *The Great Duty of Charity Recommended*, *Works*, Vol. 6, pp. 239–40.

Chapter 11

Theologian and Churchman

It has been said that unlike many of his contemporary preachers in America Whitefield tended to place less emphasis on doctrine in his preaching. Whether or not that was the reality of the situation, Whitefield's spirituality, preaching, and writing were undergirded with a clear theological framework. Although he was very often inordinately busy he took the opportunity to read in depth during his long sea voyages and doubtless also when there were safe opportunities during his travels over land. In a letter to a fellow clergyman dated 21 June 1750 Whitefield related that on his journey to Kendal in Cumbria, "he had read Mr Law's second part of *The Spirit of Prayer* in which are many things which I pray God to write on the tables of my heart".[1] There are many references in his journal, sermons, and pamphlets to authors and titles of books which he found to be helpful and commended to others. From these it soon becomes clear that he stood firmly in the Puritan and Reformed theological tradition.

The impact of Oxford

As we noted earlier, among the many books Whitefield read, William Law's *A Serious Call to a Devout and Holy Life* came to have a profound and lasting influence on him. Indeed a great deal of what Law wrote came to be played out in his life and worship.

Whitefield began to pray and sing the psalms three times a day, as Law advocated, as well as to fast each Friday, and regularly receive the sacrament of Communion. Whitefield's reading of Law's description of Ouranius who represents the ideal "holy priest" clearly became a major inspiration to him. Ouranius, Law wrote, "learned the great value of souls, by so often appearing before God as an intercessor for them. He never thinks he can love or do enough for his flock". In his desire to bring men and women to experience forgiveness and the new birth it is clear that Whitefield totally subscribed to "the great value of souls" which was of supreme importance to Ouranius.

Ouranius also visits his people "to encourage their virtues, to assist them with his advice and counsel and to know the estate of their souls".[2] Whitefield was totally committed to doing the very same. He continually returned to the societies he had formed to encourage and instruct them. To the end of his days he wrote enormous numbers of letters urging people he had met to seek the Lord, overcome temptations, give themselves more fully to prayer, avoid dysfunctional relationships, shun heretical doctrine, and correct erroneous behaviour. Ouranius had "a haughtiness in his temper when he was first ordained" but he prayed that spirit away and came to have "great tenderness even for the most obstinate sinners". Over time Whitefield, likewise, became increasingly mellow and humbly respectful of people. Following Ouranius he gave "close application to his studies, attended to the needs of the poorest and prayed often and fervently".[3] Whitefield was in total agreement with Law that "all prayer and devotion, fastings and repentance, meditation and retirement, all sacraments and ordinances, are but so many means to render the soul conformable with God." He wrote in his journal in November 1736 that his reading Mr Law's excellent character of Ouranius in his *A Serious Call to a Devout and Holy Life* brought him to care for the poor and stirred in him a greater commitment to prayer.[4] He also recorded that in his struggle to free himself from the love of stage plays he was stirred up by Mr Law's excellent treatise entitled *The Absolute Unlawfulness of Stage Plays*.[5]

Whitefield wrote that reading Joseph Alleine's *An Alarm to the Unconverted* (1672) and Richard Baxter's *A Call to the Unconverted to Turn and Live* (1669) "much benefited me". He also found William Birkitt's *Expository Notes* and the Presbyterian Matthew Henry's *Exposition of the Old and New Testaments* (1708–10) "were admirable to lead him into Gospel truths".[6] He purchased a copy of Henry's Commentary in November 1736.[7]

The magisterial Reformers

At an early point in his time in Oxford Whitefield recorded in his journal that God enlightened his soul and brought him to see the necessity of being justified in his sight by *faith only*. At the time when he first reached this conviction he related that most of his friends were inclined to a "mystic divinity". But soon afterwards he was able to bless God that most of them had come to share his view of the matter. "It is," he wrote, "the doctrine of Christ" and "the good old doctrine of the Church of England for which I hope I shall be willing to die."[8]

Whitefield, along with the Wesleys and others of the Holy Club, soon became well-versed in the writings of the magisterial Reformers. He frequently mentions his debt to them and his reading of them in letters to his friends and fellow clergy. In March 1754 Whitefield was in Lisbon where he was disturbed by what he saw of Roman Catholicism. He wrote in a letter to a dear friend, "What a spirit must Martin Luther, and the first Reformers be endued with, that dared to appear as they did for God! Lord hasten that blessed time, when others, excited by the same spirit, shall perform like wonders."[9] A week later, still in Lisbon, he wrote again of "the mighty power from on high" with which "Luther, Calvin, Melancthon, Zwinglius [sic] be necessarily endued with, who dared first openly to oppose and stem such a torrent of superstition and spiritual tyranny, and such blind obedience to a papal power."[10] Whitefield's reading of the Reformers sharpened his antipathy towards the Roman Church. In November 1755 he wrote, "I shall always think it my bounden duty, next to inviting sinners to the blessed Jesus, to exhort my hearers to exert themselves against the first approaches of popish tyranny and arbitrary power. O that we may be able to watch and pray against all the opposition of *Antichrist* in our hearts."[11] Whitefield read John Foxe's *Book of Martyrs* while bound for America on board the *Elizabeth* in the summer of 1739 and found much challenge from it.[12]

John Calvin

Whitefield always had great respect for the Wesleys, since it was they who had first brought him to faith and nurtured his spiritual life. However he came to have a strong difference with them over Calvin's position on predestination. This was a conflict, as Henry Rack pointed out, that was "as old as Augustine and Pelagius and older".[13] Wesley's theology was more in keeping with the views of the Dutch theologian Jacob Arminius. In 1740 Wesley published his sermon entitled "Free Grace", which he had earlier preached in Bristol in August 1739.[14] In it he totally rejected the view that a section of mankind by virtue of an unchangeable and irresistible divine decree was inevitably damned.

At the time when Wesley published his sermon Whitefield was in America. There he had made strong friendships with William Tennent (1673–1746), his eldest son Gilbert Tennent (1703–64), and had become acquainted with Jonathan Edwards. As a result of their influence Whitefield became convinced that the doctrine of election was the only sure safeguard against the view that people are saved by their own decision.[15] The result of all this was that Whitefield reached the opinion that Wesley's view smacked of universal redemption. In consequence they were soon engaged in a strongly worded exchange of letters which at times strained their friendship to the limits. From 1743 onwards the followers of Whitefield had become known as Calvinistic Methodists to distinguish them from the Wesleyans. With the passing of time some of the wounds were healed, though never completely, and they were able to work and preach together in a number of places.

Whitefield responded forcefully and at length to Wesley in a letter sent from Bethesda dated 24 December 1740. He then published it on his return to England in March 1741 under the title "A letter to the Rev. Mr. John Wesley in Answer to His Sermon entitled Free Grace". He began by stating that he believed it to be his duty "to bear an humble testimony, and earnestly to plead for the truths, which I am convinced, are clearly revealed in the word of God". He frankly acknowledged his belief in the doctrine of reprobation and in the view "that God intends to give saving grace, through Jesus Christ only to a certain number and that the rest of mankind, after the fall of Adam… will at last suffer that eternal death, which is its proper wages." Wesley had argued in response that if this teaching was asserted "then all preaching is vain: it is needless to them that are elected" and "it is useless to them that are not elected for they cannot possibly be saved". Whitefield's reply was simply that God who had appointed that a certain number must be saved "has also appointed that the preaching of the word is also a means to bring them to it". He also suggested that preaching "might be useful even to those who were not elected in restraining them from much wickedness and sin". Wesley held strongly that election and reprobation tend to take away the motive for holiness, indeed even to destroy it. To this Whitefield retorted that "the

Apostle preached" that people are chosen through sanctification and that many of God's dear children who are elect "yet are meek, lowly, pitiful, courteous, tender-hearted, kind, of a Catholic spirit, and hope to see the most vile and profligate converted".[16]

Wesley further insisted that predestination "tends to destroy the comforts of religion, the happiness of Christianity, &c" but Whitefield reminded him that the 17th Article asserted "that the godly consideration of predestination, and election in Christ, is full of sweet, pleasant, unspeakable comfort to godly persons". Whitefield went on to comment that the article plainly demonstrated that "our godly reformers did not think election destroyed holiness or the comforts of religion". Whitefield was insistent that without a belief in election and the unchangeable love of God "it was simply not possible for anyone to have a comfortable assurance of salvation" arguing that "assurance could only arise from a belief of God's electing everlasting love".[17]

Whitefield felt that "electing love" would prevent believers from "trying to build on their own faithfulness" and that every small lapse of behaviour might throw believers into doubts, fears, and darkness. Wesley, it seems, remained unconvinced and in his sermon declared how uncomfortable it was to think that "thousands and millions of men, without any preceding offence or fault of theirs, were unchangeably doomed to everlasting burnings". Whitefield's response to that was that no one could be presumed to be without fault since after his fall Adam passed on his fallen nature to all his posterity. "If God might justly impute Adam's sin to all… he might also justly pass by some."[18]

Whitefield was also decidedly uneasy with Wesley's view that perfection was possible in this life and that it could be obtained by faith. It seemed to Whitefield and the Calvinists that this was making salvation dependent on human effort. It was largely for this reason that he had earlier begged Wesley to "never speak against election in your sermons".[19] He also recognized that public disputations over points of Christian doctrine might well turn people away from the faith. In another letter to Wesley he again urged his long-standing friend "not to be strenuous in opposing the doctrines of election and final perseverance", adding that "I cannot bear the thoughts of opposing you: but how can I avoid it, if you go about (as your brother C– once said) to drive John Calvin out of Bristol."[20]

Wesley had also made the further point that predestination meant that "God is merciful only to some men" – namely the elect. Whitefield replied that "the Lord is loving to every man, and his mercy is over all his works". In addition, following Matthew 5:45, "he sends his rain on the just and the unjust".[21]

Whitefield drew his reply to a conclusion by insisting that by denying election "you plainly make salvation depend not on God's free grace, but on man's free will". That said, he struck a final note of humility in writing that "we shall never in this life be able to search out God's decrees to perfection. No, we must humbly adore what we cannot comprehend, and with the great apostle at the end of all inquiries cry out, 'O the depth, &c' or with our Lord, when he was admiring God's sovereignty, 'Even so Father, for so it seemed good in thy sight.'"[22] The nub of the dispute was that Whitefield maintained that Wesley's doctrine of "free grace" inevitably led to good works contributing to salvation while Wesley asserted that eternal election was bound to cause antinomianism.

In his major study on John Wesley, Henry Rack pointed out that the evangelist continued to argue against predestination in all his subsequent controversies with more or less these same arguments.[23] On the other hand, he commended Whitefield who has often been regarded as something of a showman or "divine dramatist" for demonstrating that he could give a well-argued defence of traditional Calvinist views.

On a number of occasions Whitefield wrote letters in which he referred to the encouragement he derived from the certainty of his final perseverance. He also spoke of the way in which the doctrines of election and free justification "afford me great confidence in God my Saviour".[24] In a letter sent from Philadelphia in November 1739 Whitefield expressed his gratitude that "God has been pleased to enlighten me more in that comfortable doctrine of *Election*."[25] On some occasions, however, Whitefield didn't seem quite so secure in his commitment to the doctrine. He wrote for example to a "Mr H", urging him in the words of a common Calvinist addage "to make his calling and election sure".[26] He counselled "John F", an orphan, "to come to Jesus by faith, and he shall embrace you in the arms of his mercy".[27] It is clear that Whitefield's concern over Arminianism was that it appeared to make a person a contributor to their own salvation. He wrote that "nothing but the doctrines of the Reformation" could avoid this dilemma.[28]

Whitefield also took strong issue with John Wesley over his teaching of the doctrine of sinless perfection, declaring that he did not expect that indwelling sin will be finished and destroyed this side of the grave. He wrote that he could not give a better answer than the words of an old and venerable Quaker, "Bring me a man that hath really arrived to this, and I will pay his expenses, let him come from where he will."[29] Whitefield felt there was a touch of inconsistency in Wesley's advocacy of perfection and his strong opposition to final perseverance.[30]

Whitefield found it hard to let the matter rest and wrote again to Wesley in November 1740, "I am yet persuaded you greatly err. You have set a mark you will never arrive at, till you come to glory. I think few enjoy such continued manifestations of God's presence as I do, and have done, for some years; but I dare not pretend to say I shall be absolutely perfect."[31] Significantly from the time of this letter the

Methodist revival divided into two main groupings: the Arminians under the Wesleys, and the Calvinists following Whitefield, Harris, and other prominent Welsh leaders. The disputation was harsh and led to the building of separate chapels. However, with the passing of the years both Whitefield and Wesley gradually mellowed and became less entrenched in their views. Some years later Whitefield was able to write in a letter to Wesley that "I rejoice to hear, that you and your brother are more moderate with respect to sinless perfection. Time and experience I believe will convince you, that attaining such a state in this life, is not a doctrine of the everlasting gospel."[32] Although the breach was never healed Whitefield's relationship with the Wesleys was much improved by the time of his death in 1770.

Whitefield had been present at a conference held by "seven true ministers of Jesus Christ, despised Methodists"[33] at Islington on 5 January 1739 where matters of doctrine and practice were still in doubt, but after prayer they were able to settle some issues by use of sacred lot. This was the only recorded instance in which Whitefield took part in the casting of lots. Tyerman cites a letter dated 22 March 1739 in which Whitefield mentioned a colleague by the name of Joseph who refused to submit to a lot as to whether he should return with Whitefield to England.[34] Whitefield had told him that if he refused his request he would never return to America but it is clear from the rest of letter that he harboured doubts as to whether he should have tried to make him submit to guidance by lot. By the close of the following year his doubts about the practice had further increased. In "A Letter to Some Church Members of the Presbyterian Persuasion" he wrote, "I am no friend to casting lots; but I believe, on extraordinary occasions, when things can be determined no other way, God, if appealed to, and waited on by prayer and fasting will answer by lot now, as well as formerly."[35] We also see Whitefield being strongly critical of Wesley's practice of casting lots with sacred dice, which he held to be "tempting the Lord".[36] Finally, in June 1748, we find him writing, "Casting lots, I do not now approve of, nor have I for several years; neither do I think it a safe way (though practised, I doubt not, by many good men) to make a lottery of the Scriptures, by dipping into them upon every occasion."[37] This latter practice involved praying for God's overruling and then opening the Bible and randomly without looking placing a finger on the page and seeing if the verse on which it landed offered any form of guidance.

Calvin's teaching was often in Whitefield's thoughts. He drew particular encouragement from Beza's *Life of Calvin*, which he read in the spring of 1741.[38] He declared shortly afterwards that "Calvin's example has been very much pressed upon me." He continued, "As we are of Calvinistical principles, I trust we shall in this respect imitate Calvin's practice, and shew all meekness to those who may oppose us."[39] He was clear that he had embraced Calvin's doctrine not because of Calvin, but because he believed that Jesus himself had taught him.[40] Despite being criticized by the Bishop of London for "reviving the old Calvinistical disputes concerning predestination, &c.", Whitefield defended himself by saying that this was simply "reviving the essential articles of the Church of England, which undoubtedly are Calvinistical".[41] Summarizing his teaching Whitefield asserted that "the principles which I maintain, are purely Scriptural, and in every way agreeable to the church of England articles".[42] He did agree with Wesley, it should be said, "in giving an universal offer to all poor sinners that will come and taste of the water of life".[43]

Whitefield's heart also lay with the early Puritans on both sides of the Atlantic. He wrote in 1741 to the Boston Congregational minister, Charles Chauncy (1705–87), "May you live to see the Spirit of scriptural Puritanism universally prevail."[44] In an address to the president, professors, and tutors at Harvard College Whitefield professed that he was "a Calvinist as to principle" and that he preached "no other doctrines than those which the [puritan] founders of Harvard College had preached long before he was born".[45] Whitefield was of the view that "the more the revival the more Puritan works are needed".[46] This conviction was probably because he recognized their solid biblical teaching was vital in order to underpin the revival. Among the Puritan writings which he published were a two-volume edition of Bunyan's works and John Foxe's, A *Sermon on Christ Crucified*.

The Scriptures

Following in the faith of both the Protestant Reformers and Puritans Whitefield's teaching was rooted in the Scriptures. He held to the inerrancy of Scripture and adhered to the Reformation assertions of Scripture alone, Christ alone, faith alone, and God's glory alone. Whitefield held the biblical books to be "written by holy men of God as they were moved by the Holy Ghost".[47] Yet when it came to interpreting the text Whitefield was aware of the importance of the context. He recognized that the Gospel of John had been "written to confound the heresy of Ebion and Cerinthus" and therefore the apostle "took all opportunities of proving, that Jesus was very God of very God".[48] He began his sermon on *The Marriage of Cana* by stating that "the chief end St John had in view when he wrote his gospel, was to prove the divinity of Jesus Christ, that the Word, (who not only was from everlasting with God, but also was really God blessed forevermore)."[49] Together with the deity of Christ Whitefield held the virgin birth, the atoning death, literal resurrection, ascension, and return of Christ as non-negotiable essentials of the Christian faith. In fact the return of Christ and future hope became Whitefield's increasing comfort in his later years. In a letter to Robert Keen in July 1765 he wrote, "I hope ere long, to have a more sudden transition into a better country. Come Lord Jesus, come quickly."[50] This particular plea referred not to the return of Christ but rather expressed hope for death and subsequent experience of a heaven without pain and suffering.

Whitefield's core doctrines

Christology

In *A Second Letter to the Right Reverend the Bishop of London* written in August 1744 Whitefield made it clear that both he and his fellow Methodists "instil into people's minds wherever they go *the great doctrines of the reformation, Homilies* and *Articles* of the church".[51] Whitefield had a high Christology and was able to explain very simply that Jesus was "truly God" and indeed God and man in one being; that God and man might be able to come together.[52] On the other hand, if the situation demanded it, he could explain his faith in Christ in more complex theological terms. In a sermon on the presence of Christ in the believer based on 2 Corinthians 13:5 he said:

> My brethren, JESUS CHRIST is coequal, coessential, coeternal, and consubstantial with the Father, very God of very God; and as there was not a moment of time in which God the Father was not, so there was not a moment of time in which God the Son was not.[53]

In this Whitefield was clearly using the arguments in support of Jesus' deity that were put forward by Athanasius and his supporters at the Council of Nicaea in AD 325. In fact Whitefield went on in this sermon to warn of the dangers of the Arians who denied the godhead of Christ, and esteemed him as "a creature and subordinate God".

If they had only humbly searched the Scriptures "they would have found divine homage was paid to Christ" and that "he shall be called mighty God, the everlasting Father", and the government will be "on his shoulders". In his sermon, *Christ the only Preservative against a Reprobate Spirit*, Whitefield spoke of the heterodox views of Jesus put forward by the Socinians who held Jesus "solely as a good man sent from God, to show the people the way they should go". They regarded the death of Jesus not as a sacrifice for sin but as "an example to the world".[54] In his sermon *What Think Ye of Christ?* Whitefield was adamant "that an Arian or Socinian cannot be a Christian". The Arians, he pointed out, would have us believe that Jesus Christ is only a created God, which is self-contradictory. The Socinians who held that Jesus was merely a good man "failed to recognise his death as an atonement for the sins of the world".[55] He went on to press home his argument that if Jesus was not truly God he must have been the vilest sinner that ever appeared in the world since he accepted divine worship from the man who had been born blind.[56]

Whitefield constantly reminded people of the full divinity of Jesus by referring to him, as we have seen, in a very many of his letters as "Our glorious Emmanuel". He was a firm believer in the return of Christ at the end of the age but unlike some revivalists he did not attempt to speculate on matters of time or seasons "which the Father hath put in his own power".[57]

Baptism

Baptism, for Whitefield, was a matter of indifference. He regarded the mode in which it was conducted as something which Christians should not "fall into disputing about".[58] There are a number of references in his journal and letters to his baptizing young children, including his own son. He did not hold to the doctrine of baptismal regeneration held by many in the High Church Party. In Chapter

2, we noted that when he arrived in Georgia in June 1738 he immediately gained favour by performing the office by "sprinkling" as opposed to "dipping".[59] This latter practice which Wesley had insisted on had created great dissatisfaction and some had even refused the sacrament for that reason.

Whitefield seems to have enjoyed good relationships with the Baptists. In England he had come to a gradual acceptance of them, while in America he had warmed to them more quickly. He preached in the Baptist meeting house at Ashley Ferry near Charleston and a short time later incurred the wrath of Secretary Stephens for allowing Mr Tilly, "a serious and lively Baptist minister", to preach in his Savannah parish church.[60] It seems he also held Mr Jones, a Philadelphia Baptist minister, in high regard.[61]

Justification

As is noted earlier in this chapter the doctrine of justification lay at the centre of Whitefield's preaching and teaching. He taught we are justified "meritoriously by the blood of Christ, instrumentally by the faith of Christ and declaratively by our good works".[62] On board a ship bound for America on Sunday 5 February 1738 he preached his sermon on justification to the officers and men in the great cabin.[63] Three years later he emphasized in a letter to "D—A—" (probably Daniel Abbot of London) that "in the Lord alone, and not in myself, have I complete righteousness and strength".[64] In his defence of *The Conduct and Behaviour of a certain Sect usually distinguished by the Name of Methodists* Whitefield supported his earlier stated view to the Bishop of London and several episcopal colleagues that the Church of England is "a leaky, sinking ship". The reason for this, he asserted, was that a number of the bishops, including "my Lord of London" were "openly pleading for good works being a condition of our justification". He therefore urged in response that justification by faith alone is "the grand point of contention between the generality of the established clergy, and the Methodist preachers". He emphasized that Methodists plead for "free justification by faith alone" and "the imputed righteousness of Jesus Christ". He then pointed out to the bishop that "Free justification was first enjoined by King Henry VIII and then established by King Edward VI and Queen Elizabeth by acts of Parliament." He was emphatic that justification is the only immediate cause and means of our peace with God and "the chief means to discover and suppress the Romish antichrist, popery, &c. and all other superstitious, sects, errors and schisms out of our land".[65]

In this defence of justification by faith alone it is abundantly clear that Whitefield was deeply attached to the faith and writings of the Protestant Reformers. He supported his arguments with a sound knowledge of Reformation history and pointed out to the bishop that this was the doctrine "for which the glorious martyrs of the Church of England burnt in Smithfield". In a second letter to Bishop Edmund Gibson penned in August 1744 Whitefield pointed out that if we are justified by faith alone "a careful and sincere observance of moral duties cannot be a condition of our acceptance with God, and our being justified in his sight."[66]

For Whitefield justification was rooted in the cross. Justification was being declared right through having trusted in the sacrificial death of Christ. In defence of the early Methodists Whitefield wrote, "Our church... says, that true faith is a "sure trust and confidence in God, that by the merits of CHRIST, his sins are forgiven, and he reconciled to God'."[67] It concerned him that London clergy too readily shunned the cross and were not bold for God.[68] Regarding the benefits of justification Whitefield was clear that "all believers are actually delivered from the guilt of both actual and original sin, from the power of their corruption here, and that at the hour of death they shall be delivered from the very inbeing of sin, and be admitted to the glorious Jesus, and the spirits of just men made perfect, hereafter."[69]

The Holy Spirit

Along with the Wesleys and other early Methodists the Holy Spirit was at the centre of Whitefield's own personal life and all of his preaching and teaching. He spoke of the Spirit in his sermon on the subject as "the third person in the ever-blessed Trinity, consubstantial and co-eternal with the Father and the Son, proceeding from them both, yet equal to them both".[70] Whitefield was insistent that the Christian believer should have the witness of God's Spirit with their spirits that they are his children. "Beg God," he wrote to a dear friend, "that you may feel his spirit working mightily in your soul, and witnessing with your spirit that you are a child of God."[71] In many Dissenting communities in the early decades of the eighteenth century conversion tended to be seen as intellectual assent to biblical doctrine. For Whitefield and the Wesleys, however, it was the note of assurance stemming from the Holy Spirit's presence in the believer, which was the all-important aspect. Whitefield was constant in his preaching and teaching that this indwelling and inward witness of the Spirit was the privilege of every Christian believer. He pointed doubters to the words spoken by Jesus shortly before his passion that those who believed in him "should experience rivers of living waters flowing from their innermost beings".[72] Writing to Lady Fanny Shirley in August 1749 Whitefield exclaimed, "Alas! To what a heaven they are strangers, who deny the influence of the Blessed Spirit, and cry down the felt and abiding joys of the Holy Ghost as fancy, enthusiasm and delusion."[73]

Despite the attempts of the Bishop of London to vilify him as an enthusiast, Whitefield stated that "I never did pretend to extraordinary operations of working of miracles, or speaking with tongues, in testimony that my mission and doctrine were from God." He was clear that he only laid claim to what he termed the ordinary gifts and influences of the Spirit.[74] He turned the tables on those clergy who fed their congregations "only with the dry husks of dead morality" and denied them the blessings of the Spirit of God. Such, he declared "are the bane of the Church of England".[75]

The new birth

At some point during the summer of 1737 Whitefield was prevailed upon to print his sermon *On the Nature and Necessity of the New Birth in Christ Jesus*, which had been used to bring about revival in London, Bristol, Gloucester, and Gloucestershire. Whitefield found that Dissenters were surprised to discover a sermon on this subject from a Church of England clergyman. It sold widely to people from all denominations in both England and overseas.[76] To those clergy who objected to people professing to experience an instantaneous new birth Whitefield reminded them that many of their number held to the doctrine of an instantaneous baptismal regeneration.[77] At the time Whitefield began his ministry the doctrine of the new birth was largely neglected or denied. By the time of his death it was increasingly accepted in the Protestant world.

Ecclesiology and church government

Whitefield was clear from the start of his ministry that there was no form of church government outlined in Scripture that excluded a toleration of all other forms of polity.[78] His view was that some things might be wrong with the Church of England but that in this life we can never expect to see a perfect church or a perfect man. It was therefore his practice not to quarrel or dispute on minor issues of practice.[79] In a word to those who supported his preaching in America Whitefield wrote, "whether Conformists, or

Nonconformists, our main concern should be, to be assured that we are called and taught of God".[80] In his dealings with the Associate Presbytery in Scotland in January 1740 Whitefield objected to their insistence on the Presbyterian system of government, exclusive of all other ways of worshipping God. He informed them that though he professed to be a minister of the Church of England he was of a "catholic spirit" and that "if he met with a person who loves the Lord Jesus in sincerity it would be of no great concern as to what communion he belonged to".[81] In the summer of 1741 he wrote again, urging them "not to trouble yourself or me in writing about the corruptions of the Church of England".[82]

Whitefield's ecclesiology wasn't confined to national churches or the major denominations. He increasingly found his heart "more and more enlarged to and more disposed to love and honour all denominations of believers".[83] It is clear that both he and Wesley believed their societies, and indeed those of the Moravians, were expressions of the church. On a number of occasions Whitefield celebrated the sacrament in private homes. He wrote from Philadelphia to "dear brother K", inquiring "how is it with you, and the church in your house. I believe though it is but a little flock, yet it will be our heavenly Father's good pleasure to give you the kingdom. How happy it is, when all are of one mind in a house; all agreed to entertain and love the Lord Jesus."[84] He wrote to a friend in Boston in July 1741 that he rejoiced that a church was about to come into being in his house.[85] In October the same year he wrote to Lord Melville rejoicing that one day he would perhaps see a church in the Melville house.[86]

The final state

Both the dangers of hell and the blessings of heaven were present in Whitefield's message. He was very ready to warn people of the dangers of hell and wrath to come to the ungodly. In June 1738 he invited a person from his parish in Georgia to breakfast with him. This man had been denying the eternity of hell's torments to come and Whitefield challenged him as to whether he believed in the everlasting punishment. The man replied that he believed wicked men would be annihilated and Whitefield challenged him on the basis of the twelfth article of the Creed regarding everlasting life. The man, however, could not be persuaded, despite Whitefield reading to him a passage from the book of Revelation.[87]

In May 1740 Whitefield put together a plain and straightforward creed for the Allegany Indians. The final section addressed Christ's return and the final judgment, after which "he that shall believe in Christ, and hath shewn forth his faith by his works, shall be saved; he that hath not believed in Christ, shall be damned for ever, and be cast into the lake of fire and brimstone".[88] The warning of hell is evident in Whitefield's sermon entitled *The Indwelling of the Spirit, the Common Privilege of all Believers*, in which he warned that when you hear Jesus say "to all that are not born again of God, 'Depart from me, ye cursed, into everlasting fire, prepared for the devil and his angels,' do not your hearts sink within you, with a secret horror?"[89] In his sermon *The Eternity of Hell-Torments* he pressed home the seriousness of everlasting punishment: "If the torments reserved for the wicked hereafter are eternal, then let this serve as a caution to such persons." He further supported the eternal nature of punishment in hell, pointing out that since God rewards his saints with everlasting happiness he will "punish sinners with eternal misery". He also added that the torments of the wicked are eternal because the devil's punishment is also eternal.[90]

In contrast to the dangers of hell Whitefield frequently found comfort "that after a short fermentation in the grave our earthly bodies will be fashioned unto Christ's glorious body".[91] In his the last years of his ministry, when his health was broken, he frequently mentioned how much he looked forward to the rest and transformations of heaven. In his sermon on *Walking with God* he spoke of the ways in which, after death, "the spirits of those who walked with God, shall return to God that gave them" and that "at the morning of the resurrection, soul and body shall ever be with the Lord". He was clear that believers' resurrection bodies will be like Christ's glorious body and their souls filled with the fullness of God's presence.[92]

Whitefield the churchman

Beginning in his teenage years when he first attended the sacrament in Gloucester Cathedral Whitefield came to have a strong attachment to the Church of England. Like Wesley he was adamant that he would never leave the established church. He encouraged the members of the Methodist societies he founded to attend Holy Communion in their nearest parish church. Whitefield greatly valued his ordination and was conscious that he had received an anointing when the bishop laid his hands upon him. On a number of occasions he spoke of having had an apostolic commission by virtue of his being an Anglican clergyman.

He was always quick to fly his establishment colours when addressing a bishop. A typical instance of this was his reply in defence of his field preaching to the Bishop of Bangor in February 1756. He began his lengthy six-folio letter to the reverend prelate stating in the words of the Prayer Book liturgy that in "fear of him to whom all hearts are open, all desires known, and from whom no secrets are hid, I desire now to sit down and give your Lordship an explicit answer". To the bishop's accusation that he had broken the canon, which said that "neither minister or church wardens, nor any other officers of the church, shall suffer any man to preach within their chapels, but such as shewing their licence to preach",

Whitefield made a robust response. He pointed out that when he applied to the Bishop of London for a license, he was pleased to say, "I was going to Georgia, and needed none." He contended that his preaching in the fields was not prescribed by the terms of the canon and reminded the bishop that "he was episcopally ordained and had very lately published a small tract (which I humbly beg your Lordship's acceptance of) on purpose to recommend the communion office of the Church of England".[93]

Whitefield had a correspondingly sacramental understanding of Communion which he often referred to in somewhat Catholic terms as "the blessed sacrament". When it came to the presence of Christ in the Eucharist, as he sometimes spoke of it, he held to Cranmer's teaching. Following the archbishop he taught that there is a spiritual feeding which takes place as the believer eats and drinks in faith, and which hopefully continues beyond the service and the walls of the church. Whitefield had a strong sense of the presence of Christ in the sacrament and maintained the Church of England view that "if we receive the sacrament worthily, we are one with Christ, and Christ with us: we dwell in Christ and He in us."[94]

As soon as Whitefield was ordained a deacon, although he was not legally allowed to lead a Communion service, it was his delight to assist in distributing the elements. This is evident from a number of references in his journal. In June 1737, for example, he was invited to preach at St Ann's and Forster Lane churches in the City of London at six o'clock in the morning and to assist in "administering the holy sacrament". He reported that "so many came we were obliged to consecrate fresh elements two or three times".[95] His journal for Sunday 28 January 1739 reads, "Received the Sacrament at Crooked Lane... I found I received Christ and fed on him in my heart by faith with thanksgiving." In his journal entry for 26 April 1739 he wrote, "Assisted in administering the

Blessed Sacrament at Islington, where the vicar in conformity to the rubric, takes care to observe the octaves of Easter."[96] Later in May Whitefield noted, "Went with our brethren from Fetter Lane Society to St Paul's and received the Holy Sacrament, as a testimony that we adhered to the Church of England"[97] and on Sunday 12 August 1739, "assisted Mr Piers in administering of the blessed Sacrament, in his own church, to nearly six hundred communicants".[98] During the voyage to America, which began two days later, Whitefield recorded that on nine Sundays he administered the sacrament in his cabin early in the day. Later on each occasion he seems to have read Morning Prayer and expounded the Scriptures to the sailors.[99]

Whitefield was not so wedded to the Church of England discipline that he was unable to share Communion with others who were outside her walls. While he was at Charleston, for instance in August 1740, he administered the sacrament in a private house and reported "Baptists, Church folks, and Presbyterians, all joined together, and received according to the Church of England, except two, who desired to have it sitting: I willingly complied knowing that it was a thing quite indifferent." Many were moved to tears and requested Whitefield to hold another sacrament on the following day and he was glad to respond to their request.[100]

When Whitefield first reached his parish in Savannah he immediately followed the Church of England best practice of house-to-house visiting and reading prayers and expounding the readings. He also set about catechizing the servants at seven in the evening on Sundays.[101] In defence of his preaching to the bishop of London Whitefield stated that "My constant way of preaching is, first, to prove my propositions by scripture, and then illustrate them by the articles and collects of the Church of England. Those that have heard me, can witness, how, how often I have exhorted them to be constant at the public service of the church."[102]

In defending himself to the bishop of Bangor who had objected to his preaching in a London chapel Whitefield robustly defended himself with his Anglican credentials. He had, he said, been ordained for twenty years and as thousands could testify had "conscientiously defended her homilies and articles, and upon all occasions spoken well of her liturgy". He went on to inform "his Lordship" that without ever having received any payment from the Church of England he would "continue to use her liturgy, where ever a church or chapel is allowed me, and preach up her articles, and enforce her homilies". He further stated that he would never leave the established church and would continue to adhere to her doctrines to his dying day.[103]

On a number of occasions Whitefield found it necessary to defend the preaching and teaching of the Methodists. The heart of his defence in all these cases was the fact that Methodists kept always to the doctrines and teaching of Cranmer and the English Reformers who had produced the Articles of Religion, the Prayer Book liturgies and the Book of Homilies. The Methodist itinerants, he declared in a second letter to the Bishop of London, "continue to this day, witnessing to small and great the grand doctrines of the Reformation, justification by faith alone in the imputed righteousness of Jesus Christ, and the necessity of the indwelling Spirit in order to make them meet to be partakers of the heavenly inheritance." Whitefield asserted that "the Methodists in general, are members of the Established Church".[104] He defended his Methodist followers stating "we are willing to frequent the church, and receive the holy sacrament, if the clergy give us leave". He was also happy for this even when the clergy were seemingly unregenerate because Article 26 stated that the grace of the sacraments is not taken away on account of the unworthiness of the clergy.[105]

In the course of a correspondence with the Revd Dr David Durell (1728–75), the vice-chancellor of the University of Oxford,

Whitefield summed up his convictions stating, "Our English liturgy is, without doubt, one of the most excellent established forms of public prayer in the world."[106] It was indeed almost his daily reading alongside the Scriptures. It formed a vital part of his private devotions and his ministry even in the midst of times of great awakening in both England and America.

In summary, it is clear that the tenor of Whitefield's theology was set at the time of his undergraduate studies at Pembroke College and his membership of the Oxford Holy Club. He was greatly influenced by the writings of Law and Francke and the importance of following an ordered and disciplined spirituality. His ordination was clearly a sacramental event in which he experienced a divine presence. This helped to anchor his doctrine to the teachings of the Articles of Religion and the Book of Common Prayer. His Anglicanism became increasingly that of the Protestant Evangelicalism of Cranmer, the magisterial Reformers and Calvin in particular. As has been noted, he staunchly adhered to Calvin's teaching on double predestination, limited atonement, and everlasting punishment. Despite his many close friendships with Dissenters in both Britain and the American colonies Whitefield always declared his theology was that of the Church of England.

Chapter 11 notes

1 *Letter to the Rev. Mr. H—*, 21 June 1750.
2 W. Law, *A Serious Call to a Devout and Holy Life* (London, Griffith, Farran, Browne & Co, undated), pp. 242–43.
3 Ibid.
4 *Journal*, about the middle of November, 1736, p. 79.
5 Whitefield, *A Short Account*, Section 3, p. 20.
6 Ibid. The authors who influenced Whitefield were Joseph Alleine (1634–68); Richard Baxter (1615–91); William Birkitt (1650–1703); Matthew Henry (1662–1714).
7 *Letter to Mr H—*, 5 November 1736.
8 Whitefield, *A Short Account*, Section 3.
9 *Letter to Mr C—*, 26 March 1754;

10 *Letter to My Dear Friend*, 3 April 1754.

11 Whitefield, *Letter to Mr B—*, 1 November 1755.

12 Whitefield *Letter to Mr—*, 16 August 1739.

13 H. D. Rack, *Reasonable Enthusiast*, p. 199.

14 See J. Telford, *Life of Wesley*, pp. 140–41; H. D. Rack, op. cit., pp. 198–201.

15 See W. S. Winthrop, *Religion in America*, p. 69; also L. Tyerman, *Life*, Vol.1, pp. 274–75.

16 Taken from *A letter to the Rev. Mr. John Wesley in Answer to His Sermon entitled Free Grace*, 1740, contained as Appendix III in Whitefield's *Journals* (London, The Banner of Truth Trust, 1965), p. 581.

17 *A Letter to the Rev. Mr John Wesley*, p. 581.

18 Ibid, p. 583.

19 Ibid, 25 June 1740.

20 Ibid, 25 August 1740.

21 Ibid.

22 All citations taken from Whitefield, *A letter to the Rev. John Wesley*.

23 H. D. Rack, op. cit., p. 200.

24 *Letters to Rev and Dear Sir*, 10 November 1739.

25 *Letter to Mr H—*, 10 November 1739.

26 Ibid, 28 November 1739.

27 *Letter to John F—, an orphan*, 27 July 1741.

28 *Letter to the Rev. Mr. P—*, 10 November 1739.

29 *A Letter to the Rev. John Wesley*, 25 September 1740.

30 Ibid.

31 Ibid, 9 November 1740.

32 Ibid, 11 September 1747.

33 Ibid, 5 January 1739.

34 *Letter from Bristol*, 22 March 1739, in L. Tyerman, op. cit., Vol. 1, p. 193.

35 *A Letter to Some Church Members of the Presbyterian Persuasion in answer to certain Scruples lately proposed, in proper Queries raised on each Remark*, 1 November 1740, *Works*, Vol. 4, p. 48.

36 *Letter to John Wesley*, 24 December 1740 in Whitefield's *Journal*, p. 572.

37 *Letter to Reverend Sir—*, 24 June 1748, *Works*, Vol. 4, p. 244.

38 *Letter to Mr J— H—*, 25 March 1741.

39 *Letter to Mr F—*, 22 September 1742.

40 *Letter to the Rev. Dr. C—*, 24 September 1742.

41 Whitefield, *An Answer to the First Part of an Anonymous Pamphlet, entitled, "Observations upon the Conduct and Behaviour of a certain Sect usually distinguished by the Name of Methodists" in a Letter to the Right Reverend the Bishop of London, and the other Right Reverend the Bishops concerned in the Publication thereof, Works*, Vol. 4, p. 115.

42 *Letter to Mr D—*, 10 November 1739.

43 *Letter to the Rev. John Wesley*, 11 September 1747.

44 *Letter to the Rev. Mr. Charles Chauncy*, 16 January 1741.

45 *A Letter to the Rev. the President, and Professors, Tutors and the Hebrew*

Instructor, of Harvard College in Cambridge in answer to a Testimony Published against the Reverend Mr George Whitefield and his Conduct, Works, Vol. 4, p. 225.

46 Lambert, F., op. cit., p. 145.

47 Whitefield, *The Duty of Searching the Scriptures, Sermons of George Whitefield*, p. 197. See also 2 Peter 1:21.

48 Whitefield, *Observations on Select Passages of Scripture Turned into Catechetical Questions, Begun, 12 March 1738, Works*, Vol. 4, p. 349.

49 Whitefield, Sermon, *The Marriage of Cana* (Peabody, Hendrickson Publishers, 2009), p. 185.

50 *Letter to Robert Keen*, 12 July 1765.

51 *A Second Letter to the Right Reverend the Bishop of London*, 25 August 1744.

52 *Letter to the Allegany Indians*, 21 May 1740.

53 *Christ the Only Preservative Against a Reprobate Spirit*, Sermon, *Works*, Vol. 6., p. 293.

54 Ibid.

55 Whitefield, *What Think Ye of Christ?*, Sermon, *Works*, Vol. 5, p. 357.

56 Ibid.

57 *Letter to My dear Brethren in Christ*, 12 June 1739. See Acts 1:7.

58 *Letter to the Rev. Mr. O——*, 27 May 1742.

59 *Collections of the Georgia Historical Society, The Journal of Secretary Stephens*, supplement to Vol. 4, entry for 18 June, cited in A. Dallimore, op. cit., Vol. 1, p. 203.

60 A. Dallimore, op. cit., vol. 1, p. 522.

61 *Journal,* 8 May 1740.

62 R. Elliot, *A Summary of Gospel Doctrine taught by George Whitefield* (London, Banner of Truth Trust, 1959), p. 37.

63 *Journal,* 5 February 1738.

64 *Letter to D——A——*, 16 May 1741.

65 Whitefield, *An Answer to The First Part of an Anonymous Pamphlet, entitled, "Observations upon the Conduct and Behaviour of a certain Sect usually distinguished by the Name of Methodists in a Letter to the Right Reverend the Bishop of London, and the Right Reverend the Bishops concerned in the Publication thereof, Works*, Vol. 4, p. 116.

66 *A Second Letter to the Right Reverend the Bishop of London*, 25 August 1744.

67 Whitefield, *Remarks on a Pamphlet entitled The Enthusiasm of Methodists and Papists Compared, Works*, Vol. 4, p. 37.

68 *Letter to Mr R——*, 26 July 1741.

69 *Letter to Mr B——*, 29 June 1750.

70 Whitefield, *The Indwelling of the Spirit, the Common Privilege of all Believers*, Sermon XXXVIII, *Works*, Vol. 6, p. 91.

71 *Letter to Mrs——*, 10 November 1739.

72 Whitefield, *Some Remarks Upon a late Charge against Enthusiasm Delivered by The Right Reverend Father in God, Richard, Lord Bishop of Lichfield and Coventry, Works*, Vol. 4, p. 188.

73 *Letter to Lady Fanny Shirley*, 26 August 1749.
74 Whitefield, *Answer to the Bishop of London's Last Pastoral Letter*, *Works*, Vol. 4, p. 9.
75 Whitefield, *The Indwelling of the Spirit, the Common Privilege of all Believers*, Sermon XXXVIII, *Works*, Vol. 6, p. 95.
76 Whitefield, *A Further Account*, Section 3.
77 *A Second Letter to the Right Reverend the Bishop of London*, 25 August 1744.
78 *Letter to Mr D—E—*, 13 August,1741.
79 *Letter to Mr S—M—*, 26 May 1742.
80 *Letter to My dear Brethren in Christ*, 10 November 1739.
81 *Letter to Reverend and dear Sir*, 16 January 1740.
82 *Letter to the Rev. Mr. W—*, 10 August 1741.
83 *Letter to Mr J—B—*, 27 May 1742.
84 *Letter to the Rev. Mr. K—*, 10 November 1739.
85 *Letter to Mr E—D—*, 26 July 1741.
86 *Letter to Lord Melville*, 26 October 1741.
87 *Journal*, 5 June 1738.
88 *Letter to the Allegany Indians*, 21 May 1740.
89 Whitefield, *The Indwelling of the Spirit, the common Privilege of all Believers*, Sermon XXXVIII, *Works*, Vol. 6, p. 98.
90 Whitefield, *The Eternity of Hell-Torments*, Sermon, *Works*, Vol. 5, p. 392.
91 *Letter to Mr P—*, 6 October 1747.
92 Whitefield, *Walking with God*, Sermon II, *Works*, Vol. 5, p. 35.
93 *Letter to Bishop of Bangor*, 16 February 1756.
94 Whitefield, *Answer to the Bishop of London's Last Pastoral Letter*, *Works*, Vol. 4, p. 8.
95 *Journal*, 21 June 1737.
96 Ibid, 12 August 1739.
97 Ibid, 20 May 1739.
98 Ibid, 12 August 1739.
99 See *Journal*, 19, 26 August; 2, 9, 16, 29 and 30 September 1739.
100 Ibid, 25 August 1740.
101 *Letter to Mr H—*, 10 June 1738.
102 Whitefield, *Answer to the Bishop of London's Last Pastoral Letter*, *Works*, Vol. 4, p. 10.
103 *Letter to the Bishop of Bangor*, 16 February 1756.
104 *Letter to the Right Reverend the Bishop of London*, March 1744, *Works*, Vol. 4, pp. 132.
105 Whitefield, *An Answer to the First Part of an Anonymous Pamphlet*, *Works*, Vol. 4, pp. 118–19.
106 Whitefield, *A Letter to the Reverend Dr Durell, Vice-Chancellor of the University of Oxford*, *Works*, Vol. 4, p. 316. Durell was installed as vice-chancellor of the University of Oxford in 1765.

Chapter 12

A Fervent Spirituality

By any standards Whitefield was one of the world's most remarkable and influential preachers and it is important now to consider the spirituality which fuelled his extraordinary life. There has been a divergence of opinion regarding the meaning and scope of the term "spirituality". James Gordon, in his book *Evangelical Spirituality*, observed that the word is frequently taken to denote "those attitudes, beliefs and practices which animate people's lives and help them to reach out towards super-sensible realities".[1] With a specific focus on Christian spirituality, Gordon emphasized that it concerns "both the interior life of the inward person" and "the implementation of the commandments of Christ, to love God and our neighbour".[2] Alister McGrath drew a distinction between the general use of the term "spirituality" which is about "the spirit" that motivates someone, and "Christian spirituality", which he defined as "the quest for a fulfilled and authentic Christian existence, involving the bringing together of the fundamental ideas of Christianity and the whole experience of living on the basis of and within the scope of the Christian faith".[3] In a further sentence he sharpened this a little stating that it "refers to the way in which the Christian life is understood, and the explicitly devotional practices which have been developed to foster and sustain that relationship with Christ".[4] Linda Wilson, in her pioneering study of nineteenth-century English Nonconformist female spirituality used the term in a similar way stating that it can refer to both "the way in which a person develops his or her relationship with God, and the outworking of that in his or her life, both public and private".[5] It is in this way that this chapter considers Whitefield's spirituality.

Methodism

Clearly, as Gillies and others have pointed out, the foundations of Whitefield's spirituality were laid when he joined with the Methodists at Oxford. He very soon began to live out his days by the rule adopted by the Wesleys and the members of their Holy Club. Whitefield and his companions sought to sustain their rule by keeping diaries. In his manuscript diary we see how he carefully charted his eating and drinking, his confession of known sins, time spent in public and private prayer, his "lectio divina", his discipline in study, and religious conversation.[6] Importantly also, he received the Communion every sabbath, visited the sick and prisoners in the city's gaol, and read to the poor.[7] Following his ordination this strict routine continued, Whitefield dividing his day into three parts. As we have already seen, Whitefield divided his day into three lots of eight hours. Whitefield's heartfelt devotion to Christ and self-discipline drew on the practices of the sixteenth- and seventeenth-century Reformers. In his manuscript diary he frequently lists his faults. For instance on 19 March 1736 he recorded, "I have been to-day in great disorder. Dull sleepless almost all nt [night]. Dejected in the morn[ing] no comfortable communion in God. Almost all I a[m] is disordered both in body and mind."[8] In another entry the following month he wrote, "Lay abed an hour too long. God for Christ's sake forgive me. I had a very odd dream. I fear the devil kept me asleep."[9] He lived simply almost to the point of destitution at times in his early days. He fasted and practised self-denial and demonstrated his faith with compassionate and loving good works. And as we have seen, he increasingly inveighed against the theatre, dancing, games of chance, taverns, and extravagance of dress.

Hindmarsh, in a chapter entitled, "Whitefield and the Emergence of Evangelical Devotion" underlined the fact that "Oxford Methodism also had obvious affinities with Puritanism". It was this that led the young undergraduate to read Joseph Alleine's *Alarm to the Unconverted*, Richard Baxter's *Call to the Unconverted*, and other later Puritan works. Shrewdly Whitefield noted in his manuscript diary, "I find I must not go too far in the dissenting books without balance, than those of our own Church."[10] Later, following his travels in America and Scotland in particular, as Hindmarsh, Dallimore, and others have pointed out, he became increasingly drawn to the writings of the Protestant Reformers and the early seventeenth-century Puritans.

Prayer

Skevington Wood wrote that "following his conversion prayer became Whitefield's vital breath and his native air". Indeed, Whitefield wrote shortly after the momentous event, "Oh, what sweet communion had I daily vouchsafed with God in prayer! How often have I been carried out beyond myself when sweetly meditating in the fields!"[11] In one of his sermons he said, "I have prayed a thousand times till the sweat dropped from my face like rain, that God in His Infinite mercy would not let me enter the Church before he thrust me forth in His work."[12]

Writing to a Mrs H in December 1737 Whitefield noted that "On Wednesday night eighteen of us continued all night in praises, and praying for you and our other friends."[13] Whitefield, as we have seen, was a strong advocate of extempore prayer in private devotion but also in society meetings and at major public occasions. He noted in his journal of 29 October 1740 that "when the spirit of prayer began to be lost then forms were invented". In an answer to the Bishop of London who regarded extempore prayer as a mark of "enthusiasm", Whitefield wrote that "the spirit of God does assist true Christians to pray extempore, now, as well as formerly". This, he asserted "is undeniable, if the Scriptures be true".[14]

Early entries in his journal provided glimpses of his determination to make prayer his top priority. "Had a love-feast with the brethren at Fetter Lane," he recorded on 1 January 1739, "and spent the whole night in prayer, psalms and thanksgiving. God supported me without sleep." A week later he jotted, "Had another love-feast, and spent the whole night in prayer and thanksgiving at Fetter Lane."[15]

Fasting

There were times when Whitefield prayed with fasting. These were often times of personal need or days of national and political crisis. In March 1744 Methodists in several Gloucestershire towns and villages suffered mobbing and several incidents of brutal persecution. At Hampton windows were broken, clods of earth were thrown, and women pulled by their hair and roughly treated. Whitefield and others took the matter to court. In an account published after the assize held in Gloucester he wrote, "Being aware of the great consequences of gaining or losing this trial, both in respect to us and the nation, we kept a day of fasting and prayer through all the societies, both in England and Wales."[16]

Faith, imagination, and thanksgiving

Whitefield spent much time on his own in secret prayer and before any major preaching it was his practice to withdraw from company to call out for divine assistance. His long sea voyages were often times when he devoted himself to praying. Shortly after his arrival back on home soil in 1738 he wrote that while he had been on board the *Whitaker* he "was praying night and day".[17] In a letter to a friend shortly after his arrival in Edinburgh by ship from a visit to London he wrote, "On board, I spent most part of my time in secret prayer."[18] During his thirteen long sea voyages across the Atlantic Whitefield wrote numerous letters, the great majority of which abound with references to people and situations he had at last had the time to pray for. On board a ship bound for America in July 1763 he wrote to a dear friend, "Through mercy I have been surprisingly kept up during the voyage, long but not tedious. Jesus hath made the ship a *Bethel*, and I enjoyed the quietness which I have fought for some years on the shore."[19]

Whitefield believed imagination and a focus on Christ to be significant aids to praying in faith. He urged the importance of endeavouring to visualize the heavens being opened when people pray. "Imagination," he wrote, "will strengthen your faith, excite a holy earnestness in your prayers, and make you wrestle with God."[20] On his arrival back on home soil in November 1738 Whitefield reflected, "God has done for me more abundantly than I could ask or think. The seed of the glorious gospel has taken root in the *American* ground, and, I hope, will grow into a great tree."[21] To a correspondent who had written to him about her fears Whitefield replied, urging her to "look up" to Jesus in faith, for "He will send you help in time of need. Indeed he will never leave you or forsake you."[22]

Another constantly recurring note in Whitefield's life and indeed in his prayer was thanksgiving. His many hundreds of published letters are filled with thankfulness for divine protection particularly from hostile mobsters and for the supply of his many material needs both in England and in America. He was mindful of God's rich material provision for his London chapels, his orphanage in

Savannah, and the needs of the poor and disadvantaged for whom he made frequent collections. He constantly expressed his gratitude to God for protection during his travels at sea and on land, as well as for the outpouring of the Holy Spirit on the lives of the thousands who came to hear his message wherever he went. He was widely reported to be genial, affable, outgoing, and positive. The root of this gracious temperament lay in his constant thankfulness.

The importance of gratitude in his life was clearly seen in a sermon he preached on 17 May 1738 entitled *Thankfulness for Mercies Received, a Necessary Duty*. "Matter for praise and adoration," he wrote, "can never be wanting to creatures redeemed by the blood of the Son of God." Again he stated, "This part of Christian perfection, though begun on earth, will be consummated only in heaven."[23] He also spoke of the "sin of ingratitude" and declared, "there is nothing we ought more earnestly to pray against."[24] It was the apostle Paul who mentioned that "one of the highest crimes of the Gentiles [was] that they were not thankful".[25] In another sermon entitled *The Great Duty of Family Religion*, Whitefield spoke of "the duty of gratitude" that is owed to God.[26]

Singing

Whitefield knew the truth of Augustine's words that "to sing is to pray twice". The value and the power of singing was a powerful reality, which he had learned from reading the writings of William Law.[27] In a letter which he wrote "To my dear friend" on 2 May 1738 while on board the *Whitaker*, Whitefield wrote, "God has been pleased graciously to visit me with a violent fever, which he notwithstanding so sweetened by divine consolations, that I was enabled to rejoice and sing in the midst of it. Indeed, I had many violent conflicts which the powers of darkness, who did all they could to disturb and distract me."[28]

Whitefield often sang as he journeyed between preaching places as well as when in the company of Christian friends. He also encouraged the societies which he formed to come together to pray, share, and sing together.[29] After having preached a sermon in the village of Brinkworth, Wiltshire, in June 1743 he sent a few lines to a close friend stating, "After sermon, I rode to Longley, in company with many dear children of God, who attended me both on horseback and on foot. We sung, and looked like person who had been at a spiritual wedding."[30] In a sermon he entitled *Christ the Only Preservative Against a Reprobate Spirit*, Whitefield urged his hearers "not to be afraid of singing of hymns, or of meeting together to build each other up in the ways of the Lord".[31]

Private and corporate worship

Martin Thornton observed in his classic, *English Spirituality*, "the foundation of Christian life is the liturgy".[32] Worship – both private and public – is clearly the *sine qua non* of all spirituality. Whitefield delighted in both. Whenever he went to towns and cities to preach it was his custom if possible to attend one of the local churches for worship. His first port of call was most often the Church of England if there was a welcome. He delighted in the Church of England liturgy and loved the collects and prayers. The Book of Common Prayer almost became his daily reading. He wrote a preface to a new edition of the Book of the Homilies. It had ten sections with one of the homilies for each preceded by a collect. As we have seen, Whitefield was comfortable with both extempore and written prayers. To the latter end he wrote a short booklet entitled *Prayers on Several Occasions*. There were prayers to say in a variety of different situations. They included "A prayer before Singing of Psalms", "A prayer for a Person in a Storm at Sea", and "A prayer for a Woman, desiring Direction, after an offer of Marriage is made to her".[33]

As has been noted the Eucharist was a very important ingredient of Whitefield's spirituality. In the days when he was a youngster growing up in Gloucester, he was profoundly moved by the presence of Christ during the Communion services in the cathedral. Later, when he was an undergraduate, he joined the members of the Holy Club in their weekly attendance at the sacrament. Their discipline led him to highly value the sacrament throughout the rest of his life.[34] For Whitefield, receiving of the bread and wine was a time when the presence of Christ was both vivid and strong. As soon as he was ordained it was his delight to assist in the distribution of the bread and wine. After his ordination as priest he often presided at Communion services in private homes and churches other than those of his own Church of England. Cranmer's liturgy and doctrine of a spiritual feeding he believed to be the most perfect understanding of the sacrament. In 1755 Whitefield produced a small Communion book entitled *A Communion Morning's Companion*. It had 140 pages and consisted of Bishop Ken's five meditations on Questions and Answers of the Church of England Catechism, the Order for the Administration of the Lord's Supper and fifty-three sacramental hymns. He wrote, "I particularly fixed on Bishop Ken because his sweet meditations on the Redeemer's passion were some of the first things that made a religious impression on my own soul."[35]

Silence and quiet

While it was the case that Whitefield was a "full-on" activist who was constantly on the go, often literally morning, noon, and night, he also knew the value of silence. He wrote to a close friend from Savannah in June 1740 and stressed the importance of making time to be alone and still.

> I have a garden near at hand, where I go particularly
> to meet and talk with my God, at the cool *of every
> day*. I often sit in silence, offering my soul as so
> much clay, to be stamped just as my heavenly potter
> pleases: and whilst I am musing, I am often filled as
> it were with the fullness of God. I am frequently at
> *Calvary*, and frequently at *Mount Tabor*; but always
> assured of my Lord's everlasting love.[36]

In one of several letters to Lord Lothian who had become one of his friends, Whitefield wrote: "Be, therefore, my Lord, much in secret retirement. Commune with your own heart in your chamber, and be still, and you will then hear the secret whisper of the Holy Ghost. As for praying in your family, I entreat you, my Lord not to neglect it."[37]

Scripture

Together with prayer, the daily and frequent reading of the Scriptures was at the heart of Whitefield's spirituality. Searching the Scriptures, he asserted "is a duty incumbent on every private person" since it is "a precept given by our blessed Lord indifferently to all".[38] The Bible was never far from Whitefield's hand. Whenever he had spare moments he opened its pages. Words that he wrote on one particular day applied to his every day, "O what a Blessed book is the Book of God. O it is heavenly manna to my soul. Feed on it, my soul feed on it."[39]

He often read the Scriptures on his knees. His practice was "to look… always for Christ in the Scripture. He is the treasure hid in the field, both of the Old and New Testament." In another paragraph he wrote: "Have Christ, then, always in view when you are reading the word of God." He aimed always to put into practice what he read. Again he urged "in order to search the Scriptures still more effectually, make an application of every thing you read to your own hearts".[40] So deeply and frequently did Whitefield engage with the text of Scripture that a large number of the many hundreds of letters that he sent to his inquirers, friends, and fellow labourers are laced with biblical texts and illustrations. Although most of those who received letters from him were very probably encouraged by his concern, a number of bishops and senior clergy took offence and accused him on this account of being "apostolic" in his speaking and writing.

As well as strongly denouncing unregenerate clergy Whitefield was also critical of those clergy who knew little of Scripture. A constant study of two things, he advised a correspondent, make an able minister of the New Testament: the "book of God, and your own heart".[41] On the evening of the night on which he died Mr Parsons with whom he was lodging "found him reading in the Bible, with Dr Watts's Psalms lying open before him".[42]

In a sermon preached on the very day of Whitefield's death the Revd Jonathan Parsons noted that "Whitefield gave himself to reading the Holy Scriptures, to meditation and prayer; and particularly, he read Mr Henry's Annotations on the Bible, upon his knees before God."[43] Matthew Henry was a Presbyterian minister and author, best known for his six-volume biblical commentary *Exposition of the Old and New Testaments*. The meaning of each verse of each chapter is carefully explained and was therefore a way of growing in spiritual knowledge and godly living. It was widely read by Christian people in the eighteenth century, Whitefield among them.

Reading

Whitefield read widely, and, as we have seen, drew spiritual encouragement from the lives of the magisterial Reformers including Luther, Calvin, and Zwingli. The influence of the nonjuror[44] William Law has already been discussed. So influential was he that in June 1748[45] Whitefield published *Law Gospelised*, which was, in his own words, "An attempt to make Mr Law's Serious Call more useful to the Children of God." Law conveyed much of his spiritual advice through imaginary characters who model the ideal Christian minister, godly woman, tradesman, and other domestic occupations or roles. In this way we meet with Eusebius, who not only knows the doctrines of grace, receives the blessed sacrament once a month, and sometimes prays extempore, but also "buys books of devotion"![46]

In chapter II the reader encounters Miranda. For her,

> Books of devotion, and especially such as enter into the heart of religion, and describe the inward holiness of the Christian life, have such a large place in her closet, that she is sometimes afraid that she lays out too much money in them, because she cannot forbear buying all the practical books of any note.[47]

In a letter to a fellow clergyman Whitefield noted that he had "recently called on good Mr Law, whose books many years ago were blessed to my soul, when the work that is now spreading, was then in embryo".[48] Whitefield read and commended many books that answered Miranda's criteria of promoting "the inward holiness of the Christian life". Among those he particularly valued were Thomas à Kempis' *The Imitation of Christ*, *The Country Parson's Advice to His Parishioners* (anon.), Bishop William Beveridge's *Sermons* and Matthew Henry's *Exposition of the Old and New Testaments*. This latter devotional commentary he purchased from his friend the Gloucester bookseller Gabriel Harris.[49] He reminded clergy Henry's books were "too voluminous for the common people" and that "I have not read them all".[50] Prominent in Whitefield's spiritual reading was The Book of Common Prayer. He delighted in its offices and read them frequently, often together with others. He delighted in the collects too, some of which he put together with Bible passages and published for others to read.

Holy Spirit

Whitefield had received the witness of the Holy Spirit at an early point during his time in Oxford. Quite possibly it was his reading of Scougal which had made him aware of the new birth and in consequence led him to experience the Holy Spirit's presence. In consequence he had an almost continuous and vivid sense of the presence of Christ in his life. "The love of Jesus shed abroad in the heart by the Holy Ghost," he wrote, "is indeed all in all; this is glory begun; this is the opening of the kingdom of heaven in the soul; this is a never failing well of water, which will at last spring up to life eternal."[51] Whitefield frequently spoke of his experience of the Holy Spirit in his life. Sometimes it was manifested as "joy in the Holy Ghost" or as "the sealing of the Spirit". He also frequently spoke of being filled with the Holy Spirit or being filled with the fullness of God. Above all it was his conscious awareness of the immediate presence of the Spirit which thrust him forward and gave him confidence to declare his faith and stand confident and firm despite opposition whether from the pens of the prelates or the clods of mud thrown by the hooligans who tried to disrupt his meetings.

Writing on 2 October 1738 on board ship returning to England from the inhabitants of his Savannah parish Whitefield emphasized that one needful thing is "the new birth in Christ, that ineffable change which must pass in our hearts, before we can see God". He gave the following counsel.

> The author of this blessed change is the Holy Ghost, the third person of the Trinity. The Father made, the Son redeemed, and the Holy Spirit is to sanctify, and so apply Christ's redemption to our hearts. The means to attain this Holy Spirit, you know, and the way you know: *self-denial,* and the *way of the cross...* Another means to attain the Holy Spirit, is public worship: for Christ promised, "where two or three are gathered together in my name, there will he, by his Spirit, be in the midst of them"... Do not forsake the assembling of yourselves together in the house of God... Many other means there are of obtaining the Holy Ghost, such as, *reading the Scriptures, secret prayer, self-examination,* and *receiving the blessed* sacrament.[52]

Whitefield spoke of the Holy Spirit's presence in the hearts of believers as "the source of all our present peace, and the only solid preparation for future comfort in the coming world". The love of Jesus shed abroad in our hearts by the Holy Spirit, Whitefield reminded an inquirer, "is indeed all in all... the opening of the kingdom of heaven in the soul" and "a never failing well of water, which will at last spring up to life eternal".[53]

When Whitefield wrote and spoke of being led in his own life by the Holy Spirit, the Bishop of London and others accused him of being an "enthusiast". Never one to meekly bow down to unjust or unsubstantiated criticism Whitefield responded by asking his bishop if he could see the wind? Yet, he continued, "your Lordship knows when it makes any impression upon your body?" In the same way it is possible for "a spiritual man to know when the Holy Spirit makes an impression upon his soul".[54]

The Bishop of London and others dubbed Whitefield an enthusiast on account of his professing to be led by the Spirit. Whitefield however was quick to point out that the word "enthusiast" simply meant "in God".[55] He reminded his Anglican critics that the Church of England "in her excellent Communion-office, tells us, that those who receive the sacrament worthily, 'dwell in Christ, and Christ in them; that they are one with Christ, and Christ with them'".[56] In a sermon entitled *The Indwelling of the Spirit, the Common Privilege of all Believers* Whitefield was clear "that the Holy Spirit is the common privilege and portion of all believers in all ages; and that we as well as the first Christians, must receive the Holy Ghost, before we can be truly called the children of God."[57] Whitefield stated that holding to this doctrine could by no means justify his being dubbed an enthusiast.[58]

In common with many revivalists it was part of Whitefield's spirituality to be guided by what were generally known as "impressions". The term was derived from the fact that most often an individual would be taken by a sudden thought which would come with unexpected intensity. Sometimes it would be a verse from the Bible that would play strongly on a person's mind. On other occasions there would be a sudden urge to take a particular course of action or to speak out on a particular matter. The recipients of these kinds of promptings often spoke of their minds being strongly urged or "impressed", hence the term impression. Impressions were clearly part and parcel of a vivid fervent and experiential religious experience. In his earlier years, shortly after his receiving the witness of the Spirit, Whitefield was of the view that the impressions he received should be promptly responded to as obedience to God's guiding hand. Whitefield frequently found that texts of Scripture were impressed on his mind and he took this to be the Lord's guidance. In a letter he penned from Gloucester to a dear friend in February, 1744 he wrote, "Pleased with the thought, and ambitious of having a son of my own, so divinely employed, Satan was permitted to give me some wrong impressions, whereby, as I now find, I misapplied several texts of Scripture. Upon these grounds I made no scruple of declaring, 'that I should have a son, and that his name was to be *John*'."[59]

In October 1740 Whitefield went to Northampton, Massachusetts where his preaching helped to rekindle the revival.[60] During his time in the town he was able to have a number of discussions with Jonathan Edwards who had warned in his *Distinguishing Marks of a Work of the Spirit of God* of the dangers "of giving too much heed to impulses and strong impressions on the mind".[61] Following this time Whitefield became more circumspect and recognized there was an irrational aspect in the matter. Subsequently Whitefield was happy to acknowledge that he had been mistaken in some of the actions he had taken in response to these seemingly forceful impulses. In later times he came to take more note of the gracious hand of God in the circumstances of his life and ministry. Witness these lines in a letter to the Countess of Huntingdon in August 1748, "As there seems to be a door opening for the nobility to hear the gospel, I will defer my journey till Thursday, and, God willing, preach at your Ladyship's on Tuesday."[62]

Relationships

A very important aspect of Whitefield's spirituality was that of keeping relationships in good repair. He fully recognized the teaching of the apostle John that people couldn't claim to love God if they didn't love their fellow men and women. He therefore constantly strove to do all he could to set matters right. He increasingly came to publicly acknowledge his wrongdoings and mistakes. He regularly asked his friends and close associates to speak to him about his faults or inappropriate behaviour. He was quick to apologize and ask for forgiveness whenever and wherever it was necessary. In 1740 he wrote, "I think it no dishonour, to retract some expressions that formerly dropped from my pen, before God was pleased to give me a more clear knowledge of the doctrines of grace." He went on to say, "I am not ashamed to own my faults... I shall be thankful to any that will point out my errors; and I promise, by divine assistance, they shall have no reason to say, 'I am the one who hates to be reformed'."[63] In a letter written in November 1742 he wrote as if bemused, "My mistakes have been so many, and my impudence so great, that I have often wondered that the glorious Jesus would employ me in his service."[64]

Whitefield recognized that forming deep relationships was a two-way process. It involved first a willingness to be corrected and admit one's faults and then out of that to be willing to correct others.

Be willing to be corrected

Whitefield was always ready to be reproved by both his friends as well as by others he encountered who hardly knew him. On his arrival in Philadelphia after his voyage from England during the autumn of 1739 Whitefield responded to a letter he had received from a fellow clergyman.

> Why so long silent during my stay in England? Why did you not write me a letter of reproof, and smite me friendly for what you thought was amiss in the discourse between me and a friend at Bristol. I should have taken it kindly at your hands. When I am unwilling to be told of my faults, dear Sir, correspond with me no more.[65]

To a minister in Monmouth he wrote, "Nothing gives me more comfort, next to the assurance of God's love, than the pleasing reflection of having so many Christian friends to watch with my soul."[66] Whitefield openly and publicly listed what he considered to be his major weaknesses of character. These included being over-fond of Scripture language, speaking and writing what he thought was from the Spirit of God but which was his own spirit, and being guided by impressions.[67] In 1748 he even went so far as apologize to the trustees of Georgia for having expressed himself "in too strong, and sometimes unbecoming terms".[68] To Mrs F Whitefield he wrote, "If we hate reproof, we are far from being true followers of the Lamb of God."[69] To the members of his Methodist societies he urged, "My brethren, content not yourselves with reading and praying together, but set some time apart to confess your faults and communicate your experiences one to another."[70]

Reproving one another

There were times when it was clear to Whitefield that some of his relationships were beginning to break because there were faults on both sides. Such was the case in the early days of his ministry. Both he and the Wesleys had learned much from the Moravians and had been encouraged by attending love feasts at their Fetter Lane Society in London. However, with the passing of time they had grown apart from the Moravians. Whitefield in particular had suffered at their hands in his Savannah parish. In a letter to their leader Peter Böhler dated 10 October 1741, Whitefield wrote, "There have been faults on both sides. I think my dear brother, you have not acted simply in some things. Let us confess our faults to one another, and pray for one another, that we may be healed."[71]

In later years tensions increased considerably in England over Moravian doctrinal and ritual matters. Finally Whitefield wrote to their leader Count Nicholas Zinzendorf.

> For many years past, I have been a silent and impartial observer of the progress and effects of Moravianism, both in England and America; but such shocking things have lately been brought to our ears, and offences have swollen to such an enormous bulk, that a real regard for my king and country, and a distinctive love for the ever-blessed Jesus, will not suffer me to be silent any longer. Pardon me, therefore, my lord, if I am constrained to inform your lordship that you, together with some of your leading brethren, have been unhappily instrumental in misguiding many simple, honest-hearted Christians; of distressing, if not totally ruining, numerous families, and of introducing a whole farrago of superstitions, not to say idolatrous fopperies into the English nation.[72]

At first reading Whitefield's words perhaps appear to be unnecessarily strong but nevertheless they still witnessed his desire to speak the truth in love to all. It was for this same reason that he challenged a fellow clergyman with the words "Does your going weekly to a club, where the company play at cards, and sit up late at night agree with your holy vocation, either as a Christian or a minister?"[73] Similarly, when in Philadelphia in November 1739, he rebuked a fellow clergyman stating, "It is no good report that I hear of you in common life. Your practice contradicts your doctrine, and what good can you do, if every one of your parishioners, whilst you are preaching, may reply, 'Physician heal thyself'?"[74]

As has been noted Whitefield found himself in conflict on a number of occasions with his respected friend and mentor, John Wesley. He wrote to him in September 1740, "I am sorry, honoured Sir, to hear by many letters, that you seem to own a *sinless perfection* in this life attainable."[75] Whitefield had also publicly taken Wesley to task for his sermon on free grace and published details of his seeking guidance by drawing lots. On 10 October 1741, however, he sent a letter to John Wesley apologizing for making public the fact that he had used the sacred lot in making some decisions. He wrote: "I am sorry now, that any such thing dropped from my pen, and I humbly ask pardon. I find I love you as much as ever, and pray God, if it be his blessed will, that we may be all united together."[76] He concluded, "In about three weeks I hope to be in Bristol. May all disputings cease, and each of us talk of nothing but Jesus, and him crucified."[77] Significantly, notwithstanding his many struggles over the doctrines of election and reprobation with John and Charles Wesley, Whitefield bequeathed his mourning ring "to my honoured friends and disinterested fellow labourers, the Rev. Messrs John and Charles Wesley, in token of my indissoluble union with them, in heart and Christian affection, notwithstanding our difference in judgment about some particular points of doctrine".[78]

Whitefield recognized that disputing served only to divide Christian communities and needed to be resisted whenever possible. His feelings in the matter were clear in a letter addressed to a close friend in Pennsylvania. Whitefield wrote: "For Jesus Christ's sake, as much as in you lies, put a stop to disputing. It embitters the spirit, ruffles the soul, and hinders it from hearing the small still voice of the Holy Ghost."[79]

Deep relationships

As well as constantly striving to maintain his relationships in good repair, Whitefield was always humble in his attitude to his fellow clergy. He didn't put himself across as the one who knew it all or had the answer as to the way things should be done. He was always willing to listen to others preach and to learn from them. He made particular efforts to establish close friendships with those who were engaged in the work of revival. In America he was especially grateful for the advice of Jonathan Edwards and William and Gilbert Tennent. In England he worked closely with Howell Harris and the Countess of Huntingdon, both of whom, as we have seen, gave him considerable support. Whitefield was ever grateful for the privilege of being appointed the Countess's chaplain.

It has been said and with justification that at times Whitefield was too self-deprecating and overly demeaning in his attitude to the nobility and the great and the good. In a number of his letters he refers to himself as an unworthy servant and other such terms. His stooping to the aristocracy is particularly apparent in many of his letters to the Countess of Huntingdon. Perhaps, however, this may in part be explained by the fact that he had been born and brought up in the relatively humble circumstances of the Bell Inn in Gloucester.

We capture glimpses of the fervent love which Whitefield felt for his friends and fellow labourers in the work. In a letter to Jonathan Barber, one of his superintendents in Savannah, Whitefield wrote, "My dear brother, I love you unfeignedly in the bowels of Jesus Christ, and heartily thank you for all your works of faith, and the care you have taken of my dear family [Bethesda]." A few sentences later he continued, "I long to be with you, to open our hearts freely, and to tell one another what good God has done for our souls."[80] Some years later Whitefield wrote in a similar very affectionate manner to another close friend that "I fully purposed to write to you before my embarkation for America, but sickness prevented. However, I dearly love you, and often remember you before the throne, who I am persuaded hath loved and given himself for you."[81] These two letters are typical of many which Whitefield wrote during his ministry on both sides of the Atlantic.

Let not your good be evil spoken of

It's important to recognize that Whitefield's warm expressions of brotherly love don't allow us to imagine he was soft when the need of the moment required him to stand up strong or defend himself against those he believed had wrongly accused him. Whitefield stood firmly behind the biblical principle "let not... your good be evil spoken of".[82]

A prominent instance of Whitefield's ability to forthrightly defend himself against accusations took place in the spring of 1744. An anonymous pamphlet entitled *Observations upon the Conduct and behaviour of a certain Sect usually distinguished by the Name of Methodists* had been published in large quantities and circulated in London and Westminster. Whitefield was uncertain who the author was but wrote, "I had reason to believe that my Lord of London was concerned in composing or revising them." However, Mr Owen, a printer in Paternoster Row, informed him that he had orders from several bishops. Whitefield therefore responded to "my Lord of London" and several other bishops in a published pamphlet entitled, *A Letter to the Bishop of London & Co*. His opening words were, "The Apostle Peter exhorts us, 'to be ready to give an answer to every one that asketh us a reason for the hope that is within us, with meekness and fear.'" He then stated his desire was "to comply with this apostolic injunction", which had compelled him to publish an open defence of the Methodists. In what followed, Whitefield underlined that Methodist loyal citizens of the crown subscribed to the Anglican formularies and were faithful attenders at the sacrament in their parish churches.

Whitefield had real ability to turn the tables on his opponents. He pointed out that many Church of England clergy were "promiscuously and carelessly allowing all sorts of people to the communion and that had it not been for me they would have left the church".[83] When it came to their Lordships' criticism of his field-preaching Whitefield was quick to point out that "our glorious Emmanuel" preached on a mount, from a ship and in a wilderness. To that he added that the apostles "preached in schools, public markets and such like places".[84]

Whitefield's defence of his part in Methodism to the Bishop of London was one of many. He vindicated himself against charges of enthusiasm made by the bishop in the earlier pastoral letter. He justified his extempore preaching to members of the New York Presbyterians.[85] He defended Methodists from the charges made against them by the Bishop of Coventry and Lichfield in his Triennial Visitation of 1741.[86] He stood up for his conduct, extempore preaching, and teaching on the Holy Spirit in a pamphlet of twelve folios published in 1745 and entitled, *A Letter to the President, Professors and Tutors at Harvard College.* And he made a robust response to a pamphlet entitled *The Enthusiasm of Methodists and Papists Compared.* In it he defended field-preaching and instant conversion but also acknowledged his faults concerning impressions, his judgmental attitudes, and use of Scripture language.[87] In 1753 Whitefield published a strong public attack against the Moravians on account of their introducing many strange ritual practices into their worship. By these, he wrote, "you have been unhappily instrumental in misguiding many, real, simple, honest-hearted Christians".[88]

In 1763 Whitefield published *Observations on some fatal mistakes* in response to a book published by William Warburton, Bishop of

Gloucester. He rebuked the prelate for "taking occasion to wound, vilify, and totally deny the all-powerful, standing operations of the Blessed Spirit, by which alone, his Lordship or any other man living can be sanctified and sealed to the day of eternal redemption".[89] In 1768 Whitefield published a highly critical response to the vice-chancellor of the University of Oxford, the Revd Dr David Durell, following the expulsion of six students from Edmund Hall. Their alleged crime was held to be the Methodist practice of singing hymns and praying extempore prayers. Whitefield was quick to point out that their faith was in fact "the faith of Cranmer, Ridley and Latimer and those glorious lights of the reformation". Never one to miss a sharp point Whitefield stated that there was something wrong when students can swear and blaspheme extempore but praying was deemed to be worthy of expulsion.[90] As late as July 1768 we find Whitefield in Edinburgh urgently requesting a friend in London for "fifty of my letters to the Archbishop to be directed to the custom-house at Leith". Clearly he felt the need to vindicate himself to the people of Scotland's capital city.[91]

These and many other similar instances reveal an important aspect of Whitefield's spirituality. Not only is spirituality about a bold and forthright Christian faith, it is also about maintaining self-worth and following the dictates of conscience.

Letter writing

There is little doubt that letter writing was a significant part of Whitefield's spirituality. John Gillies published nearly 1,500 of his letters in the early 1770s. Susan O'Brien, commenting on them appositely, wrote that "when Whitefield sent letters from the colonies to London for distribution, he did so by the trunk-load".[92] Letter writing was a means by which Whitefield strengthened bonds of friendship with those he regarded as soulmates and whom he trusted to hold him to account and help to build him up in the faith. Letters were also a medium by which Whitefield shared his experiences and articulated lessons that he had learned by reflecting on God's provision and sustaining presence in trials, sickness, and hostility. Whitefield's letter writing was as wide-ranging as his travels. He received so many letters that he was more than grateful to receive the secretarial help of lay Evangelicals but replies were nearly always his own. Through his writing he also stimulated and encouraged many churches which organized letter-reading concerts. These occasions began as early as 1739 and were gatherings where people sang, prayed, and listened to some of Whitefield's letters being read out. O'Brien helpfully pointed out that Whitefield's huge correspondence helped to create "a letter-writing network" that had a core of leading ministers which included such individuals as Edwards and Colman in America and James Robe and William McCulloch in Scotland.

Whitefield wrote letters because he recognized that people's faith grew through interaction and writing their stories to him. For this reason he was ever ready to correspond with people he met or counselled at the conclusion of his preaching. He wrote words of encouragement and shared lessons he had learned from his own experience or discovered from his reading. The growing "epistolary network" was a major means by which the revival spread.

The significance of Whitefield's spirituality

Whitefield's spirituality had its weak points. The obsessive austerity and rigid lifestyle of his Oxford days was played out in an extreme and arduous workload in which he gave himself very little time for rest and relaxation. The impact of living by the strict rules of the Holy Club where even wrong thoughts were recorded in diaries and journals and brought into submission caused him to have a very puritanical outlook on life. Whitefield's was not a spirituality which could have embraced the erotic or celebrated the love expressed in the Song of Songs. That said, the fervent and experiential faith and those of his fellow Methodists was a marked reaction against the rationalism and laxity of the times. It was for that reason that the Georgian bishops in particular found Whitefield's spirituality hard to come to terms with and dubbed him an "enthusiast".

Whitefield gave the church in England and America a disciplined spirituality which had come to him through the writings of William Law and perhaps owed something for that reason to the ascetic disciplines of St Francis and St Bernard. Above all Whitefield's spirituality was of the heart and feelings. It stood in contrast to eighteenth-century latitudinarian piety and theology which was more overtly grounded in liturgy and a sense of duty. His spirituality embraced the whole of life and particularly the importance of pursuing one's work and calling with wholehearted determination and perseverance. In this respect it could almost be seen as an extension of the work ethic of the seventeenth-century Puritans who regarded the conscientious labour of six days each week as living before and in the presence of God. Indeed, Whitefield himself declared on the night of his death, "I would rather wear out, than rust out."[93] Hindmarsh's suggestion that the image of fire best embraces all the aspects Whitefield's spirituality is helpful.[94] It was indeed the fire of the Spirit which warmed his heart, personalized his private devotion, generated his compassion and care, and thrust him forward to preach and contend for the faith with a confident and determined boldness.

A significant proportion of the evidence used in this chapter, although by no means all, to illustrate Whitefield's spirituality has been drawn from the earlier years of his life and ministry. There are reasons for this. The number of letters he wrote gradually appear to have decreased with the passing of the years. In the last twelve months of his life, when his health was in steep decline, there were only forty-two published letters. During the last decade of his life he seemed to have less opposition and there was therefore less need to defend himself. Prayer, reading, and meditating on Scripture was part of his daily routine until the very last days. Gillies recorded that right at the end of his life it was still his constant custom every evening to "be offering up prayers, intercessions, with hymns and spiritual songs in every house to which he was invited".[95]

Chapter 12 notes

1   J. Gordon, *Evangelical Spirituality* (London, SPCK, 1991), p. vii.
2   Ibid.
3   A. McGrath, *Christian Spirituality: An Introduction* (Oxford, Blackwell, 1999), p. 2.
4   Ibid, p. 3.
5   L. Wilson, *Constrained by Zeal: Female Spirituality Amongst Non-conformists 1825–1875* (Carlisle, Paternoster Press, 2000), p. 4.
6   D. B. Hindmarsh, *The Spirit of Early Evangelicalism*, p. 17.
7   See for example J. Gillies, op. cit., p. 7; L. Tyerman; op. cit., Vol. 2, p. 26; Whitefield, *A Short Account*, Section 1, p.19.
8   Whitefield, *Manuscript Diary*, 19 March 1736, p. 21.
9   Ibid, 18 April 1736, p. 48.
10 Ibid, 18 March 1735/6 cited in D. B. Hindmarsh, *The Spirit of Early Evangelicalism*, p. 28.
11 Whitefield, *A Short Account of God's Dealings*, Section 3, p.13.
12 Whitefield, *A Short Account*, cited in A. Skevington Wood, *The Inextinguishable Blaze* (Grand Rapids, Wm B. Eerdmans Publishing Company, 1968), p. 89.
13 *Letter to Mrs H—*, 23 December 1737.
14 Whitefield, *Answer to the Bishop of London's Last Pastoral Letter*, *Works*, Vol. 4, p. 11.
15 *Journal*, 7 January 1739.
16 *A Brief Account of the Occasion, Process, and Issue of a Late Trial at the Assize held at Gloucester*, 1744, *Works*, Vol. 4, p. 105.
17 *Letter to Mr H—*, 30 December 1738.
18 *Letter to My dear Brother A—*, 4 June 1742.
19 *Letter to Mr S—S—*, 15 July 1763.
20 Sermon, *Intercession Every Christian's Duty*, *Works*, Vol. 6, p. 340.
21 *Letter to Mr—*, 16 November 1738.

22 *Letter to Dear Madam—*, 23 July 1739).
23 Sermon, *Thankfulness for Mercies Received, a Necessary Duty*, *Works*, Vol. 5, p. 95.
24 Ibid, p 96.
25 Ibid.
26 *The Great Duty of Family Religion*, *Works*, Vol. 5, p. 60.
27 See previous chapter.
28 *Letter to My Dear Friend*, 2 May 1738.
29 D. C. Jones et al., op. cit., p. 55.
30 *Letter to Mr S—*, 27 June 1743.
31 Sermon, *Christ the Only Preservative Against a Reprobate Spirit*, *Works*, Vol. 6, p. 296.
32 M. Thornton, *English Spirituality* (London, SPCK, 1963), p. 50.
33 *Prayers on Several Occasions*, *Works*, Vol. 5, pp. 455–90.
34 D. B. Hindmarsh, T*he Spirit of Early Evangelicalism*, p. 34 noted Whitefield "had a high sense of encountering God at Holy Communion".
35 L. Tyerman, op. cit., Vol. 2, p. 344.
36 *Letter to Mr W—D—*, 28 June 1740.
37 *Letter to Lord Lothian*, 26 October 1741. See also L. Tyerman, op. cit., Vol. 1, p. 515.
38 Sermon, *The Duty of Family Religion*, *Works*, Vol. 5, p. 56.
39 D. B. Hindmarsh, op. cit., p. 30.
40 Sermon, *The Duty of Family Religion*, *Works*, Vol. 5, p. 56.
41 *Letter to Mr J. E.—*, 23 November 1742.
42 J. Gillies, op. cit., p. 271.
43 Ibid, p. 295.
44 A title given to members of the Church of England who after 1688 refused to give allegiance to William and Mary on the grounds that they would thereby break their oath to James II and their successors.
45 See *Letter to The Rev. Mr. S—*, 24 June 1748, "My health I think has improved, and I have finished my abridgement of Mr Law's Serious Call, which I have endeavoured to gospelise."
46 *Law Gospelised or, An Address to all Christians concerning Holiness of Heart and Life* (June, 1748), *Works*, Vol. 4, p. 382.
47 Ibid, p. 391.
48 *Letter to the Rev. Mr. H—*, 1 March 1749.
49 D. B. Hindmarsh, op. cit., p. 29 points out that Whitefield paid seven pounds for the volumes, "a tremendous amount of money by any measure".
50 *Letter to Mr—*, 22 August 1748.
51 *Letter to Mr G—P—*, 30 September 1752.
52 *Address to the Inhabitants of Savannah*, October 1738, *Works*, Vol. 3, pp. 428–29.
53 *Letter to G—P—*, 30 September 1752.
54 Whitefield, *Answer to the Bishop of London's Last Pastoral Letter*, *Works*, Vol. 4, p. 10.

55 Sermon, *An Exhortation to the People of God not to be discouraged in their Way, by the Scoffs and Contempts of wicked Men, Works*, Vol. 6, p. 362.
56 Sermon, *The Indwelling of the Spirit, the Common Privilege of all Believers, Works*, Vol. 6, p. 93.
57 Ibid, p. 90.
58 *Answer to the Bishop of London, Works*, Vol. 4, p. 13.
59 *Letter to Mr D—T—*, 9 February 1744.
60 J. Edwards, *An Account of the Revival in Northampton in 1740–1742*, p. 148.
61 J. Edwards, *Distinguishing Marks of a Work of the Spirit of God*, p. 137.
62 *Letter to Lady Huntingdon*, 22 August 1748.
63 *A Letter to some members of the Presbyterian Persuasion, Works*, p. 47.
64 *Letter to Mr P—*, 27 November 1742.
65 *Letter to Rev. and Dear Sir*, 10 November 1739.
66 Ibid.
67 *Letter to the Rev. Mr. S—*, 24 June 1748.
68 *Letter to the Honourable Trustees of Georgia*, 6 December 1748.
69 *Letter to Dear Mrs F—*, 10 November 1739.
70 *A Letter to the Religious Societies of England, Works*, Vol. 5, p 31.
71 *Letter to Peter Böhler*, 10 October 1741.
72 L. Tyerman, op. cit., Vol. 2, p. 301.
73 *Letter to Rev. and dear Sir*, 10 November 1739.
74 *Letter to Reverend Sir*, 28 November 1739.
75 *A Letter to the Rev. John Wesley*, 25 September 1740.
76 Ibid, 10 October 1741.
77 Ibid.
78 J. Gillies, op. cit., p. 355.
79 *Letter to Mr F—*, 22 September 1742.
80 *Letter to Jonathan Barber*, 21 May 1743.
81 *Letter to My dear Mr P—*, 24 August 1763.
82 Romans 14:16.
83 See Whitefield, *Answer to the Bishop of London's Last Pastoral Letter, Works*, Vol. 4, pp. 5–19.
84 Ibid, pp. 125–140.
85 Whitefield, *A Letter to Some Church Members of the Presbyterian Persuasion, Works*, Vol. 4, pp. 45–49.
86 *Some Remarks upon a late Charge against Enthusiasm delivered by The Right Reverend Father in God, Richard Lord Bishop of Lichfield and Coventry* (1744).
87 *Remarks on a Pamphlet entitled The Enthusiasm of Methodists and Papists Compared, Works*, Vol. 4, pp. 229–48.
88 *An Expostulatory Letter Addressed to Nicholas Lewis, Count Zinzendorf, Works*, Vol. 4, p. 254.
89 G. Whitefield, *Observations on some fatal mistakes in a Book Lately Published, and intitled, The Office and Operations of the Holy Spirit vindicated from Insults of Infidelity, and the Abuses of Fanaticism. By William Lord Bishop of Gloucester, Works*, Vol. 4, p. 301.

90 *A Letter to the Reverend Dr Durell, Works,* Vol. 4, pp. 318, 329.
91 *Letter to Mr A—K—,* 2 July 1768.
92 S. O'Brien, "A Transatlantic Community of Saints: The Great Awakening and the First Evangelical Network, 1735–1755", *American History Review,* 91, October 1986, p. 817.
93 J. Gillies, op. cit., p. 271.
94 D. B. Hindmarsh, op. cit., p. 7.
95 J. Gillies, op. cit., p. 330.

Chapter 13

Last Days and Assessment

Final labours

Whitefield's final voyage to America began on 4 September 1769. As he was about to sail he asserted, "all the world is my parish".[1] Boarding the *Friendship* he reported that "I have not been in better spirits for some years: and am persuaded this voyage will be for the Redeemer's glory".[2] He reported that the captain and passengers were civil and ready to attend divine worship.[3] The voyage, however, proved to be frustratingly long, as the ship did not finally leave New Romney, Kent, until 28 September,[4] eventually reaching Charleston on 1 December.[5] There, Whitefield preached for a week and expressed the hope that "some South Carolina souls [were] beginning to look heavenward".[6]

On 9 December he set off by sea for Georgia, the roads being impassable owing to the inclement weather. He preached at Savannah and checked on the affairs at his orphan house. Some of his time he devoted to his plan to transform it into an academic college. He discussed the matter with the governor who was supportive of the project. On 12 April Whitefield embarked ship for Philadelphia and stated that it was his intention to preach in the northern parts during the hot summer season and return to Georgia in the winter.[7]

After three weeks of preaching in the City of Brotherly Love Whitefield felt "a wide and effectual door was opened" with people of all ranks clamouring to hear him preach. On 14 June he penned a letter to his close friend Robert Keen telling him that he had "just returned from a hundred and fifty mile circuit, in which, blessed be God! I have been enabled to preach every day". He also noted that he was receiving so many invitations to preach "that I know not which way to turn".[8] Encouraged and feeling well he rode on to New York, arriving on 21 June and preaching to "congregations larger than ever".[9] He spent the month of July "riding above five hundred miles" and preaching in twelve towns. After returning to New York he took a brief rest before travelling on to Boston,[10] where from 17 to 20 September he preached daily.[11]

Living life at such an extraordinary demanding pace it was inevitable that his health would suffer once more. Such proved to be the case. On 17 September he reported that "two or three evenings ago I was taken in with a violent lax, attended with reaching and shivering". After a short rest he felt well enough to continue his planned itinerary and set out once more, this time to Portsmouth and New Hampshire. Returning from there to Boston he stopped at Exeter where Gillies related that he preached "for two hours in the open air, to accommodate the multitudes that came to hear him".[12] In the afternoon he set out "greatly fatigued" to return to Boston. En route he arrived at Newburyport on the evening of Saturday 29 September intending to preach there the next day. Being exhausted Whitefield went early to bed. He was awake several times during the night and complained of difficulties in breathing. At six o'clock on the Lord's Day morning, he expired in a fit of asthma.

Whitefield died as he had lived – exhausted by much speaking. His English travelling companion, Richard Smith, was with him and left a detailed account of his death. The Revd Jonathan Parsons, in whose house they were staying, took care of the funeral arrangements with the help of his elders and deacons. At the funeral in Newburyport the Revd Daniel Rogers led a powerful prayer in which he confessed he owed his conversion to Whitefield's ministry. The sermon was given by the Revd Mr Jewel. Whitefield was buried at his request before the pulpit in Mr Parson's church. The news of Whitefield's death finally reached London on 5 November 1770. His close friend Robert Keen brought the news to the Tabernacle and Tottenham Court Road Chapel. Whitefield had made it known on several occasions that if he should die abroad John Wesley should preach his funeral sermon. Accordingly Keen made the necessary arrangements and the sermon was preached on Sunday 18 November. In his tribute Wesley declared:

> What honour hath it pleased God to put on his faithful servant! Have we read or heard of any person since the apostles, who testified the gospel of the grace of God, through so widely extended a space, through so large a part of the habitable world? Have we read or heard of any person, who called many thousands, so many myriads of sinners to repentance. Above all, have we seen or heard of any who has been a blessed instrument in his hand of bringing so many sinners from dark, and from darkness to light, and from the power of Satan to God.[13]

An assessment

So the question arises how shall we assess George Whitefield and his role in the eighteenth-century transatlantic revival? Clearly by any standards he was a very remarkable man. Ronald Knox, in his critical assessments of revival movements, wrote of Whitefield, "Any man with a reasonable capacity for admiration must stand awestruck at the record of both his labours and success."[14] Any estimate of his impact and influence must include the following.

An outstanding leader

Whitefield undoubtedly stands alongside the Wesleys as the co-leader of eighteenth-century Methodism. Dallimore calls him the central figure of the revival.[15] Rupert Davies described him as "the originator of the Methodist revival", pointing out that for a considerable time this is how he was known, at any rate to the public.[16] J. C. Ryle, the nineteenth-century Bishop of Liverpool, was of the opinion that "Whitefield was the foremost of the Christian leaders in the previous century." Further, "I place him," Ryle wrote, "first in the order of merit, without any hesitation."[17] Whitefield inspired a great many clergy in England, Scotland, Wales, and the American colonies to proclaim the message of the gospel with boldness and confidence. Many of their number assisted him, rode alongside him to places where he had arranged to speak, and looked to him for advice. Several hundred of his published letters were written to fellow clergy in both Britain and America, offering encouragement, advice, and guidance.

Skevington Wood's assessment that "Whitefield was no planner. He could gather souls, but he had no scheme for keeping them"[18] probably needs correction, or at the very least, some modification. Whitefield managed three major churches in London and recent research has demonstrated that in 1747 there were twenty-eight societies across the country in his care.[19] He also served as moderator of the Welsh Calvinistic Methodists. The fact of the matter was that with his ever-expanding preaching ministry he had insufficient time to organize his societies and other preaching places. Wise leader that he was he gradually transferred the pastoral care of most of them to others including Harris, Rowland, and the Countess of

Huntingdon. Criticisms of Whitefield for this reason may therefore be a little harsh. After all, there is only so much one person can do and Whitefield constantly well and truly overstretched himself.

Preacher like no other

By any assessment Whitefield was clearly one of the most remarkable and effective preachers that the world has ever seen. He preached extensively in the north, south, and west of England. He proclaimed the good news of Jesus' kingdom in Wales, Scotland, Ireland, and thousands of miles across America. He also spoke in Holland, Bermuda, and Gibraltar. He impacted more people with the gospel message unaided by the airwaves than anyone else in history. The largest churches in both England and America were unable to accommodate the huge number of people who wanted to hear him preach. The result of this was that he took to the fields and became the great pioneer and promoter of open-air preaching. It must also be said that Whitefield's exclusion from parish churches in both England and America also contributed to his taking to the great outdoors. It meant that along with the Wesleys, he no longer felt tied to parish or church boundaries.

The open-air preaching which Whitefield pioneered was peculiarly suited to the needs of the age. It was clearly a form of popular entertainment and it greatly attracted the poor who were often alienated by the clerically dominated established and denominational churches. These institutions frequently asserted there was such a thing as "honourable poverty", which was indeed divinely ordained. What amazed Whitefield's contemporaries was the huge numbers of all ranks, all denominations, and all characters who constantly came to hear him preach. But Whitefield's appeal was far more than just to the poor and the middle orders. Quite early on in his ministry eighty coaches were counted at Moorfields where he was preaching.[20] Twelve years later in America his appeal was on the very same scale. Between May and July on a tour in America in 1750 he preached over ninety sermons to congregations and gatherings which totalled above 240,000 people.[21] Augustus Toplady estimated from a small account book that Whitefield kept that he preached 18,000 sermons from his ordination to the time of his death. Others have computed a much higher number. Sir James Stephen, for example, suggested 30 or 40,000.[22] If all the exhortations and expositions he gave at society meetings and in private homes were included the larger figure is probably a fairer representation. Whitefield preached extempore with passion, fervour, and focus. He gave free vent to his emotions and knew how to move his hearers by the variation of his voice and dramatic gestures.

John Wesley spoke of the power of Whitefield's preaching:

> He cried out with a voice audible to an amazing distance: hence, in a thousand instances, where the cause of God more coolly pleaded, would have been neglected, he gained it a hearing, and carried the day: for the unusual earnestness of the speaker roused the most stupid and lethargic: it compelled them to feel; the matter must be momentous indeed, which the speaker was urging as a man would plead for his own life.[23]

John Newton, the one time slave-trader, later turned clergyman, went to hear Whitefield preach at the Tabernacle on a number of occasions. He later wrote that Whitefield "exceeded every other popular preacher of my time". He was, Newton asserted, "the originator of popular preaching, and all our popular ministers are only his copies."[24] With a gift of being able to use a poignant illustration to explain a doctrine or to provide a challenge to action on the part of his hearers, Whitefield was able to tell captivating stories which could catch the attention of rich and poor alike.

Among the positives that flowed from Whitefield's preaching there were two important consequences. First of all, the huge early successes of his open-air proclamations at Bristol, Kingswood, Moorfields, and Blackheath, followed by immediate acclamation in America raised the Methodist movement from being a small, Oxford-based sectarian group to a public national movement, which immediately impacted culture and society. Second, the sovereignty of God was at the very centre of Whitefield's faith and yet at the same time no one laboured more strenuously than Whitefield to bring about revival. Whitefield's Calvinistic convictions and his evangelistic endeavours formed a bridge between those who regarded revival as a sovereign work of God and those who believed that revival could be promoted by human endeavour. Although he believed that not all could be saved he nevertheless declared that he "offered Christ to all". In this regard he was opening up the way to the revivalism of the Second Great Awakening which was to follow at the turn of the century. Indeed, a strong argument could be made that Whitefield was the "Father of revivalism" since he embodied the characteristics of so many later revivalists. He used publicity of various kinds. He preached salvation to Christ for all though in practice he believed only the elect could access it. He exhorted those who were touched or disturbed by his preaching to put their trust in the Saviour. He made use of singing, especially Isaac Watts' hymns, at his gatherings. He was comfortable with emotional phenomena such as falling, tears, and crying out aloud. Indeed he often wept during his own sermons.

Any assessment of Whitefield must without question acknowledge him as the one through whom revival began in England, and the preacher who brought fresh outpourings of God's Spirit to many thousands in the American colonies. In particular, it was Whitefield who, with his informal style, recaptured the hearts and minds of people and rekindled the revival in Northampton, Massachusetts, just at the point at which it was beginning to wane. Although open-air preaching was not new, it was Whitefield who first saw its potential and used it to powerful effect. As a result of his successes field-preaching became a dominant feature of the revival. Once excluded from public church buildings Whitefield felt entirely free to preach wherever he believed he was called or invited. He also developed a strategy of revisiting the places where he had preached before in order to strengthen and encourage those who had originally professed faith in Christ.

Very soon after his ordination he began forming societies consisting of small groups of converts who were encouraged to share their faith and sing and pray for one another. Such societies were to emerge as another prominent feature of the Evangelical world. Whitefield, as has been noted, early developed a strategy whereby he based himself in a large town or city and then at some point during his stay made a circular preaching tour through the surrounding countryside. In this way he established a strategy which eventually became the Methodist circuit system. It was this structure that subsequently enabled the revival to make such effective inroads into the more isolated and rural communities in both America and the British Isles.

Undoubtedly Whitefield was one of the first evangelists to make extensive and effective use of print media. Through his journal and the publication of his sermons he was able to trail and promote the revival by means of publicity. He also printed his journal in small extracts and sent them on ahead to be circulated in the towns or places he was about to visit. Using the printed word in this way played a significant role in helping to promote his preaching as well as creating a mutually supportive transatlantic inter-denominational movement with English and American revivalists being able to encourage and support each other. It seems almost a contradiction that Whitefield, a Calvinist, was more than happy to market religion by what later Calvinists termed "means". In this case the "means" were his widespread use of the printed page and populist journalist techniques. Along with later revivalists, Whitefield collected and published statistics which he used to promote his forthcoming meetings. He also presented himself as a "champion of the laity who had long suffered under heavy handed ministers".[25] Perhaps he, more than Charles Finney, deserves to be credited with the title the "Father of Modern Revivalism". Indeed, Finney acknowledged Whitefield "as an innovator in propagating the gospel and a progenitor of his own revival techniques".[26]

Whitefield wrote tracts and pamphlets in defence of both Methodism and the biblical faith. He adhered strongly to the biblical principle in Paul's letter to the Romans, "Let not then your good be evil spoken of."[27] This was perhaps nowhere more apparent than in his spirited and public defences against the charge of enthusiasm. In this regard Whitefield proved himself to be a forthright and able apologist. Central to the charge against him was the doctrine of the new birth which he preached continuously. He defended it along with his teaching on the witness of the Holy Spirit to bishops and other critics on the ground that both were taught in the Book of Common Prayer. The former he defended from the baptism services and the latter he found in the service for the ordering of deacons. Whitefield was also charged with "enthusiasm" on account of his rash denunciation of those clergy he felt were unconverted and for the fact that people fell to the ground in consequence of his preaching. For the former he apologized and the latter he explained as part of a general awakening. Jonathan Parsons, in his address at Whitefield's funeral, referred to him as "a very searching, puritanical writer".[28]

Contribution to education

Important among the positive impacts of Whitefield's life was his significant promotion and support for education. Coming from a section of society where few were fortunate if they mastered the basics of the three Rs, Whitefield clearly greatly valued the privilege of his higher education at the University of Oxford, which had given him a grounding in the classics and a working knowledge of Latin and Greek. During his times of ministry in America he became keenly aware of the importance of higher education for the clergy. He made a number of visits to Harvard and Yale and did his utmost to encourage the faculty and students in the pursuit of the new birth and Protestant theology. He preached at the Philadelphia College commencement in October 1764,[29] gave considerable time and effort to raising funds for New Jersey College (which later became Princeton University); and paid particular attention to the education of the children in his own Bethesda orphanage. Later he had cherished hopes that it too might have become a college of higher education for Georgia and drew up plans and sought to obtain a charter to that end. Whitefield was a strong supporter of the Countess of Huntingdon's Trevecca College in Wales which had been established to train ministers for her chapels. He had also been much concerned about the education of slaves and the Native Americans, and had preached numerous charity sermons on behalf of schools in the British Isles.

Whitefield's contributions in the field of education played an important part in establishing Evangelical concern for learning at all levels. Methodists in particular set a high value on reading and learning to read. Even their hymns were written in order to inculcate Protestant biblical truths which was why Wesley wrote that their hymns were "a little body of practical divinity".[30] Methodist book rooms in England produced huge quantities of tracts for those who could read or were learning to read.[31] Significantly, Bebbington observed, by the mid-eighteenth century some 60 per cent of men in England and 65 per cent in Scotland were literate according to the gauge of the ability to sign their names, together with some 40 per cent of women in England and 15 per cent in Scotland.[32] In America a number of Colleges of Higher Education, although not directly connected with Whitefield, were founded in the wake of the revival. Among them were the University of Pennsylvania in 1751, the College of Rhode Island (later Brown University) in 1764, and Dartmouth College at Hanover in New Hampshire in 1769.

A pattern for caring for the poor and marginalized

It was the case that Whitefield "constantly enforced upon his audience every moral duty, particularly industry in their several callings, and obedience to their superiors".[33] It could also be argued that he treated the results of poverty rather than its causes. That said it would be a mistake to criticize the great preacher for reinforcing the social hierarchy or spending his time preaching charity sermons and making public collections for those in need. Such remedies were simply a part of the church's teaching and a reflection of the age. Whitefield gave a huge amount of publicity to his Bethesda orphan house by writing about its affairs in his journal, raising collections for it in churches, and at his open-air preachings. Additionally, he looked for gifts and bequests from the Countess of Huntingdon's circle and members of the aristocracy. In so doing he instilled the churches and Christian men and women with a godly concern to reach out and care for the needy.

Whitefield's endorsement of slavery, which he justified by citing Abraham as a precedent, and his personal owning, buying, and using slaves on his land are not easy to excuse. His plea was that both the colony of Georgia and his orphan house needed slavery in order to prosper. The fact was that even at this point in the eighteenth century many voices were being raised against what Wesley condemned as "the execrable sum of all villainies".[34] In a partial defence of Whitefield is the fact that he strongly advocated the humane treatment of all slaves and condemned those who treated their slaves with less respect than their animals. Whitefield was adamant that slaves should be properly clothed, housed, and fed, and have adequate time to rest and worship on the sabbath.

However, when it came to meeting the needs of the poor and marginalized Whitefield's was an exemplary role model. He certainly merited the title of "God's steward of the poor". The Revd D. Edwards of London spoke of him as "being full of generous philanthropy".[35] Having been brought up in the noise and bustle of the Bell Inn in Gloucester where large numbers of working men and women gathered to drink ale and play cards and board games, his sympathies, having witnessed their plight at home and abroad, were naturally with the marginalized. He was always tender-hearted and charitable toward the poor. There were numerous occasions, particularly in the city of London, when he preached charitable sermons. He made extensive pleas for money for refugees during the conflicts in Europe. Tyerman noted that "his enormous collections were to a great extent, the beginning of the marvellous beneficence which now [1870s] distinguishes the British churches".[36] He frequently preached in the prisons of London and Bristol and even on one occasion in America walked with a condemned man to the place of execution. His example and practice in this regard greatly stimulated Evangelical concern to care for the poor.

Whitefield was therefore prominent among the revival preachers in his assertion and constant practice of compassionate practical social care. Such outgoing practical love was one of four key defining aspects of Evangelicalism analysed by David Bebbington and termed "activism".[37] It became a marked feature of the Evangelical world in the later eighteenth century in both England and America.

Irenical ecumenist

The established Church of England during the time of Whitefield's ministry was a privileged institution, which in terms of law and practice was a cut above all other denominational expressions of the Christian faith. In England dissenting farmers were still forced to pay tithes to the parish priest and dissenting property owners were required to subscribe to an annual church rate to their parish vestry. In addition, their meeting houses were required to be licensed by the bishop of the diocese in which they were situated. In those American colonies where the Church of England was the established church it was still regarded by many as part and parcel of an oppressive British government.

One of Whitefield's great strengths was that he did not align himself with any one church party or set himself up as head of any church or denomination. As Stout put it, "he balked at their petty institutional rivalries".[38] Wherever he went he immediately endeared himself to a wide cross-section of people. He acknowledged and respected the clergy of other denominations and treated them as his equals. In America he befriended ministers of the Congregational, Baptist, and Presbyterian churches and worked with them and learned from them. Once excluded from Church of England pulpits he felt himself free from parochial boundaries and other denominational regulations became of little concern to him. In consequence Whitefield's preaching stirred the spiritual life of all the major Protestant denominations in both England and America. It was the case that this resulted in ructions among sections of Congregational and Presbyterian churches and yet many of their number who eschewed the extremer aspects of the revival began to experience a religion of the heart. Wesley rightly said of Whitefield that "he was truly cordial and catholic in his love for all who appeared to love the Lord Jesus".[39]

By his irenical ecumenism Whitefield brought together the members and adherents of the churches in the different colonies, raised their confidence in themselves, and created a common bond of solidarity among them. By so doing he helped to generate what with the passing of time became a national consciousness in which the colonists began to see their interests as being over against those of the British government. The awakening in which Whitefield played a major role deepened the piety, spiritual life, and commitment of the colonists but by the same token it also increased their spiritual dissatisfaction with the Church of England in those colonies where it was the establishment religion. Evangelical revivalism was of course grounded in the revolutionary principle of spiritual equality. As the colonists found a new spiritual freedom they began in turn to think in terms of political freedoms.

As we have seen, Whitefield's one major dispute was with Wesley over the issues of predestination, reprobation, and free grace, all of which came to a head in 1740. Despite their major disagreements they both recognized that the revival would quickly lose the strength of its appeal if they remained at loggerheads. In 1749 the Countess of Huntingdon made earnest efforts to bring the two leaders together. In 1753 Wesley preached in a new church built for Whitefield in Plymouth and in 1755 reported, "Mr Whitefield called on me; disputings are now no more; we love one another."[40] That said, their theological dispute was never truly resolved. The fragile accord lasted until 1770 when Wesley broke the peace having been troubled by antinomian behaviour, including drunkenness and blasphemy, on the part of predestinarians at Wednesbury, Dudley, and Birmingham. At Wesley's conference in the same year a resolution was drawn up and approved stating that they had "leaned too much to Calvinism".[41] Despite Wesley's reactivating of the conflict Whitefield had nevertheless underlined the importance of unity and of agreeing to differ if revival was to flourish.

Integrity and general bearing

Cornelius Winter wrote of Whitefield that "all who knew and were acquainted with him, soon discovered in him every mark of good sense and good manners; his company and conversation was so enlivening and entertaining, and at the same time so instructive and edifying, that no person with the least degree of common sense, could behave improperly in his presence."[42] He was always humble in bearing and cheerful in his manner and disposition.[43] J. C. Ryle rightly stated that Whitefield "was a man of singularly happy and cheerful spirit. No one who saw him could ever doubt that he enjoyed his religion."[44]

In his sermon on the occasion of Whitfield's death, John Wesley stated that though in the pulpit "he often found it needful, by the terrors of the Lord, to persuade men", he was also "singularly cheerful, as well as charitable and tender-hearted".[45] Noted by those who knew him well, Whitefield had an unblemished modesty. James Hervey recorded of his friend, "I have seen lately that most excellent minister of the ever-blessed Jesus, Mr Whitefield. I dined and supped with him at *Northampton*, in company with Dr Doddridge". He continued, "And surely, I never spent a more delightful evening, or saw one that seemed to make nearer approaches to the felicity of heaven... For my part, I never beheld so fair a copy of our Lord, such a living image of the Saviour, such exalted delight in God, such enlarged benevolence to man."[46]

Despite the famous squint which led to his sometimes being called "Dr Squintum", many seem to have found him an attractive personality – almost angelical in appearance to his admirers. As usual with sermons, the printed versions are only a faint, skeletal ghost of the originals, which were undoubtedly laced with illustrations, the use of incidents during preaching, and above all enlivened by a fine voice and dramatic manner. Like most great preachers, Whitefield had the gifts of an actor, as several well-worn anecdotes show. He was a man who could charm money out of Benjamin Franklin's pocket and move Lord Bolingbroke to compare him favourably with the bishops and declare that "he had uncommon powers".[47]

Relationships with women

Like John Wesley, Whitefield was not the best when it came to his relationships with women. As has been noted he found it hard to express his feelings – either for Elizabeth Delamotte who rejected his proposal of marriage or for Elizabeth James whom he married a year later. For Whitefield marriage seemed primarily about having an additional helper for his ministry. He must, however, at least have experienced some measure of sexual attraction to Elizabeth since she gave birth to a son (who sadly died shortly after birth) and she also suffered four miscarriages,[48] but he appears to have been unable to express his feelings. Perhaps Cornelius Winter, who lived in George and Elizabeth's home for a short period toward the end of their lives, offers us the truest picture of their marriage.

> He was not happy in his wife, but I fear some who
> had not all the religion they professed, contributed
> to his infelicity. He did not intentionally make his
> wife unhappy. He always preserved great decency

and decorum in his conduct towards her. Her
death set his mind at liberty. She certainly did not
behave in all respects as she ought. She could be
under no temptation from his conduct towards the
[opposite] sex, for he was a very pure man, a strict
example of the chastity he inculcated in others.[49]

Winter's remark "that she did not behave in all respects as she ought"
was reflected in a prayer request she made to a friend in 1746 that
she could "begin to be a helpmate for him for I have been nothing
but a load and burden to him yet and pray that all our trials may be
sanctified".[50] It is difficult not to feel sympathy for Elizabeth who
had to cope with the pain of the death of their infant son, several
miscarriages, and long periods of separation. She was a godly woman
of faith who did what she could to support her ever over-burdened
husband who was always on the move and constantly worn out by
preaching, pastoral concerns, the business of the orphanage house
and the care of his churches, chapels, and societies. Whitefield for his
part appears not to have been warm and affectionate toward her but
he always treated her with respect and honoured her in public.

Whitefield's relationships with other women, particularly those
of the aristocracy, among them the Countess of Huntingdon, Lady
Dartmouth, and Lady Fanny Shirley,[51] seem to have been strictly
confined to chapel business, Christian missions, and enterprise.
Whitefield clearly had a long and close relationship in particular
with the Countess of Huntingdon, whose chaplain he became in
1747. However, there is no evidence that their relationship was
anything other than upright fellowship as they shared in the work of
advancing God's kingdom. Stout appositely observed of Whitefield
that "the same Methodist culture that opened Whitefield up to
personal experience in religion closed his eyes to it in human love

and marriage. The very passion that brought stunning successes in public remained closed off and unexpressed in private. In this he proved himself a true Methodist."[52]

It is important to note at this point that Whitefield has received a good deal of criticism for his self-deprecating posturing to the nobility. R. A. Knox even compared him to the sycophantic Uriah Heep in Charles Dickens' *David Copperfield*.[53] Why, it may be wondered, did Whitefield feel the need to express such deference particularly in his later years when he was so widely known and admired on both sides of the Atlantic? The answer may lie in two areas. First, Whitefield had been brought up in humble circumstances in Gloucester's Bell Inn, where no doubt many of the customers were drawn from the lower ranks of society and had been taught to look up to their "betters". Add to that he had only been able to enter his Oxford college by being a "servitor", which involved looking after the needs of the students of rank and wealth. Second, the eighteenth century was an age in which the social hierarchy was still believed to be a fixed and divinely appointed order. Whitefield would have been well aware of the Church of England catechism which taught each person "to order myself lowly and reverently to all my betters".[54] Hindmarsh helpfully makes the point that Whitefield's self-abasement may in part have been a response to his strong conviction and experience of the sovereignty of God.[55]

Devotion to Christ

Above all Whitefield had a remarkable and ardent love for Christ. He was content to be a fool for Christ's sake. He had a powerful sense of the incomparable excellence of his Lord. He loved the souls of all mankind. His attachment to the great doctrines of the gospel was inflexible. He did not attempt to sweeten or attempt to make Jesus' teaching more palatable. The clergy of Boston reported in a joint letter that Whitefield "appears full of the love of God, and fired by an extraordinary zeal for the cause of Christ, and applies himself with the most indefatigable diligence, that ever was seen among us, for the promoting the good of souls."[56]

Reading through many hundreds of Whitefield's letters it is plain that he was wholly focused and taken up with Jesus. He demonstrated to a darkening England, which was known for its gin shops, brothels, and squalor that the gospel message still had a power which could bring transformation to individuals and change the course of nations.

Sheer hard work

Whatever Whitefield did he followed the biblical injunctions "to do it with all your might" and "wholeheartedly as unto the Lord". He grossly overworked such that his physical health was constantly frail resulting in frequent periods when he was forced to cease from his labours. Yet he was always too quick to return to the action spurred on by a vivid sense of Jesus' presence. Wesley observed that Whitefield's body suffered on account of "the violent exertion of his strength" and the fact that he would give himself no rest.[57] Whitefield was fully aware of his excessive workload and the frailty, vomiting and nervous stress that resulted from it. In a letter dated 11 October 1747 he wrote, "Weak as I am, I am willing to spend and be spent for the ever-loving Jesus, who has done so much for, and borne so long with me... Lord Jesus keep me from going off like a snuff!"[58] The following year he wrote to a friend and Scottish cleric that "excess of business, not want of respect, has prevented my writing to you".[59] Dr John Gillies of Glasgow, who knew Whitefield well, wrote of "his unwearied diligence in the offices of religion and his conscientious improvement of every portion of his time. Early in the morning he rose to his Master's work, and all day long was employed in a continual succession of different duties". Gillies went on to add in a later paragraph that he "felt the greatest enjoyment when engaged in a constant round of social and religious duties".[60]

Despite his having many opportunities to accumulate wealth both from the collections at his preaching and bequests from the nobility he was never tempted to avarice or spending on himself. Dr Ebenezer Pemberton in his memorial sermon at Boston on 11 October 1770 said: "The longer he lived, the more he evidently increased in purity of doctrine, prudence, patience, and the other amiable virtues of the Christian life."[61]

Last word

George Whitefield, as with all others, was a child of his age, and clearly, like them, he had his faults and weaknesses. That said, his strengths and positive influence far and away exceeded and overshadowed them. Whitefield was the man who significantly and lastingly changed the life and history of both Britain and America. Kidd has rightly called him "America's Spiritual Founding Father"[62] but he was more than that. He was certainly a celebrity on both sides of the Atlantic. In his later years Whitefield was increasingly seen by the colonists as one who sympathized with them in their growing struggles with the British government. This fact was well illustrated in his shared opposition to the Stamp Act of 1765 by which parliament required the colonists to pay for British troops stationed in their colonies. Whitefield was one of the truly influential figures who helped to fuel the democratic spirit that eventually birthed the War of Independence (1775–83) and the founding of the American nation that followed it. He had a significant impact on his friend Benjamin Franklin who was later to be one of a committee of five that helped to draft the Declaration of Independence.[63]

Whitefield was the co-founder of Methodism alongside John and Charles Wesley. But as we have discussed it was Whitefield who transformed Methodism from being a small pietistic sect within the Church of England known as the Holy Club into an international movement. By his constant travel, his powerful preaching, his poignant writing and his skilful use of print media Whitefield was a major factor in bringing divine light into the life, worship, and culture of England, Wales, Scotland, Ireland, and the American colonies in what would otherwise have been a bleak age. Whitefield was truly the first transatlantic revivalist.

Perhaps the last words should come from one who knew him very well and who was one of his greatest friends – Selina Countess of Huntingdon. She sent them to Charles Wesley to be read at his funeral service at Tottenham Court Road Chapel.

> I wish I could say anything to add to the best impressions of my late dear friend Mr Whitefield. One part of his character, ever the most to be admired by me, was the most artless mind – an Israelite in whom there was no guile… There is not one soul living either in temporals or spirituals who [he] ever meant to deceive for any purpose, and that it was his great point ever in godly sincerity and simplicity to have his whole life approved in this world. No prospect of pretended good could make him do evil – this is my testimony of respect. I account this from the clear revelation of Jesus Christ to his soul by the Holy Ghost… He had a single eye for the Lord and whatever was mistaken for this end was deficiency in judgement, considered rationally and temporally. Anyone that knew as well as I his true spiritual knowledge of eternal things must be absolutely sure of this.[64]

Chapter 13 notes

1 Whitefield et al., *Sermons on Important Subjects* (London, 1825), p. 684.
2 *Letter to Mr T—*, 5 September 1769.
3 *Letter to Mr Robert Keen*, 8 September 1769.
4 Ibid, 28 September 1769.
5 Ibid, 1 December 1769.
6 *Letter to Miss H—*, 6 December 1769.
7 *Letter to Mr Robert Keen*, 9 May 1770.
8 Ibid, 14 June 1770.
9 Ibid, 30 June 1770.
10 Ibid, 17 September 1770.
11 J. Gillies, op. cit., p. 269.
12 Ibid.
13 Ibid, pp. 288–89.
14 R. Knox, *Enthusiasm* (Oxford, Clarendon Press, 1950), p. 491.
15 A. Dallimore, op. cit., Vol. 1, p. 380.
16 R. Davies, *Methodism* (Harmondsworth, Penguin Books, 1964), p. 65.
17 J. C. Ryle, *The Christian Leaders of the Last Century* (London, T. Nelson and Sons, 1872), p. 2.
18 A. Skevington Wood, *The Inextinguishable Blaze* p. 79.
19 D. C. Jones et al., op. cit., pp. 243–44.
20 A. Belden, *George Whitefield, the Awakener* (London, undated), p. 71.
21 Ibid, p. 187.
22 A. Toplady, *The Works of Augustus Toplady* (London, 1844), p. 495, cited in A. Dallimore, op. cit., Vol. 2, p. 522.
23 J. Gillies, op. cit., p. 331.
24 L. Tyerman, op. cit., Vol. 2, p. 625.
25 See *Boston Evening Post*, 19 November 1754 in F. Lambert, op. cit., p. 195.
26 C. G. Finney, *Lectures on Revival*, ed. W. G. McLoughlin (Cambridge, Mass, 1960), pp. 250–76 in F. Lambert, op. cit., p. 227. Charles Finney (1792–1875) was a Presbyterian lawyer turned preacher who in later years became a Congregational pastor. He was a powerful preacher and effective revivalist in the 1820s and 1830s and wrote extensively about revivals and how to achieve them. For this reason he has often been lauded as the "Father of Modern Revivalism".
27 Romans 14:16.
28 J. Gillies, op. cit., p. 293.
29 *Letter to Mr Robert Keen*, 19 October 1764.
30 J. Wesley, *Wesley's Hymns* (London, Wesleyan Book Room), Preface.
31 D. Bebbinton, *Evangelicalism in Modern Britain* (London, Unwin Hyman, 1988), p. 69.
32 Ibid, p. 123.
33 J. Gillies, op. cit., p. 323.
34 J. Wesley, *Thoughts on Slavery*, 1774.

35 J. Gillies, op. cit., p. 320.
36 See L. Tyerman, *The Life of the Rev. George Whitefield*, Vol. 2 , p. 400 and 621-23.
37 D. Bebbington, op. cit., pp. 12–19.
38 H. Stout, *The Divine Dramatist*, p. 17.
39 J. Gillies, op. cit., p. 310.
40 R. A. Knox, *Enthusiasm* (Oxford, Clarendon Press, 1950), p. 497.
41 Ibid.
42 See L. Tyerman, op. cit., Vol. 2, p. 623 and J. Gillies, op. cit., p. 310.
43 *A Letter to the Religious Societies of England*, 1739, *Works*, Vol. 4, p. 33.
44 J. C. Ryle, George *Whitefield*, p. 29.
45 J. Gillies, op. cit., p. 323.
46 Ibid, p. 185.
47 H. Rack, *Reasonable Enthusiast*, p. 193.
48 A. Dallimore, op. cit., Vol. 2, p. 472.
49 *Memoirs of Cornelius Winter* (Bath, 1808), p. 80, cited in A. Dallimore, *George Whitefield*, Vol. 2, p. 472.
50 A. Dallimore, op. cit., Vol. 2, p. 472.
51 For other female friends see F. Cook, *Selina*, pp. 119–28.
52 H. Stout, *The Divine Dramatist*, p. 173.
53 R. A. Knox, op. cit., p. 480.
54 Church of England catechism, answer to the question, "What is thy duty towards their Neighbour?" *The Book of Common Prayer* (Oxford, University Press, undated), p. 343.
55 D. B. Hindmarsh, op. cit., p. 40.
56 J. Gillies, op. cit., p. 65.
57 Ibid, p. 331.
58 *Letter to Mr P—*, 11October 1747.
59 *Letter to Rev. Mr. M—*, 6 August 1748.
60 Cited in A. Dallimore, op. cit., Vol. 2, p. 513.
61 J. Gillies, op. cit., p. 310.
62 T. S. Kidd, *George Whitefield America's Spiritual Founding Father* (Yale University Press, 2014).
63 See H. Stout, "George Whitefield and Benjamin Franklin: Thoughts on a Peculiar Friendship", *Proceedings of the Massachusetts Historical Society*, Third Series, Vol. 103 (1991), pp. 9–23; and Holland, D., Review of "When Benjamin Franklin met the Reverend Whitefield; Enlightenment and the Power of the Printed Word", by Hoffer, Peter Charles, *Journal of Religion*, Vol. 94, No 2 (April, 2014), pp. 248–50.
64 Countess of Huntingdon, Tribute to be read at George Whitefield's funeral service, cited in F. Cook, *Selina*, p. 283.

Bibliography

Abbey, C. J., and Overton, J. H., *The English Church in the Nineteenth Century* (London, Longmans, Green and Company, 1878), 2 vols

Allen. W. O. B. and E. McClure, E., *Two Hundred years: The History of the Society for Promoting Christian Knowledge 1698–1898* (London, 1898)

Andrew, J. R., *George Whitefield: A Light Rising in Obscurity* (London, Marshall, Morgan and Scott Ltd, 1879)

Anon., *A Brief View of the Conduct of Pennsylvania for the Year 1755* (London, R. Griffiths, 1756)

Anon., *An Additional Scene to the Comedy of the Minor* (London, 1761)

Anon., *The Country Parson's Advice to his Parishioners* (London, 1680; London, Monarch, 1998)

Anon., *The Methodist: a Comedy: being a Continuation and Completion of the Plan of the Minor written by Mr Foote* (London, 1761)

Anon., *The Register Office: a Farce in Two Acts* (London, 1761)

Baker, F., *Methodism and the Love Feast* (London, Epworth, 1956)

Baker, F., *William Grimshaw* (London, Epworth Press, 1963)

Bebbington, D., *Evangelicalism in Modern Britain: A History from* the 1730s to the 1980s (London, Unwin Hyman, 1988)

Beebe, K. E., *The McCulloch Examinations of the Cambuslang Revival* (First published Scottish Historical Society, 1742, then Boydell Press, 2013), 2 vols

Belcher, J., *George Whitefield: A Biography with special reference to his Labors in America* (New York, American Tract Society, 1857)

Belden, A., *George Whitefield, the Awakener* (London, undated)

Cole, N., "The Spiritual Travels of Nathan Cole", reprinted in *The William and Mary Quarterly*, 3rd Series, VII (1950)

Cook, F., *Selina Countess of Huntingdon* (Edinburgh, The Banner of Truth Trust, 2001)

Copeland, D. A., *Debating Issues in Colonial Newspapers* (Westport, CT., Greenwood Press, 2000)

Currie, J., *New Testimony and Vindication of the Extraordinary Work of God at Cambuslang, Kilsyth and other places in the West of Scotland* (Robert Smith and Alexander Hutchinson in Company, 1743)

Davies, R., *Methodism* (Harmondsworth, Penguin Books, 1964)

Downes, J., *Methodism Examined and Exposed* (London, 1759)

Edwards, J., *An Account of the Revival of Religion in Northampton in 1740–1742, as Communicated in a Letter to a Minister in Boston* (Edinburgh, The Banner of Truth Trust, 1991)

Elliott, R. A., *Summary of Whitefield's Doctrine* (London, Banner of Truth Trust, 1959)

Erskine, J., *THE SIGNS OF THE TIMES CONSIDERED, or the high PROBABILITY that the present APPEARANCES in New England, and the West of Scotland, are a PRELUDE of the Glorious THINGS promised to the CHURCH in the latter age* (Edinburgh, T. Lumisden and J. Robertson, 1742)

Fawcett, A., *The Cambuslang Revival* (London, The Banner of Truth Trust, 1971)

Field, C. D., "The social composition of English Methodism to 1830: a membership analysis", *Bulletin of John Rylands University Manchester Library*, 76 (Spring 1994)

Franklin, B., *Memoirs of the Life and Writings of Benjamin Franklin* (London, 1818), 2 vols

Gib, A. A., *Warning Against the Ministrations of Mr George Whitefield* (Edinburgh, David Duncan, 1742)

Gibson, F., *The Bishop of London's Pastoral Letter to the People of His Diocese: Especially Those of the Two Great Cities of London and Westminster: By Way of Caution, Against Lukewarmness on the One Hand, and Enthusiasm on the Other* (London, S. Buckley, 1739)

Gibson, W. and Smith, T. W. (eds), *George Whitefield Tercentenary Essays* (University of Wales Press, 2015)

Gillies, J., *Historical Collections of Accounts of Revival* (First published 1754, London, James Nesbit & Co, 1845)

Gillies, J. *Memoirs of the Life of the Reverend George Whitefield* (London, Edward and Charles Dilly, 1772)

Gordon, J., *Evangelical Spirituality* (London, SPCK, 1991)

Green J., *The Principals and Practices of the Methodists farther considered, in a Letter to the Reverend Mr George Whitefield* (Cambridge, 1761)

Grumet, R. S., *The Munsee Indians: A History* (Norman, University of Oklahoma, 2009)

Haykin, M. A. G., *The Revived Puritan: The Spirituality of George Whitefield* (Evangelical Press, 2004)

Hempton, D., *Methodism: Empire of the Spirit* (New Haven, CT, Yale University Press, 2005)

Holland, D., Review of *When Benjamin Franklin met the Reverend George Whitefield: Enlightenment and the Power of the Printed Word*, by Peter Charles Hoffer, *Journal of Religion*, Vol. 94, No 2 (April, 2014)

Hudson, W. S., *Religion in America* (New York, Charles Scribner's Sons, 1965)

Hughes, H. J., *Life of Howell Harris the Welsh Reformer* (London, James Nesbit, 1892)

Hyatt, E. L., *Pilgrims and Patriots: The Radical Roots of American Democracy and Freedom* (Hyatt Press, 2006)

Jay, W., *Memoirs of the Late Reverend Cornelius Winter* (Bath, 1808)

Johnson, E. A., *George Whitefield: A Definitive Biography* (Tentmaker Publications, 2009)

Jones, D. C., Schlenther, B. S., and White, E. M. et al., *The Elect Methodists: Calvinistic Methodism in England and Wales 1735–1811* (Cardiff, University of Wales, 2016)

Jones, M. H., *The Trevecca Letters* (C.M. Book Agency, Caernarvon, 1932)

Kidd, T. S., *George Whitefield, America's Spiritual Founding Father* (New Haven, Yale University Press, 2014)

Kidd, T. S., *God of Liberty: A Religious History of the American Revolution* (New York, Basic Books, 2010)

Kirby, G. W., *The Elect Lady* (Trustees of the Countess of Huntingdon's Connexion, 1972)

Knox, R. A., *Enthusiasm* (Oxford, Clarendon Press, 1950)

Lambert, F., *Pedlar in Divinity: George Whitefield and the Great Awakening, 1737–1745* (Princeton, University Press, 1994)

Law, W., *A Serious Call to a Devout and Holy Life* (London, Griffith, Farran, Browne, Undated)

Lawson, S. J., *The Evangelical Zeal of George Whitefield* (Reformation Trust Publishing, 2014)

Lester, J. (ed.), "The Spirit with the Word: The Reformation Revivalism of George Whitefield", Packer, J. I., in *The Collected Shorter Writings of J. I. Packer* (Carlisle, Paternoster

Macfarlan, D., *Revivals of the Eighteenth Century* (London and Edinburgh, undated)

Macfarlan, D., *The Revivals of the Eighteenth Century with Three Sermons by the Rev George Whitefield* (London, John Johnstone, 1800)

Mahaffey, J. D., *The Accidental Revolutionary* (Baylor, 2011)

Marsden, G., *Jonathan Edwards: A Life* (New Haven, Yale University Press, 2003)

McGrath, A., *Christian Spirituality: An Introduction* (Oxford, Blackwell, 1999)

Murray, I., *Revival and Revivalism* (Edinburgh, The Banner of Truth Trust, 1994).

Nash, G. B., T*he Unknown American Revolution: The Unruly Birth of Democracy and the Struggle to Create America* (New York, Penguin Books, 2006)

Nichols, J., *Literary Anecdotes of the Eighteenth Century* (London, Nichols, Son, and Bentley, 1812)

Noll, M. A., *The Old Religion in a New World* (Grand Rapids, William B. Eerdmans Publishing Company, 2002)

O'Brien, S., "A Transatlantic Community of Saints: The Great Awakening and the First Evangelical Network, 1735–1755", *American History Review*, 91, October, 1986

Occum, W., "Occum Circle Personography", Dartmouth College Press, 1999)

Philip, R., *Life and Times of George Whitefield* (London, George Virtue, 1838)

Podmore, C. J., "'The Fetter Lane Society", *Proceedings of the Wesley Historical Society*, Volume XLVI, pp. 125–53.

Podmore, C. J., *The Moravian Church in England* (Oxford, Clarendon Press, 1998)

Rack, H. D., *Reasonable Enthusiast* (London, Epworth Press, 2002)

Ripper, J., *American Stories: Living American History* (London, Routledge, 2008) 2 vols

Robe, J. A., *A Faithful Narrative of the Extraordinary Work of the Spirit of God* (London, S. Mason, 1742–43)

Rowell, G., *Hell and the Victorians* (Oxford, University Press, 1974)

Ryle, J. C., *George Whitefield and His Ministry* (London, Banner of Truth Trust, 1959)

Ryle, J. C., *The Christian Leaders of the Last Century* (London, T. Nelson and Sons, 1872)

Seymour, A C. H., *The Life and Times of Selina, Countess of Huntingdon* (London, 1839), 2 vols

Smith, J. H., *The First Great Awakening: Redefining Religion in British America 1725–1775* (Madison, Farleigh Dickinson University Press, 2015)

Stephen, Sir J., *Essays in Ecclesiastical Biography* (London, Longmans, Green, Reader and Dyer, 1872)

Stephens, W., *A Journal of the Proceedings in Georgia*, 2 vols, beginning October 1737, Georgia Records (1906)

Stout, H. S., "George Whitefield and Benjamin Franklin: Thoughts on a Peculiar Friendship", *Proceedings of the Massachusetts Historical Society*, Third Series, Vol. 103, pp. 9–23

Stout, H. S., *The Divine Dramatist* (Grand Rapids, William B. Eerdman Publishing Company, 1991, reprinted 1994)

Telford, J., *The Life of John Wesley* (London, Epworth, 1960)

Thornton, M., *English Spirituality* (London, SPCK, 1963)

Toplady, A., *The Works of Augustus Toplady* (London, 1844)

Tyerman, L., *The Life of the Rev. George Whitefield* (London, Hodder and Stoughton, 1877), 2 vols

Wakeley, J. B., *Anecdotes of the Rev George Whitefield* (London, Hodder, 1900)

Wesley, *Journal* (London, Kelly, 1909–1916) 8 vols

Whitefield, G., *A Short Account of God's Dealings With the Reverend Mr George Whitefield* (London, The Banner of Truth Trust, 1965)

Whitefield, G., *Published Letters, Works*, Vols 2 and 3

Wilson, L., *Constrained by Zeal: Female Spirituality Amongst Non-conformists 1825–1875* (Carlisle, Paternoster Press, 2000)

Wood, A. S., *The Inextinguishable Blaze* (Grand Rapids, Wm B. Eerdmans Publishing Company, 1968).

Select manuscripts, documents and papers consulted

Boston Evening Post, July 1745

Boston Evening Post, November 1754

Boston Gazette, January 1764

Boston Gazette, February 1764

Christian History, 15 November 1744.

Gloucester Journal, May 1729

Lloyd's Evening Post, 17 March 1760

The Monthly Review, July 1760

Seward, W., *Diary of William Seward*, MS, Mun. A.2.116 (Chetham's Library, Manchester), 1702–40

Whitefield, G., *MS Diary 1736*, Reference ADDMS 34068, British Library

Whitefield, G., *Sermons on Important Subjects* (London, 1825)

Whitefield, G., *The Works of the Reverend George Whitefield* (London, Edward and Charles Dilly, 1771), 6 vols

Whitefield, G., *A Letter to the Rev. Mr John Wesley*, Appendix, *Whitefield's Journals* (London, Banner of Truth Trust, undated)

Index